M000312890

Western Foreign Fighters

Western Foreign Fighters

The Threat to Homeland and International Security

Phil Gurski

ROWMAN & LITTLEFIELD
Lanham • Boulder • New York • London

Published by Rowman & Littlefield
A wholly owned subsidiary of The Rowman & Littlefield Publishing Group, Inc.
4501 Forbes Boulevard, Suite 200, Lanham, Maryland 20706
www.rowman.com

Unit A, Whitacre Mews, 26-34 Stannary Street, London SE11 4AB

Copyright © 2017 by Rowman & Littlefield

All rights reserved. No part of this book may be reproduced in any form or by any electronic or mechanical means, including information storage and retrieval systems, without written permission from the publisher, except by a reviewer who may quote passages in a review.

British Library Cataloguing in Publication Information Available

Library of Congress Cataloging-in-Publication Data

Names: Gurski, Phil
Title: Western foreign fighters : The threat to homeland and international security / Phil Gurski.
Description: Lanham : Rowman & Littlefield, 2017. | Includes bibliographical references and index.
ISBN 9781442273795 (cloth : alkaline paper) | ISBN 9781442273801 (paper : alkaline paper) | ISBN 9781442273818 (electronic)

∞ ™ The paper used in this publication meets the minimum requirements of American National Standard for Information Sciences Permanence of Paper for Printed Library Materials, ANSI/NISO Z39.48-1992.

Printed in the United States of America

To the men of Newfoundland who helped me to understand both the zeal of fighting and the carnage that is war

To all who have lost loved ones through war or terrorism

Contents

Preface

A PERSONAL NOTE

While I was nearing the end of the first draft of this book, I was involved in two events that profoundly affected me and the message I am trying to convey here. In early November 2015 I spent two weeks in the north of France on a tour of World War I and World War II sites, including four days at a bed-and-breakfast in the Somme region of Picardy (Ocean Villas, named after the pronunciation given by Welsh soldiers to the town they were stationed in, Auchonvillers). This particular hostel was located on the Western Front (there was even an old trench running through it), and within a few minutes' drive one can find Commonwealth War Graves Commission cemeteries filled with tens of thousands of graves, the remains of British, Canadian, Australian, South African, and other young men who fought and died between 1914 and 1918.

Less than a kilometer from that B&B is a monument to the sacrifice made by men who enlisted in the Royal Newfoundland Regiment and fought at Beaumont-Hamel, a small part of the Battle of the Somme in 1916. On July 1, 1916—Canada Day (then known as Dominion Day, though not for the Newfoundlanders, whose country would not join the Canadian Confederation until 1949)—the regiment sent forth its finest young men against the German trenches shortly after dawn. The slaughter was immediate and catastrophic: of the 780 men who left the trenches that morning, only 68 answered roll call the following day. Newfoundland has never forgotten the carnage.

Back in that B&B in Auchonvillers among many mementos of the war is a photograph on the wall of ten young men: the Newfoundland Regimental hockey team of 1917. Two of their members died in France in later years. I found the photo haunting. These men were in the bloom of youth and lived life to the fullest, playing organized hockey in the early days of a sport that would quickly become Canada's national game. They came from an island country where small fishing villages dominated. And yet they volunteered en masse to fight in a war across the very ocean where they made their living. They died in the hundreds: It is said that no community in Newfoundland— where there are probably at most two degrees of separation between any two residents—escaped the tragedy of the death of at least one of its young men; many communities lost several. In the capital, St. John's, it has been claimed that no street was left untouched by death on the battlefield.

As I looked at the young men in that photo, aside from feeling a deep sense of loss and sadness, I asked myself, Why? Why did these individuals with so much to live for, choose—*voluntarily*—to leave their island home-land and elect to fight in a war that was not theirs? Newfoundland was, after all, not under threat. There was a huge ocean between the imperial designs of Kaiser Wilhelm II's Germany and their country. And yet volunteer they did.

Beyond Newfoundland, hundreds of thousands of Canadians made the same choice: Over six hundred thousand fought in World War I, and 10 percent did not return. Like Newfoundland, Canada was not threatened by the madness that was the war in Europe. And although the United States did not enter the war until 1917, thousands of its citizens volunteered to travel to France to help beforehand. The question remains, Why did they agree to fight?

The second event that deeply impacted me and the writing of this book was much more real to me, as it was contemporary and involved acts of terrorism, which I studied as an intelligence analyst in Canada for over three decades. The day I left Paris, ten hours later that day, to be precise, the city was rocked by terrorist attacks at the national stadium and several restaurants and bars. Hundreds were killed or wounded. The attacks were initially be-lieved to have been carried out by Islamic State (IS), and the next few days revealed that several of the assailants were French and Belgian citizens who had radicalized in the West and traveled to join IS. They had returned to wreak havoc on their compatriots. Why? Why did they go to Syria in the first place? Why did they come back? What is the impact of their return from conflict zones and that of the thousands of others who have made similar journeys?

Different eras, different wars, different calls to fight, but similar out-comes—death and destruction. It is my sincere hope that this book provides some answers to the questions we all have about humankind and the desire to join conflict, whether that conflict is sanctioned war or terrorism.

Chapter One

Introduction

Foreign Fighters as a Security Issue

During the long 2015 federal-election campaign, Canadian prime minister Stephen Harper announced that if his Conservative Party were to maintain power it would introduce legislation making it illegal to travel to regions of the world that are hotbeds of "Islamic terrorism." This law would seek to address what the government calls the "threat from within": Canadians seeking to engage with terrorist groups abroad. As the prime minister put it, people traveling to these areas could eventually return to Canada and bring their "terrorist training" with them. There are individuals, he said, "who for reasons you and I will never understand turn their back on our country and, indeed, turn their backs on civilization itself to travel overseas to join jihadist causes."[1]

Well, Prime Minister (well, *former* PM, as his party lost the election), this book will seek to provide that understanding—or at least in part.

It seems that almost every day we awaken to another story of a Canadian or Western citizen who has chosen to leave their country and go fight in Syria. Some sign up to fight with Kurdish forces, while the majority seem to be drawn to terrorist groups like Islamic State and Jabhat al-Nusra. Others elect to join groups in Somalia such as Al-Shabaab or in Afghanistan such as the Taliban. And we are getting more and more accounts of shattered families asking why their children and siblings left them behind.

Why do they go? What do they hope to achieve? What will happen to them when they get there? When they get back? What are the implications for Canada and Canadians or other countries once (if?) they return? Should we let them go or stop them from leaving?

This book explores the difficult challenges facing us from those who elect to fight wars in which Canada and other Western nations either have no official presence or that involve parties representing a clear threat to the West (i.e., terrorist groups). These are conflicts in which we in the West "have no dog." Building on my last book—*The Threat from Within: Recognizing Al Qaeda–Inspired Terrorism and Radicalization in the West*—the focus here will be on Canadians, and other Westerners, who see violent jihad as a divine obligation. We will examine their motivations and their reasons for traveling to foreign battlefields. Most importantly, we will discuss what, if any, security threat they pose to our country.

I hope that this book will contribute to our collective understanding of why our fellow citizens, many of whom have much to live for here and appear at least on the outside to be fully integrated and well-adjusted individuals, make decisions that to the majority seem to defy sense. The implications for all of us—government officials as well as ordinary citizens—are significant.

It is my intention to challenge accepted wisdom when it comes to foreign fighters. They are not all "brainwashed." They are all not "losers." They are not all mentally ill. In most cases they believe fervently in what they are doing and that they are making a difference. We may not agree with their choices—for they are indeed choices, made for the most part voluntarily—but they do correspond to some form of internal logic. Failure to recognize this leads to inaccurate analysis and shortsighted and ineffective policies and solutions.

Young men have been joining up for centuries, of course. War has appealed to many across the years. And we in Canada have heard many stories of why eighteen-year-olds elected to leave the farm or their family to fight in wars far away. Some of these conflicts—World War I, for example—were endorsed by the Canadian government. Others—like the Spanish Civil War—were not. Regardless of state sanction or an absence thereof, people threw their hats in the ring. Most returned; some did not. In this book I hope to uncover some of the reasons why these men made the decision to fight.

I must also stress that by looking at individual motivations for electing to fight in conflicts across the decades I am not equating the justifiability or "rightness" of these conflicts. We in Canada recognize the sacrifice of our citizens in a number of wars: World Wars I and II, Afghanistan, and Korea: We do not see those who join the Islamic State or Al-Shabaab in the same light. Nor should we, as the groups to which Westerners are scurrying are listed terrorist entities. Some conflicts, on the other hand, occupy a gray zone, at least in Canada: Spain in the 1930s and Vietnam in the 1960s. The varying levels of "acceptability" should not stand in the way of an analysis of decision making. The purpose here is to see whether what drove an eighteen-year old to sign up in 1914 to go to Europe to fight the Hun has anything in common with why a similar eighteen-year-old a century later leaves Canada, flies to Turkey, makes his way to the border, and joins Islamic State. Drawing lessons across history does not imply that these lessons are the same in every instance. After we examine motivations, we will look at whether or not these warriors present any threat to their societies once the conflict ends and they come home. Even if these motivations are similar across "good" wars and "terrorist" wars, can we not still condone the former and condemn the latter?

To the extent possible, I will rely on the very words and rationales provided by fighters themselves. Whether or not this is a reliable metric—are people always capable of understanding why they do things?—I see it as the best available source of information. These justifications will be taken from media stories and interviews, personal accounts, and videos and texts issued by terrorist groups.

In light of my career as an intelligence analyst for the Canadian government over a thirty-plus-year period, I believed it unwise to carry out field research, specifically getting into contact with current foreign fighters. My previous work—and the fact that I worked in intelligence is not secret—would have precluded honest disclosure on their part, and it would have been nigh impossible to establish a relationship based on trust. In addition, communication may have been dangerous, either for me or for my interlocutors. It is for those reasons that I have chosen to use already published material as my data source and to provide the analysis derived from my career as value added.

The approach adopted here is also consistent with an intelligence background. In intelligence we seek to collect information, analyze that information, and provide advice to the government of the day. Here I am seeking to provide what is of interest to intelligence and law-enforcement agencies as well as the general public and what would be useful for these agencies providing advice to governments. Hence, as with my first book, I do not intend to adopt an academic tone (while recognizing and using the tremendous work and contribution made by academic researchers), starting with a literature review and proposing a hypothesis and testing it. As well, this book will be relatively short and will not rehash the many excellent books on foreign fighters, Islamic State, and other terrorist groups. There are several available, and I will not summarize what has been already analyzed. I am all too aware that writing a book entails placing an end date on events and that by the time this manuscript reaches the public much will have changed. It is my hope that what will be different will be largely quantitative and not qualitative and that the points made here will still be highly relevant.

A career in intelligence also led me to include a chapter on what we are doing about foreign fighters and what else we could do to deal with this phenomenon. I intend to discuss which policies and practices strike me as useful and effective and which may be more problematic. As I had an opportunity to work both sides of the counterterrorism divide—investigation and enforcement as well as early intervention and counter-radicalization—I believe I am somewhat uniquely qualified to speak to the spectrum of responses. My career took me from SIGINT to HUMINT to PREVENT, and I have learned much from all three spheres over the years.[2]

In essence I will attempt to provide an initial response to two main questions: Why do people decide to abandon their homelands and join terrorist groups, and are their reasons any different than those proffered by soldiers across the centuries? And do these individuals pose a significant threat to their societies if they survive and return? There are undoubtedly other important issues surrounding the foreign-fighter phenomenon, but I will limit my discussion to these two.

STRUCTURE OF THE BOOK

This book consists of eight chapters, an appendix, a glossary, and a suggested-reading list. In the next chapter, I explore very briefly the nature of war and why nations resort to conflict. This is to set the stage for a more in-depth examination of personal motivation by looking at state motivation. In chapter 3 I discuss why Canadians and other Westerners volunteered to join the military in wars to which Canada or other nations were a party as determined by the government of the day, as well as wars where the country was not officially involved. For reasons of succinctness, I limit the analysis on the first set to Canada's participation in World War I and the United States post–9/11, while for the second I examine the rationale behind decisions to fight in the Spanish Civil War and the Vietnam War, as well as in Israel and the war in Iraq and Syria on the side of the Kurds. Where possible I present evidence drawn from the very words of the participants, some of whom will be residents of other Western nations beyond Canada and the United States. In chapter 4 I present data on why Canadians and other Westerners are flocking to Iraq and Syria to fight alongside groups such as the Islamic State and contrast their rationales with those of the soldiers examined in chapter 3. Chapter 5 follows the debate among extremists regarding whether women can engage in warfare and looks at the substantial rise in female participation, a phenomenon not seen to a similar extent in other conflicts to date. In chapter 6 we look at the security implications behind these mujahedeen, ranging from their radicalization in Canada and the West to their possible return to their home countries. Chapter 7 discusses what we can do in the face of this challenge. I wrap up with a few concluding and forward-looking thoughts in chapter 8. The appendix is an overview of jihad as war, from the early days of Islam to the current conflicts in Africa and the Middle East.

This section provides background for the concepts that have inspired individuals to seek jihad and given them the justification for doing so. A glossary of terms, a suggested-reading list, and a bibliography complete the book.

NOTES

1. Gloria Galloway, "Tories Vow Ban on Travel to Terror Havens If Re-elected," *Globe and Mail* (Toronto), August 9, 2015, http://www.theglobeandmail.com/news/politics/harper-promises-travel-ban-to-places-that-are-ground-zero-for-terrorist-activity/article25897926/.

2. SIGINT is "signals intelligence," HUMINT is "human intelligence," and PREVENT is part of the UK's CONTEST counterterrorism program.

Chapter Two

Why War?

Now Abel kept flocks, and Cain worked the soil. In the course of time Cain brought some of the fruits of the soil as an offering to th Lord. And Abel also brought an offering—fat portions from some of the firstborn of his flock. The Lord looked with favor on Abel and his offering, but on Cain and his offering he did not look with favor. So Cain was very angry, and his face was downcast.

Then the Lord said to Cain, "Why are you angry? Why is your face downcast? If you do what is right, will you not be accepted? But if you do not do what is right, sin is crouching at your door; it desires to have you, but you must rule over it."

Now Cain said to his brother Abel, "Let's go out to the field." While they were in the field, Cain attacked his brother Abel and killed him.

—Genesis 4:3–8

War is not healthy for children and other living things.
—slogan designed by Another Mother for Peace,
an anti–Vietnam War group

War is diplomacy by other means.

—Carl von Clausewitz

War—what is it good for? Absolutely nothin'.
—Edwin Starr, lyric from his former Billboard #1 song, "War"

Jihad and the rifle alone; no negotiations, no conferences, and no dialogues.
—Abdullah Azzam

7

CHAPTER ABSTRACT

This brief chapter will discuss the nature and history of war and begin to answer the question of why we are so keen to enter into it. Starting with prehistory, examples will be provided to demonstrate that war has long been part of our species and how we condone killing on a mass scale through state-offered justifications.

WHAT IS WAR?

As noted in Genesis, which purports to be the story of humanity and its relationship with God, serious violence has been with us since the very beginning. Cain and Abel were the sons of the first humans, Adam and Eve. It is hard to get any earlier in history than that. Whether you believe that the Bible is the word of God or that it is myth, it speaks volumes about us that, after the Creation sequence as told in a book that has spawned three major world religions, the first story deals with serious violence.

War and serious violence may be in fact part of the human condition. War in a sense is simply serious violence on a grand scale. Whereas individuals can cause great harm and death in a very limited way (ignoring the possibility of the use of a particularly lethal weapon), lots of individuals with lots of weapons can wound and kill many (the horrendous casualty numbers of the world wars have shown us this).

It is instructive that an act long condemned by most people as wrong, except in the most extreme circumstances, has also been sanctioned at the highest level. We punish those who kill with the tools that we have developed in our laws (including, paradoxically, the killing of those who kill—i.e., capital punishment), and yet we allow our governments to declare killing on massive scales okay.

In this book I will define *war* as the use of armed aggression by one group against another for some larger purpose (territory, resources, defense, ideology, etc.). More specifically, state actors (or nonstate actors) engaged in armed action against another state actor. I will ignore armed conflict between or among nonstate actors (gangs, criminal networks, etc.).

Terrorism lies somewhere in the middle, since extremist groups can kill many more than any given individual can but generally not as many as a state at war (again, events such as the terrorist attacks of September 11, 2001, are the exception, not the rule), unless a group gets its hand on a weapon of mass destruction. While my focus is on terrorism, we need to look at war in general to gain a fuller understanding of terrorists' motivations.

Every time you open a newspaper or read news online, it seems that someone somewhere is at war with someone else. People die in violent conflict, ranging from acts of terrorism to interstate or intrastate warfare every day. (Try this test: Read any reputable daily paper, online or in print, for a month, and count the days on which there is *not* a report on the death of someone in these circumstances. I will be highly surprised if you find a single day with no such reportage.) And what is more troubling, I think—and I am not alone in this—is that times were much more violent in the past when there was no CNN or BBC to report events. The average citizen of the fourteenth and fifteenth centuries would have been hard pressed to keep up with the daily carnage during the Hundred Years' War, for instance.

Some scientists have suggested that humans cannot help but engage in armed aggression with one another, and there has been research that may show that our prehuman ancestors and mammalian cousins also engaged in war. Studies in Africa, for instance, appear to indicate that groups of chimpanzees will organize violent raids against other groups of chimpanzees.

In the January 2015 issue of *National Geographic* Glenn Hodges wrote that, "by all appearances, the earliest Americans were a rough bunch. If you look at the skeletal remains of Paleo-Americans, more than half the men have injuries caused by violence, and four out of ten have skull fractures. The wounds don't appear to have been the result of hunting mishaps, and they don't bear telltale signs of warfare, like blows suffered while fleeing an attacker. Instead it appears that these men fought among themselves—often and violently."[1] Even if it is difficult to distinguish battle wounds from run-of-the-mill violence twelve thousand years ago, there is little doubt that life was brutish and short back then.

Even further back in time, Neolithic society, as it has been shown, was extremely violent. German researchers reported in August 2015 that they had found evidence of an "apocalyptic nightmare of violence, warfare, and cannibalism" in which the bodies of twelve- to thirteen-year-old boys were found with cranial injuries.[2] Scientists interpreted this as evidence of "collective violence."

In the Lake Turkana region of Kenya, scientists have found evidence of a "massacre" dating back ten thousand years. Apparently one group of hunter-gatherers attacked another, leaving the dead with crushed skulls and spear wounds. The dead included a pregnant woman whose unborn child remained inside, its bones still intact in her abdomen. Scientists believe this is the first solid evidence of warfare within a foraging society.[3]

And one more. Curtis Marean of the School of Human Evolution and Social Change at Arizona State University wrote in the August 2015 issue of *Scientific American* that the exploitation of "dense, predictable, and valuable" food resources led to high levels of territoriality among humans and that this territoriality led to intergroup conflict.[4] These conflicts were aided by two contemporaneous developments: the growing ability to operate in groups of unrelated people and the creation of projectile weaponry. All this occurred as much as seventy-four thousand years ago or even earlier. It thus confirms the hypothesis that warfare and intergroup violent conflict has a long history indeed.

Looking forward, will organized violence always be with us? The 2013 film *The Purge* takes place in a future United States where the government (the "new founding fathers") has sanctioned a twelve-hour period once a year where citizens can "purge" themselves of their violent thoughts and anger by engaging in any crime, including murder, with the sanction—and encouragement—of the state, suggesting that humans have a deeply instilled violent streak that must be satisfied to ensure peace at other times. Yes, this is fiction, but it may speak to an underlying truth: It is beyond doubt that warfare and violence have been the norm throughout human history, and it is likely that they will remain so for the foreseeable future.

Other cultures and societies across time have shown that warfare and violence appear to be the rule and not the exception. Here are a few examples:

- Hawaii after the eleventh century: "If chiefs were not at court, then they were probably at war, for hostilities were *endemic* both within the islands that made up the Hawaiian archipelago and among them, as chiefs and warriors battled for ascendancy. Tension and fear became the defining features of Hawaiian society, and even sleep brought no relaxation, for it was dangerous to sleep next to the walls of the grass houses in case of a lethal spear thrust through the thatch."[5]
- Europe: Between 1560 and 1715, Europe knew only thirty years of peace.[6] This period was marked by the Thirty Years' War, in which 7.5 million are thought to have died (three centuries earlier, the Hundred Years' War resulted in three million dead).[7]
- China: When the Qing Dynasty replaced the Ming Dynasty from 1618 to 1683, an estimated twenty-five million people were killed.[8]

War has been with us a very long time. But, as we move forward as a global society and need to cultivate better cooperation in order to face truly catastrophic issues like global warming, will wars still be part of our human ways? In other words, will things get better or worse? On the positive side of the ledger, consider the findings of Canadian linguist and cognitive scientist Steven Pinker, who wrote an epic book on war and violence back in 2011 called *Better Angels of our Nature*.[9] I have no intention of summarizing an eight hundred-plus-page book here. Suffice to say that Pinker showed, through a meticulous and comprehensive look at historical records (which were far from complete), that we are much less violent than we used to be. Despite a massive increase in weapons lethality (from stones to nuclear weapons), fewer people die in war today than did in earlier millennia. And violence once thought normal, if not condoned—against women, children, and animals—is now universally condemned. Pinker convincingly shows that violence is down but is not making the claim that it is gone for good. Interestingly, as crime rates plummet, society's fears of violence rise. Even if Pinker is right, and it is hard to argue with his data, it is nevertheless true that violence and war has been a characteristic of human society for a very long time.

But perhaps we are making progress. As Joshua Goldstein put it in his book *Winning the War on War*,

> In the first half of the twentieth century, world wars killed tens of millions and left whole continents in ruins. In the second half of that century, during the Cold War, proxy wars killed millions , and the world feared a nuclear war that could have wiped out our species. Now, in the early twenty-first century, the worst wars, such as Iraq, kill hundreds of thousands. We fear terrorist attacks that could destroy a city, but not life on the planet. The fatalities still represent a large number, and the impacts of wars are still catastrophic for those caught in them, but, overall, war has diminished dramatically. [10]

Taking the other side of the argument, *The Economist*, in its "World in 2016" preview, agreed that after World War II the trend in war-related deaths was downward: from 180,000 a year during the four decades of the Cold War to one hundred thousand a year in the 1990s and lower further to fifty-five thousand in the first decade of the third millennium. In its view, 2016 will confirm that the trend has reversed itself, noting that the civil war in Syria alone has claimed 250,000 lives since 2011, while the war in South Sudan has killed fifty thousand since December 2013. *The Economist* is anything but sanguine for 2016, stating that five years after the Arab Spring "much of the Middle East will still be a battlefield for Islamist extremists. . . . Islamic State will remain undefeated, as will Boko Haram in Nigeria." It goes on to write that Afghanistan will still be seeking peace and stability while Thailand, Myanmar, and the Philippines will continue to face stubborn guerrilla movements. [11]

War has been so ubiquitous throughout human history that its language has invaded (pun intended) our speech. Militaristic terms have been adopted and modified to the point that they become common metaphors. In English, for example, you can *attack* someone's position in a debate. We talk about *battleground* electoral districts. Candidates *come under fire*. In the 1960s we talked of the British *invasion* in music and fashion. People will *fire the first salvo* in an argument. In a one-sided hockey game it can seem that one team is *coming in waves*.

Some have argued that there is actually a benefit—or rather a series of benefits—to war. In *War! What Is It Good For?* Ian Morris writes that millennia of war have made humanity richer and safer in four main ways:

- By fighting wars, people have created larger and more organized societies that have reduced the risk that their members will die violently.
- War is the only way people have found to create larger, more peaceful societies.
- The larger societies created through war have made us collectively richer.
- We have become so good at waging war, using more and more lethal means, that it is now getting harder to start conflict (for fear of total destruction, à la the mutual assured destruction of the Cold War). [12]

While some of these arguments seem unconvincing and circular to me—"We have created larger societies and we have had war since the beginning, ergo war was a necessary condition for creating these larger societies"—nevertheless, Morris does underscore the point that war appears to be an inevitable practice of humans. Good, bad, or somewhere in between, it is with us to stay (even if as Pinker has shown it is less common than in the past).

WHY WAR?

States of course rely on individuals to carry out war on their behalf. These individuals have to be motivated to fight and kill (despite the fact that humans have been killing one another since the dawn of time, there may in fact be an inherent aversion to doing so most of the time). Motivations as we shall see in later chapters may include an appeal to nationalism or patriotism, religious injunction, or a sense of grievance, among others. Should the state fail to gain enough adherents to willingly join its cause, the result is forced enrollment (conscription).

There is inevitably some overlap between state and individual rationales for war. We will examine individual motivations beginning in chapter 3. It is important, nevertheless, to look at why states decide to engage in mass killing of identified enemies. I do not intend to provide an exhaustive account of why nations go to war: whole books—rather, whole collections of books—have been written on any given conflict. The following section may strike some as simplistic, but it serves merely to set the stage for a larger examination of individual choice in the decision to fight.

What is it about war that appeals to us? Why do we decide to engage in it (assuming that it is not entirely genetically programmed)? What factors underlie the decision to send millions of people into situations where there is a good chance they will be seriously injured or die?

States go to war for a variety of reasons. The following list, though certainly not exhaustive, gives us an idea of how states rationalize war:

- Naked aggression
- Nationalism/ideology
- Resource acquisition
- Territorial expansion/greed/arrogance/hubris
- Defense
- Coming to the aid of an ally
- "Preventative" wars
- "Higher" cause—that is, religion
- Humanitarianism—that is, helping a population against an aggressor

There are undoubtedly other justifications, and it is probable that in some wars multiple drivers are at play.

We can see these factors by looking at specific conflicts. The following section is illustrative in nature and does not pretend to be a comprehensive look at any one war. There are far too many contradictory theses as to why wars start: The recent plethora of books to mark the centenary of World War I only emphasizes this morass. However, if we just consider the major wars (some, not all) in the twentieth and twenty-first centuries alone, we can see how these factors affect the decision to launch war.

- World War I: A combination of imperial hubris (Germany), coming to the aid of an ally (Britain and Germany, as well as Canada and other Commonwealth members), and defense (France). There is also an interesting religious aspect that is often overlooked but that was covered in *The Great and Holy War* by Philip Jenkins. [13]
- World War II: A combination of naked aggression, nationalism, and territorial expansion (all Germany, Japan, and Italy), defense (Britain, Russia, and China), and coming to an ally's defense (United States, Canada, and others).
- Korea: Naked aggression (North Korea), defense (South Korea), alliance (the United Nations—Canada, the United States, and others).
- Vietnam: Ideology (many sides) and defense (the United States for South Vietnam).
- Gulf War I (1980–1988): Naked aggression (Iraq) and defense (Iran).
- Gulf War II (1991–1992): Naked aggression (Iraq) and alliance (the United States for Kuwait).
- Balkans: Territorial aggression, ethnoreligious nationalism, and protection of populations (all sides).
- Gulf War III (2003–2008?): Preventative (United States), defense (Iraq), and religious (foreign fighters).
- Syria: Nationalism (the Assad regime and main non-Islamist opposition groups), religious cause (Islamist groups), and defense (Kurds).

It should be underscored again that any given war may have multiple drivers.

So, why do *individuals* go to war? Assuming that we are not talking about conscription, where the state forces individuals to join armies, what are the reasons individuals willingly place themselves in situations that could cause them grievous harm or death? Not surprisingly, some of the rationales mirror those seen above for state actors.

- Nationalism
- Sense of adventure/thrill
- Money (mercenaries)
- Sense of duty/desire to come to the aid of others
- Higher cause
- Something to do/a job

We will see examples of these motivations and more in later chapters.

WAR AND TERRORISM

Why am I juxtaposing wars and terrorist groups? Simply stated, most terrorist groups frame their actions and ideologies in terms of war. This war may be based on religion, class, social inequality, a desire for a better world, or other justifications—all seen through the filters created by the groups themselves, of course. If we look at the literature of these groups, we see references to their raisons d'être through the lens of war.

Whether or not we should also refer to counterterrorism operations as war is controversial. Many have suggested that by using martial vocabulary we are inflating the importance of terrorist groups, very few of which can muster any kind of "army" and even fewer of which have any hope of taking and holding territory, as regularly happens in wartime. This debate was particularly heated in the wake of the November 2015 Islamic State–directed (or at least inspired) attacks in Paris and the subsequent declaration of war on IS by French president François Hollande. In the first quarter of 2016 major Canadian media pundits argued back and forth as to whether or not the new Trudeau government should overtly declare that Canada is at war with IS.

Here are a few examples of how terrorist groups see themselves as armies engaged in actual warfare:

- Horst Mahler of the German Rote Armee Fraktion described his group's actions thus: "We were from our point of view in something like a war. It was in order to be able to face the problem of death that we defined ourselves as soldiers."[14]

- Former Al Qaeda leader Osama Bin Laden, in his declaration of the creation of the World Islamic Front in February 1996, said that "All these American crimes and sins are a clear pronouncement of war against God, his Messenger, and the Muslims. Religious scholars throughout Islamic history have agreed that jihad is an individual duty when an enemy attacks Muslim countries."[15]
- According to Daniel Baracskay, the Palestinian Liberation Organization's "ideological platform rests on the concept of armed struggle by the masses designed to advance a popular liberation war and worldwide revolution."[16] And of course IS, which sees itself as a state and the kernel of the worldwide caliphate, regularly uses war metaphors to justify its actions. The following quotations were taken from one single issue of its flagship magazine, *Dabiq*, issue no. 8, "Shari'ah Alone Will Rule Africa":

  - "We perform jihad so that Allah's word becomes supreme and that the religion becomes completely for Allah . . . everyone who opposes this goal or stands in the path of this goal is an enemy for us and a target for our swords."
  - "War is entirely predictable in that it can only lead to one of two outcomes. Either one side emerges victorious while the other is vanquished, or some kind of truce is reached. It is the only way wars end, and America and its allies will never win this war."
  - "As the battle in Libya continues to intensify, the Islamic State enjoys greater consolidation . . . the armies of the Khilafah continue marching forward to liberate new regions."

Again, terrorist groups are convinced that they are at war and that their cause is just or evenly divinely ordained. War, they say, is a necessary phase that will usher in a better world (recall that US president Thomas Jefferson famously said, "The tree of liberty must be refreshed from time to time with the blood of patriots and tyrants."). Furthermore, groups like IS and AQ see their participation in war as a response to aggression on the part of the enemy. In what has been called the single (or common) narrative, these groups have claimed that it is the West that has initiated a grand war on Islam and on Muslims. As a consequence, "true" Muslims are merely defending themselves from a host bent on their destruction. They add that their war has divine sanction and, as we shall see in the next chapter, fighting is a divine obligation placed on all good Muslims.

Chapter 2

THE ROLE OF IDEOLOGY

No matter how we choose to define *terrorism*—and there are many, many definitions worldwide—one element of our understanding of the term that must be present is ideology. Terrorism is an act of serious violence—usually against people but sometimes against inanimate objects, such as buildings or infrastructure—that is carried out for an idea. It can be any idea—religious, political, socioeconomic, etc. If you remove the ideological basis of terrorism, you are simply left with violence. The vast majority of crimes of a violent nature are not terrorism, because they are not executed to further a cause. They may be motivated by passion or money, or perhaps they are executed under the influence of drugs or alcohol, or in some cases people are violent "for the hell of it"—but they are not also ideological in nature.

A whole range of ideologies can be found underlying terrorist movements. Far-right terrorism is usually aimed at those deemed to belong to an inferior race or religion in the belief that one race (usually but not exclusively white) is superior. Leftist terrorism often targets capitalism or greed. Extremist settler movements in Israel will kill to protect the land they believed God gave to the Jewish people. Single-issue terrorism will attack abortion clinics or mink farms. And of course there is the Al Qaeda brand of terrorism, which most people will agree poses the single greatest threat today.

By the time this book is published, and even while the research was ongoing, Al Qaeda will have been supplanted by Islamic State as an inspiration for many, including those in the West, to adopt violent extremist ideology (although it is a mistake to count AQ out). But, while there are minor differences between the groups, especially on an operational footing, the bulk of the underpinning worldview is the same. Whether we call it Al Qaeda–inspired or Islamic State–inspired is irrelevant to our discussion.

This type of terrorism is based on the notion that the Islamic world is under attack from the West, which has been its sworn enemy for almost a millennium and a half. In response to this Western aggression, "true" Muslims have a divine mandate to fight back. It is this divine sanction that is the crux of Islamist terrorism. Yes, it is true that there are also political and socioeconomic issues behind the violence, but the religious motivation is primary. Fail to understand it and you fail to grasp this particular brand of terrorism.

Jihad is the term the extremists use to describe this type of violence. I do not intend to rehash the longstanding debate on the "true" meaning of jihad. Suffice to say that it has multiple aspects and that agreement on any one is not forthcoming. In the end, in a book on violence it is sufficient to deal solely with the violent definition and ignore the others.

There is no doubt that extremist groups see jihad as war. They are quick to eschew the interpretation that there is a nonviolent aspect to jihad, rejecting these meanings as false and un-Islamic. We see this obsession in the very names they give themselves, either through the use of the word *jihad* itself or some reference to war. Here are but a few examples:

- Egyptian Islamic Jihad
- Harakat ul-Jihad-i-Islami (Islamic Jihad Movement)—Bangladesh
- Indian Mujahideen
- Islamic Jihad Union—Afghanistan
- Jaish-e-Mohammed (Army of Mohammed)—Pakistan
- Jama'at at-Tawhid wal-Jihad (Organization of Monotheism and Jihad)—Iraq (former group led by Abu Musab al-Zarqawi)
- Jundallah (Army of God)—Baluchistan (in southwest Iran)
- Lashkar-e-Jhangvi (Army of Jhangvi)—Pakistan
- Lashkar-e-Taiba (Army of the Pure)—Pakistan
- Palestinian Islamic Jihad

In order to help justify violence in the name of Allah, extremist ideologues and leaders need to present authentic texts that support their arguments. Fortunately—for the extremists, that is—there is no shortage of material. This documentation stretches back all the way to the Quran and extends to the Islamic State's *Dabiq* magazine. This chapter examines some of these sources (others can be found in the appendix) and shows how they demonstrate that (violent) jihad *fi sabilallah* (in the name of God) is mandatory for all Muslims.

Some might say that none of this is important and that it's all just words. No one today pays attention to what some guy said back in the early fourteenth century CE, do they, let alone seventh-century revelations? In issue 14 of *Inspire* magazine, the chief online organ of Al Qaeda in the Arabian Peninsula, the editors offered "Words of Wisdom" from such "luminaries" as Anwar al-Awlaki (killed in 2011 in a US drone strike in Yemen), Sayyid Qutb (hanged by the Egyptian government in 1966), and Abu Musab al-Zarqawi (killed in a US airstrike in Iraq in 2006). Death seems to have had little impact on their messaging. It is as important now as it was when first uttered or written. Other groups cite the Quran or thirteenth-century ideologues or eighteenth-century like-minded scholars who helped frame the violent aspects of jihad. Words and concepts do matter.

What is clear is that a long history of exegesis on the meaning and importance of jihad still has an impact today. In my more than thirty years of experience as an intelligence analyst I came across references to individuals long dead whose views and writings influence today's extremists. It is thus critical to examine that history. Even if each individual traveling along a path to violent radicalization did not have access to, or consume, this material, chances are strong that someone in that person's ambit probably did. It is frequent that a "radicalizer" will use the material we are about to examine to convince others that what they are doing is justified.

Even when limiting oneself to the violent aspects of jihad, there is much latitude in what is acceptable and what is not, what is mandatory and what is optional. We shall see these differences as we move through the centuries. Violent groups are, however, very adept at cherry-picking justifications for their actions and intentions. You may have heard the term *cafeteria Catholics*—those who elect what doctrine to follow as if they were at a buffet line. Islamist extremists are "cafeteria Muslims."

The appendix to this book contains a very detailed survey of religious sources for jihad, ranging from Quranic verses to the words of the Islamic State. Here a few examples to provide context for what we encounter in chapter 3.

THE QURAN

The Quran, the divinely dictated message to the Prophet Muhammad from 610 to 632 CE, is the bulwark of Islam and has guided and inspired billions since the middle of the seventh century CE. This holy text is not very long: a mere 114 chapters (called *suras*) of varying length, and not listed in chronological order (this becomes very important, as we shall see below).

The text covers events both contemporary—that is, during the lifetime of the Prophet Muhammad—as well as atemporal. Believers of Judaism and Christianity will see many stories and characters familiar from the Torah and the Old and New Testaments (e.g., Adam and Eve, Abraham, Moses, Jesus, and Mary, among others).

But when it comes to jihad or fighting, there are actually few verses that can be used, or have frequently been used, by extremists to justify violence. Some of these verses are listed below (the usual method of citing a Quranic verse is to list the sura—or chapter—followed by the ayah—the verse). Note that there are more verses that mention jihad to one extent or another.[17] This list should be seen as representative and not exhaustive. A larger list can be found in the appendix.

- [8:39] "*Shakir*: And fight with them until there is no more persecution and religion should be only for *Allah*; but if they desist, then surely *Allah* sees what they do."
- [9:029] "Fight those who do not believe in *Allah*, nor in the latter day, nor do they prohibit what *Allah* and His Apostle have prohibited, nor follow the religion of truth, out of those who have been given the Book, until they pay the tax in acknowledgment of superiority and they are in a state of subjection."

- [22:039] "Permission (to fight) is given to those upon whom war is made because they are oppressed, and most surely *Allah* is well able to assist them."
- [47:004] "So when you meet in battle those who disbelieve, then smite the necks until when you have overcome them, then make (them) prisoners, and afterwards either set them free as a favor or let them ransom (themselves) until the war terminates. That (shall be so); and if *Allah* had pleased He would certainly have exacted what is due from them, but that He may try some of you by means of others; and (as for) those who are slain in the way of *Allah*, He will by no means allow their deeds to perish."

There is a tremendous amount of material here, and in the appendix and it would take an entire volume to discuss all the meaning and implications of each verse. Nevertheless, there are three aspects I wish to briefly touch on, as they relate to how violent extremists are able to use the Quran to justify to themselves, and to others, that jihad is divinely ordained.

- Like all (religious) texts, context is very important. (To cite but two examples from other faiths, in Matthew 10:34 Jesus says, "Think not that I am come to send peace on earth: I came not to send peace, but a sword," while in 2 Chronicles 15:12–13 we are told that "they entered into a covenant to seek the Lord , the God of their fathers, with all their heart and with all their soul, but that whoever would not seek the Lord, the God of Israel, should be put to death, whether young or old, man or woman.") The Quran was revealed over a twenty-plus-year span, and events unfolding at the time must be taken into consideration. Nevertheless, the Quran is seen by Muslims as an eternal message and thus should be applied in a continuous manner. So, while some scholars will argue that a given verse refers only to a historic event and should be seen through a historic lens, extremists counter that the book applies everywhere and at every time and that current circumstances dictate the need for jihad. There is also no single consensus as to what a given verse means, and extremists exploit this lack of unanimity.
- Scholars have determined that there are two principle types of suras in the Quran: those revealed while the Prophet Muhammad was in Mecca and those revealed while he was in Medina. The former do not talk about fighting as much as the latter. This difference should be seen in the context of concurrent events: the embryonic Muslim community was much stronger in Medina than in Mecca, and a series of successful battles following the displacement of the Muslim community to Medina led to growth in confidence and power. Jihad began to be seen as a divinely inspired way to both defend and expand the Muslim faith vis-à-vis its

enemies. Not surprisingly, extremists will focus on those verses revealed during a time of strength.

- There is much in the Quran that is contradictory. Allah will say one thing in one sura and appear to reverse His position in another. Scholars have devised a concept called *Naskh* ("abrogation") in which one (later) verse supersedes another (earlier) verse. Extremists have taken advantage of this when faced with criticism over their use of violence.

When you read material from violent groups like Al Qaeda or the Islamic State you will see many Quranic verses spread through the texts. It is important for these groups that they can prove that their use of violence is divinely sanctioned. Their use of the Quran is not trivial.

THE HADITHS

Another primary source of inspiration and guidance for Muslims is the hadiths. These are sayings and actions related to the life of the Prophet Muhammad. As the Quran is relatively short, the hadiths supplement the revealed text and provide wisdom on topics not (fully) covered in the Quran. Here is a sampling of hadiths that speak of jihad (a longer list can be found in the appendix):

- "Upon his return from battle Muhammad said, 'We have returned from the lesser *jihad* to the greater *jihad* [i.e., the struggle against the evil of one's soul].'"
- "A man came to the Prophet and asked, 'A man fights for war booty; another fights for fame and a third fights for showing off; which of them fights in Allah's Cause?' The Prophet said, 'He who fights that Allah's Word [i.e., Islam] should be superior, fights in Allah's Cause.'"
- "I asked the Prophet, 'What is the best deed?' He replied, 'To believe in Allah and to fight for His Cause.'"

Again, as with the verses of the Quran, it is not the intent here to go into a detailed discussion on these hadiths or any others. It is important to note, however, that the nature of hadith collection and interpretation does provide extremists with an opportunity to quote the authority of the Prophet Muhammad when they speak of the necessity of jihad.

There are tens of thousands of hadiths. Most Muslims recognize a few collections as more authoritative than others (Al Muslim and Al Bukhari collections are the most commonly cited). Nevertheless, there are many more. Complicating matters is the lack of agreement as to which hadiths are valid and which are not. Again, the vast majority of Muslims adhere to a strict line of reporting (called *isnad*) tying a hadith to a reliable witness/ reporter. There remains serious disagreement, however, over which source is more reliable than another. Extremists exploit this gray zone to use the words of the Prophet Muhammad to condone their actions.

Taking the first hadith I mentioned as an example—"Upon his return from battle Muhammad said, 'We have returned from the lesser *jihad* to the greater *jihad* (i.e., the struggle against the evil of one's soul)'"—it seems that the Prophet saw one's efforts (remember that at its root *jihad* means "effort" or "struggle") to be a better Muslim as more important than one's efforts in battle. This of course has huge implications for how Muslims run their lives. Extremists counter that the Prophet never said this and that, hence, the advice is invalid. According to them, the hadith is weak and cannot be attributed to the Prophet. If this particular hadith is seen as invalid, "true" Muslims (as seen through the lens of violent extremists) will focus on violent jihad.

It is the combination of the Quran and the hadith that provides much ammunition to extremists. The ability to cite divine and prophetic authority to show that violent jihad is ordained can be used to convince hundreds or thousands that they should fight. The battle to counter these interpretations is a difficult one.

ISLAMIC STATE

As much of the focus in this book relates to Islamic State (IS), it is illustrative to examine how this terrorist group sees jihad as war and uses sources, both authentic and some less so, to recruit fighters. It is no exaggeration that IS has exploited social media and the Internet more than any other terrorist group in history. Part of this is mere juxtaposition: IS soared onto the international scene as social-media platforms proliferated. IS has used YouTube, Facebook, Twitter, WhatsApp, and probably every other tool to spread its message, claim victory, boast of its prowess, and recruit. Whole books have been dedicated to what has been called "e-jihad." There is no easy way to treat IS's use of these media, so I will limit the discussion to their views on jihad as expressed in their magazine, *Dabiq*.

DABIQ

As of October 2015, eleven issues of *Dabiq* have appeared. The word "Dabiq" refers to a site in northern Syria where an important battle was fought between the Ottomans and the Mamluk Sultanate in 1516 and is also where an epic battle of good versus evil will be fought between Christians and Muslims leading to End Times. *Dabiq* is professionally edited and has high production values. Most issues contain a combination of text and imagery and cover topics ranging from Islamic jurisprudence to accounts of IS military victories to interviews with mujahideen.

Not surprisingly, in view of the IS interpretation of Islam and its interpretation of history and world events, combined with its vision of the future, jihad features frequently in the pages of *Dabiq*. Here are a few excerpts:

- [Issue 8] "We do not perform jihad here for a fistful of dirt or an illusory border drawn up by Sykes and Picot. Similarly, we do not perform jihad for a Western *taghut* ["evil ruler"] to take the place of an Arab *taghut*. Rather our jihad is loftier and more superior. We perform jihad so that Allah's word becomes supreme and that the religion (i.e., Islam) becomes completely for Allah. . . . Everyone who opposes this goal or stands in the path of this goal is an enemy for us."
- [Issue 8, cont.] "The mujahideen in West Africa continue to wage jihad against the enemies of Allah in a land that contains a large population of hostile crusaders. The Christian masses in Nigeria, mostly contained in the southern portion of the country and comprising less than half the population, have not shied away from massacring the Muslims of West Africa."
- [Issue 8, cont.] "The Islamic State has taken it upon itself to fulfill the *Ummah*'s duty . . . to face the crusaders and their allies in defense of Islam and to raise high the word of Allah in every land."
- [Issue 8, cont., interview with Abu Muqatil, regarding French Muslims] "I call them to wake up and fight the enemies of Allah for Allah's cause. . . . Kill anybody. All the *kuffar* ["unbelievers"] over there are targets. Don't tire yourself and look for difficult targets. Kill whoever is over there from the *kuffar*."
- [Issue 3] "As for the Muslim students who use this same pretense now to continue abandoning the obligation of the era, then they should know that their *hijrah* ["migration"] from the *darul-kuffar* ["land of disbelief"] to the *darul islam* ["Islamic world"] and jihad are obligatory and urgent."
- [Issue 3, cont.] "So abandoning *hijrah*—the path to jihad—is a dangerous matter."
- [Issue 3, cont.] "There is no solution for it except by taking the first step towards jihad—*hijrah*."
- [Issue 3, cont.] "Jihad not only grants life on the larger scale of the *Ummah*, it also grants a fuller life on the scale of the individual."
- [Issue 11] "Message to the people of the Balkans: Honor is in jihad."
- [Issue 11, cont.] "This is Ramadan! This is how as-Salaf as-Salih ["the Righteous Predecessors"] were in it! Jihad, battles, and action, as well as support and victory from Allah."
- [Issue 11, cont.] "The months of Ramadan were days of jihad and battles. In these months many Islamic expeditions, battles and victories occurred that history would never forget."

- [Issue 10] "If jihad becomes obligatory upon him then the permission of his parents is not taken into consideration because the jihad has become *fard ` ayn* ["individual obligation"] and abandonment of it is a sin. There is no obedience to anyone in disobedience of Allah."
- [Issue 10, cont.] "The scholars mentioned numerous cases that make jihad against the *kuffar fard 'ayn*, including the imprisonment of Muslims, the imminent threat of attack against the Muslims, and the faceoff of the opposing armies."
- [Issue 1] "The sun of jihad has risen. The glad tidings of good are shining. Triumph looms on the horizon. The signs of victory have appeared."

This is but a very small sample of what IS puts out as propaganda. While *Dabiq* is an important vehicle, it is dwarfed by the tweets followers put out every day. (By mid-2015, Twitter had shut down more than 125,000 accounts, most of them linked to IS, that were used to promote terrorism.[18]) All these media use religious imagery to entice Muslims to join IS and engage in violent jihad.

SUMMARY

States and organizations will go to war for a variety of reasons. Some combatants are the aggressors: others see themselves as the victims of aggression, forced to resort to war to defend their lands and their ways of life. It is not uncommon to see recruitment drives that urge people to join the cause in order to "protect our freedoms" or "defeat evil." Terrorist groups in particular emphasize their position as the aggrieved, engaging in war reluctantly in response to violence visited upon them by states and societies.

Whatever the proffered reason for war, governments and organizations also need to convince their citizens and members to sign up. I recall a TV commercial in the 1960s or early 1970s produced by an antiwar group in which the leaders of two countries that wanted to wage war were forced to square off in a boxing ring to decide the victor rather than send millions of men to their deaths (shades of David and Goliath). Such an event would of course be preferable to the wanton loss of life in modern warfare, but states would not want to see that happen. As a result, they need to develop propaganda and other ways to elicit interest in their populations to agree to fight (note that we will not talk about coercive methods like conscription here). Terrorist groups are no different: Islamic State in particular has been very effective in using social media to attract followers.

It is not the intent of this book to examine propaganda and recruitment strategies used by either governments or terrorist organizations. The focus here will lie with why individuals make the choices they do and elect to volunteer for war. The next two chapters will do exactly that, delving into why ordinary men (actually mostly but not exclusively men) take up arms, whether they do so for a recognized state in a sanctioned war or for an extremist group.

NOTES

1. Glenn Hodges, "Tracking the First Americans," *National Geographic* 227, no. 1 (January 2015): 127, http://ngm.nationalgeographic.com/2015/01/first-americans/hodges-text.

2. Zulfikar Abbany, "Early Neolithic Mass Grave Reveals New Evidence of a Violent Age in Central Europe," Deutsche Welle, August 17, 2015, http://www.dw.com/en/early-neolithic-mass-grave-reveals-new-evidence-of-a-violent-age-in-central-europe/a-18654313.

3. James Gorman, "Prehistoric Massacre Hints at War among Hunter-Gatherers," *New York Times*, January 20, 2016, http://www.nytimes.com/2016/01/21/science/prehistoric-massacre-ancient-humans-lake-turkana-kenya.html.

4. Curtis W. Marean, "The Most Invasive Species of All," *Scientific American* 313 (August 1, 2015): 32–39, doi:10.1038/scientificamerican0815-32.

5. Glyn Williams, "Trouble in Paradise," review of *Paradise of the Pacific*, by Susanna Moore, *Wall Street Journal*, August 28, 2015, C8, http://www.wsj.com/articles/trouble-in-paradise-1440790094. Emphasis added.

6. Steven Kreis, "Lecture 6: Europe in the Age of Religious Wars, 1560–1715," The History Guide, accessed June 23, 2015, http://www.historyguide.org/earlymod/lecture6c.html.

7. Matthew White, "Selected Death Tolls for Wars, Massacres, and Atrocities before the 20th Century," Necrometrics, accessed June 24, 2015, http://necrometrics.com/pre1700a.htm.

8. Jeremy Bender and Amanda Macias, "5 of the 10 Deadliest Wars Began in China," Business Insider, October 6, 2014, http://www.businessinsider.com/bloodiest-conflicts-in-chinese-history-2014-10.

9. Steven Pinker, *Better Angels of Our Nature: Why Violence Has Declined* (New York: Viking, 2011).

10. Joshua S. Goldstein, *Winning the War on War* (New York: Penguin Books, 2011), 4, emphasis original.

11. John Andrews, "More War than Peace," in "The World in 2016," ed. Daniel Franklin, special issue, *The Economist* (2015): 88, entire issue available online at http://www.theworldin.com/article/10447/world-2016.

12. Ian Morris, *War! What Is It Good For? Conflict and the Progress of Civilization from Primates and Robots* (New York: Farrar, Straus and Giroux, 2014).

13. Philip Jenkins, *The Great and Holy War: How World War I Became a Religious Crusade* (San Francisco: HarperOne, 2014).

14. Mikkel Thorup, *An Intellectual History of Terror: War, Violence and the State* (New York: Routledge, 2010), 23.

15. Bruce Lawrence, ed., *Messages to the World: The Statements of Osama Bin Laden*, intro. Bruce Lawrence, trans. James Howarth (London and New York: Verso, 2005), 60.

16. Daniel Baracskay, *The Palestine Liberation Organization: Terrorism and Prospects for Peace in the Holy Land* (Santa Barbara, CA: Praeger, 2011), 8.

17. For a complete list of 164 that deal with the topic, see Yoel Natan, "164 Jihad Verses in the Koran," compiled 2004, accessed July 6, 2015, Answering Islam, http://www.answering-islam.org/Quran/Themes/jihad_passages.html.

18. Yasmeen Abutaleb, "Twitter Suspends Over 125,000 Accounts for 'Promoting Terrorist Acts,'" Reuters, February 5, 2016, http://www.reuters.com/article/us-twitter-islamic-state-idUSKCN0VE2GM.

Chapter Three

The Decision to Volunteer for War

THE GLORY OF WAR

Thus came the war. For Canada it came out of a clear sky—the clear sky of vacation time, of the glory of the Canadian summer, of summer cottages and bush camps; and for the city population the soft evening sky, the canopy of stars over the merry-go-round resorts in the cool of the summer evening.
—Stephen Leacock, Canadian humorist

Nobody fights for a flag. . . . Nobody fights for a king. You fight for your sergeant. You fight for your squad. You fight for your land. That's what you're taught.
—Matt Liness, Canadian War of 1812 reenactor

CHAPTER ABSTRACT

In this chapter we examine the reasons why individuals made the decision to enlist in military action, whether or not the war was sanctioned or encouraged by the state. We exclude mercenaries or conscripted soldiers from our discussion: the former join up largely for money as professional fighters, and the latter do not choose to fight (they do not volunteer: they are "voluntold"). The wars discussed in this section include World War I, wars post–9/11, the Spanish Civil War, the Vietnam War, and various actions that involved volunteers with Kurdish battalions in Iraq as well as those with the Israeli Defense Forces.

CAUTIONARY NOTE

Why do people radicalize to violence? It's a question without an easy answer. There are "too many whys," as I have stated, and the individual nature of violent radicalization precludes simple modeling. Thus asking *how* is superior—and partially answerable—to asking *why*.

If this is true, as I still believe it to be, then how can I ask *why* in this book? Surely the reasons a person would have for traveling to a foreign country to fight with a terrorist organization are as complex as the steps in the radicalization process, which usually precedes this mobilization. Right? Probably. And yet I think there is a subtle difference. Radicalization is a process; buying a ticket to join IS in Syria is a decision. The latter is somewhat easier to understand from a motivational perspective than the former, at least in my view. As we shall see, however, there will be some difficulty in drawing large-scale conclusions from the data we have. As when studying violent radicalization, there will be occasions where determining a specific reason why fighters choose to fight will be found wanting. After all, radicalization precedes signing up with IS and is clearly a part of that decision-making process. This field of study is not easy. At times we have to accept that we are dealing with how and why humans make choices, an area difficult if not impossible to predict.

On another matter, what can be gained by looking at conflicts divided by over a century? How can examining the Boer Wars of the late nineteenth century have anything interesting to say about today's war against IS? On the surface one could conclude that there is nothing similar in wars that span such a variety of societies, customs, mores, and eras. But wouldn't it be fascinating if there were commonalities in the reasons proffered by those who fought? If men elect to go to war for reasons that don't change over time, then that tells us something very interesting about the nature of enlistment, does it not? Then again, perhaps motivations have changed significantly. That too would be a valuable finding. So let us look at these very different wars to see if this is true.

SANCTIONED WARS: CANADA AND THE UNITED STATES AT WAR

Canada in World War I

Wherever you go in Canada—large cities, small towns, hamlets—you will find a cenotaph commemorating those who died in war. While most will mark all the wars Canada has fought, they were initially raised to mark the "Great War," and it is the World War I sections of these memorials that strike me most. Many surnames appear several times in the commemorations, suggesting that some families lost several sons to the battlefields of Europe. And it is important to underscore that the two terrorist attacks two days apart in October 2014 singled out military personnel, including the October 22 shooting of Corporal Nathan Cirillo as he stood honor guard at the Canadian National War Memorial in Ottawa, a memorial originally designed to mark on a national scale the sacrifice of Canadian soldiers in World War I. An attack on the *national* cenotaph is indeed iconic.

My November 2015 visit to northern France showed that the sacrifice of France's youth in World War I dwarfed that of Canada. Every town in France, no matter how small, has a memorial to those who perished between 1914 and 1918. I drove through tiny villages in Bretagne where the names on those granite markers probably outnumbered the extant population. Thousands of towns, hundreds of thousands of names.

Canada is not normally a militaristic nation. While we have participated—and sacrificed much blood and treasure—in a number of twentieth- and twenty-first-century wars, the period after the Korean War saw a shift from fighting to peacekeeping. My generation (I was born in 1960) viewed the Canadian military through the participation of the United Nations' "Blue Helmets," as Canada seemed to be at the forefront of peacekeeping operations around the globe. I remember that my uncle, who served in Europe in World War II, used to participate in the annual Warriors' Day Parade in Toronto; the use of the term *warrior* used to strike me as anachronistic. The post–9/11 era, however, has witnessed a reversal to a more aggressive image as Canada sent soldiers to Afghanistan and, more recently, Iraq. Members of the military are regularly feted at hockey, football, and baseball games, where they are accorded standing ovations, and iconic Hockey Night in Canada commentator Don Cherry never misses an opportunity to recognize soldiers who have fallen in battle. The former Harper government made every effort to recognize both Canada's military past as well as the sacrifices of current armed-forces personnel.

These recent shifts notwithstanding, a century ago things were very different. The importance of the First World War for Canada as a nation cannot be overemphasized. The battles still ring loud for Canadians a century later: Ypres, the Somme, Passchendaele, Vimy, Beaumont-Hamel. It has often been said that Canada became a country on the fields of Flanders and France. In April 2017, Canada will commemorate the Battle of Vimy Ridge: there is probably no more symbolic moment in our history.

And yet the cost was high. More than six hundred thousand Canadians fought in Europe. Sixty-one thousand died, and four-fifths of the total Canadian Expeditionary Force were listed as casualties (dead and wounded). The nation was divided over the issue of conscription in 1917 when the government realized that the number of volunteers did not meet its goals. And yet tens of thousands did volunteer. This section examines why.

Canada was a dominion within the British Empire and did not have the authority to act independently in international affairs in 1914 (it earned that right with the Statute of Westminster in 1931). Thus, when Great Britain declared war on Germany in August of that year, Canada was automatically included. If Britain was at war, Canada was at war. Not that the government of Prime Minister Robert Borden would have protested too much, since love for the empire was very strong in 1914. But as an "independent" dominion, Canada would determine the size and scale of its commitment. In Montreal, citizens sang both "Rule, Britannia!" and "La Marseillaise," and Canada had a vested interest in maintaining the prestige and power of both Britain and France.[1] When Minister of Militia Sam Hughes set an initial goal of twenty-five thousand volunteers, thirty-three thousand showed up. Although Canada was not well prepared for such a vast mobilization, the excitement over war had been growing throughout the summer of 1914 as conflict seemed inevitable.

As the horrors of trench warfare, gas, high-powered shells, and machine guns were still months away, a fever gripped Canada as thousands sought to sign up. Renowned Canadian historian Tim Cook described an "orgy of military pageantry" in streets across Canada as tens of thousands came out in support.[2] Eighteen-year-old Bert Remington said that "the country went mad! People were singing on the streets and roads."[3] The war was portrayed as one of good versus evil, liberty against despotic militarism, and British justice against German *kultur*.[4] Long lines of men sought to enlist, eager for a chance to serve king and country.[5] Many were turned away, as they did not meet the physical requirements: with so many clamoring to join, the authorities could be choosy. Some complained that a mere cough or flat feet should not be enough to keep them from participating in this "war for civilization."[6] There is even an apocryphal story of a toothless rejected recruit barking at officials that he wanted to "shoot Germans, not bite them."[7]

According to Cook, there was no single reason why Canadians decided to enlist by the tens of thousands. He describes a "range of allegiances" that overlapped: the excitement of war and the need to serve; a young man's desire for adventure; the justness of Canada's war effort; the pull of empire; and more mundane reasons—such as a rash decision in the wake of a few drinks with the boys.[8]

Cook provides a few quotations from volunteers that are particularly illustrative in this regard.

- Robert Christopherson: "I wanted to see the world, and I thought this would be a great opportunity. . . . I didn't see how else I was going to ever get out of Yorkton, Saskatchewan."
- Anonymous: "All idea of war and soldiering had long gone out of my mind, but it came to me like a flash that if ever there was a war that

appealed to the chivalry and patriotism of right-minded men, this one was."

- Alfred Andrews, a lawyer from Qu'Appelle, Saskatchewan, was railroaded by friends who pointed out that "I was Canadian born and had no ties; it was my duty to enlist."

- J. M. MacDonnell: "It seemed not only the natural thing to do but the inevitable thing to do."[9]

Men under the age of eighteen needed parental permission, and many tried to enlist, having been weaned on stories of military bravery. There was also an incentive to escape unhappy home situations, get a break from manual labor in the factories or mines, or merely embrace their "emerging masculinity."[10] According to Cook, "hungerscription" led some to enlist as men sought employment after several economically depressed years.[11]

Many of the first volunteers were recent British immigrants who presumably had close ties to their country of birth and may have come to regret the harshness of their new life in Canada. According to Cook, almost two-thirds of the thirty thousand–plus men in the first contingent of the Canadian Expeditionary Force were born in Britain,[12] many of whom had previous military experience and would have been welcomed by recruiting officers.

Some were moved by the accounts of atrocities—true or not—committed by the Germans on the Belgian population. In what may be an incredible—and horrific—foreshadowing of the actions of Islamic State, stories abounded about burned libraries (IS destruction of ancient sites), outrages against women (IS use of slavery and rape), babies skewered on bayonets and summary executions (for which IS is all too well known). Georges Vanier, who later became governor-general, wrote, "I could not read the accounts of Belgian sufferings without a deep compassion and an active desire to right, as far as it was in my power, the heinous wrong done."[13]

Canadian First Nations also felt the allure of war, whether as an extension of their warrior traditions or in the hope that by serving they would win greater rights for their people.[14] By the end of the conflict, four thousand First Nation volunteers had enlisted.

Even the National Hockey Association, the precursor to the National Hockey League, got involved. Propaganda posters appeared in which soldiers at the front urged their hockey buddies to come and join the fray. Men were encouraged to show the same tenacity in the trenches as they did on the ice. One-eyed Frank McGee, an early superstar who played for the famous Ottawa Silver Seven, enlisted in 1915 and died in 1916 near Courcelette in the Battle of the Somme.

In the end, the war was seen as a war of defense, "both to keep the Hun at bay and to defend the liberal, democratic ideals that underpinned the sovereignty of the nation and the British Empire."[15]

The Canadian Letters and Images Project[16] locates, preserves, and presents to the Canadian public the experiences of Canadians at war. They have a collection of letters written by Canadian soldiers from all wars dating back to the nineteenth-century Riel Rebellion. The men describe conditions and challenges of the fight overseas. On occasion, the letters offer explanations for why they enlisted. In some ways, it is surprising that we can learn anything in light of wartime censorship of letters from the front.[17] Here are some excerpts from the letters collected by the Canadian Letters and Images Project:

- Alfred Herbert John Andrews: "When war broke out on August 4th, 1914, I was spending holidays at Gimli, Manitoba. The papers were full of the 'Calls for Men.' I did not think very seriously of it, till a conference was held in the office at which it was pointed out that as I was Canadian born and had no ties, it was my duty to enlist. I was suffering from a rupture, sustained playing football, and gave that as an excuse for not enlisting. However, people kept asking me to enlist with and others asked if I intended to go, until I couldn't stand it any longer and on August 27th, 1914, I made up my mind to enlist. I was at a party at Mrs. St. Louis' home that evening when someone made a statement about enlisting. Theo. Gunn said, 'I'd enlist if anyone would go with me.' I told him I was going to join the Fort Garry Horse in the morning and he said he'd come with me. I don't think he wanted to go but he was game and wouldn't back down."[18]
- Reverend William Beattie, "My work as chaplain is most gratifying, I am more than ever satisfied that I have done what God wanted me to do in coming with these boys. I have had more opportunity of doing good here in three weeks than I could have in Cobourg in a year. These weeks at sea are giving me a chance to get into personal touch with the boys and to bring spiritual truth and comfort to them, which will be hard to repeat when the busy life ashore begins. Every night I go below and have a service or spend the time in leading them individually to Christ. God has given me scores of souls for my hire."[19]
- William Howard Curtis: "The Germans got pretty close to England last week and fired on defenceless places. It's murder, not war, the way they fight and their spies are everywhere. A large number of the killed and wounded were children and women. This will show the rest of the world what barbarians the Germans are. This war is no picnic for England. The Kaiser cannot frighten the people so that they will keep their troops home. Instead he has only inspired more and more recruits to enlist."[20]
- John "Jack" Davey: "I hope you are not mad at me for joining this crowd I had no idea of joining when I left you on the Tuesday night or at least not so soon, but when I got in town I went around to see the bulletins the

crowd were so excited & the notice was in the window saying the 88th wanted recruits so I went down & enlisted."[21]

- Kenneth Walter Foster: "It was in April of 1915 that the good ship 'Lusitania' was torpedoed by a German submarine and many persons lost their lives and a lot of ill feeling was created amongst the people of Victoria against the German element residing there; for no sooner had the so-called victory been made known when they began celebrating on behalf of their fellow-countrymen, a very foolish thing to do for the troops stationed there were very indignant over the affair and proved that such a thing was quite out of order by raiding and putting them out of business forever. It was now my one ambition to join up right away so that I could get to France before the war was over, so I went to the recruiting station and offered by services to my country and to help right a great wrong which we believe had been done by the War Lords of the warring nations."[22]

- Alexander Matier: "You say you wondered why I broke off all communication, which I can explain, I felt that I was not only making a fool out of myself, but bringing trouble to my people and it would be better for everybody concerned if I was to make myself scarce, so after I lost my position in Boston, I applied to an employment agent in Boston, who was a Spanish-American War Veteran, he secured me a position in Canada on the Trans-continental Rly. which was then building, I done well there, as I was away from all temptation, it was something like 300 miles to the nearest town when I came down the line I felt sure my old failing would not bother me, and I had planned to return to the States but in three weeks I was as bad as ever, I will not go into details and tell you my experiences after that, but I can assure you that I have profited by them, and now have myself well in hand, you might think it a late day for me to wake up & realize I was ruining my life, and really I do not blame you, but while there is life there is hope, and I am sure the future will find me a different living man in every respect."[23]

One of the more interesting accounts—written in hindsight—explaining why Canadians volunteered in World War I can be found in the memoirs of Charles Henry Savage, who was born in 1892 and enlisted in Quebec in February 1915. His words are worth citing at length.

> It is always interesting to ask a volunteer why he enlisted. Probably the only answer that you will not get is that he did it out of patriotism. One seldom hears a soldier use that word. King and country, the Old Flag, the mighty British Empire are phrases that slip so readily from some people's lips that one is inclined to think that they come from no great depth—certainly not from as far down as the heart. The average man may feel deeply about these matters but he does not like to hear them shouted from the housetop. Generally he despises the shouters: he is embarrassed for them: they make him slightly sick.

Some enlisted for adventure, or because they were fed up and wanted a change; while the fear of being thought afraid probably consciously or unconsciously influenced many. I think, however, that the great majority of us enlisted because we felt that—whether we liked it or not—we were committed to a great war, and that other men were being killed doing a job that was as much our duty as theirs. It is all very well to be protected by a regular army, but no able-bodied red-blooded man can sit contentedly at home while his neighbour goes out to do his fighting for him. And so we "joined the army."[24]

Those Who Refused to Fight

Not everyone was excited about the prospect of war. Aside from farmers worried about their crops and a general lack of interest in francophone Canada, World War I was remarkable for the number of conscientious objectors. In her book *Crisis of Conscience: Conscientious Objection in Canada during the First World War*, Amy J. Shaw noted that many young men refused to enlist when conscription was enacted in 1917 "because of religious or ethical beliefs that forbade killing or, often, joining the military in any capacity."[25] Some Canadians belonged to sects that had protection under orders-in-council for their pacifist beliefs, including the Society of Friends, the Mennonites, and the Doukhobors.[26] In Canada, membership in a recognized pacifist sect trumped personal belief, and as a result many who made exemption claims were rejected.[27] Local tribunals set up to hear cases of conscientious objection were often staffed by local prominent people who had sons at the front in Europe, thus creating another obstacle to those seeking understanding and support for their beliefs.

Objectors tended to use language such as "Ambassador of Christ," "citizen of heaven," or "only temporarily here on Earth."[28] Some officials were skeptical about the applications of those who did not want to fight. One tribunal member commented that an affidavit was "on a printed form. That looks too much like an organized attempt to evade military service."[29] Despite the difficulties in the appeals process, in addition to the personal attacks on character and masculinity (see below), the vast majority of those conscripted sought exemption. By the end of 1917 (the first year of conscription), of the 404,395 Canadians who reported for duty, 380,510 had sought exemption (almost 95 percent). In Quebec, where conscription was most hated, one hundred fifteen thousand of one hundred seventeen thousand draftees sought a way out (98 percent).[30] All in all, by the end of the war, of the more than three hundred thousand cases heard, eighty-six thousand Canadians were granted exemption.[31]

Given the reception that conscientious objectors had at the hands—and lips—of other Canadians, it is a wonder that any went public with their beliefs. Those unwilling to fight were called many uncharitable names, including coward, unpatriotic, effeminate, antidemocratic, and "too proud to fight." Some were even accused of being pro-German; some were given a white feather, which was a sign of cowardice. Accounts in leading Canadian journals at the time illustrate just how unworthy these objectors were seen. *Saturday Night* wrote that "They're a long-haired, weak-chinned, narrow-shouldered, open-jawed lot. Physical development has been retarded by the overwhelming demands of mental turgescence. The only evidence of physical growth is in their hair. . . . The spiritual exaltation induced by such a mass of airy-fairy inflation enervates the other muscles by disuse. The conscientious objector is a human fish—largely air bladder, without need for arms and legs."[32]

The allusion to arrogance can be seen in a *Manitoba Free Press* article from 1917. "It seems to me," the author of the article wrote, "that the conscientious objectors are suffering from the same mental malady that afflicts the Germans. In one case the patients think so highly of their spiritual and mental attainments that they want to force their habit of thought and style of living on the whole world."[33]

What can we say then about the hundreds of thousands that willingly went to the Western Front at the outbreak of war? The main drivers appear to be patriotism, a sense of duty to the king and the British Empire, and a desire for adventure. Pro-British feeling was strong in Canada in 1914, and for many that would have been enough to sign up for the army. As with most things, however, it is likely that most men had mixed motivations for volunteering.

WAR POST–9/11

For my brothers' generation their I-remember-where-I-was-when event was the assassination of US president John F. Kennedy. His death has been described by some as the day America lost its innocence. For me, that moment was the attack on the World Trade Center's twin towers on September 11, 2001.[34] A lot has changed since then.

This act of war against the United States led to the decision to send troops to Afghanistan to seek and destroy Al Qaeda, the perpetrators of that infamy, as well as to the beginning of the "War on Terror." It was certainly not the first attack against US interests from Islamist extremists led or inspired by AQ. The US embassies in Kenya and Tanzania had been bombed in 1998, and a US naval vessel, the USS *Cole* had been targeted in Aden harbor in October 2000. And yet a brazen strike in the heart of the United States demanded a heightened reply.

The US military was, of course, already huge on 9/11. It certainly was large enough to go after Osama Bin Laden in Afghanistan. And yet the destruction and death of that day led many to sign up to join the army. Here are a few of their stories.

- Casey Owens of South Carolina was inspired by 9/11. "That's one of the main reasons I want to go into the military," he said. "To help fight for freedom and make sure it doesn't happen again."[35]
- Tim Freeman, also of South Carolina, promised himself he would join the military when he came of age. "9/11 brought me closer to my country," said Freeman. "It showed me the door to the Marine Corps."[36]
- Stewart Gaskins of Bowie, Maryland, lost an uncle at the World Trade Center that day. He decided to become a Marine when he was thirteen. His reasons? "9/11 changed my mindset. . . . It changed something inside of me. It made me want to fight for my country. We all became vulnerable. It became real."[37]
- Army Sergeant Cheri Depenbrock has had a lot of experience in recruiting. Prior to 9/11, recruits would tell her that they were signing up "for college, for money, and for having a full-time job." Post–9/11 she found that "it was all about the patriotism. . . . They didn't care about anything else. Money had nothing do with it. I swear, I think half those kids would have joined if we hadn't paid them."[38]

There seems to be little question that those who volunteered to join the military after 9/11 did so in part because they felt the attacks personally; their homeland had been attacked, and their fellow citizens had been killed. War was necessary to seek the perpetrators and bring them to justice—or kill them. This war was very different from the war in Vietnam, where the military had been harder pressed to convince Americans that their country was at risk (hence the draft).

A terrorist attack had led to a surge in nationalism and a desire to get the bad guys. Have terrorist incidents since 9/11 been followed by similar hikes in enlistment? Interestingly, no. In the wake of the terrorist attacks in Paris in November 2015, the so-called millennials were in favor of sending US forces to battle IS (60 percent according to one poll) but much less keen to join the military themselves (16 percent, according to the same poll).[39] It will be interesting to see, moving forward, if this is part of a larger trend.

UNSANCTIONED WARS

Not all wars are ones in which nation-states pledge official support or in which a country sees vital interests at stake. In a country such as Canada, the government can declare war without the approval of Parliament, although it often will seek such backing. Nevertheless, Canadians have fought in wars where Canada neither had an official role nor saw its interests at risk. Governments have reacted in various ways to these conflicts, ranging from ignorance and disinterest to drafting legislation to prevent the departure of Canadians. These conflicts present an interesting insight into why people join wars absent government sanction or promotion. Volunteers make decisions knowing that what they are embarking upon is either illegal or frowned upon. And yet they take up arms.

In this section we examine five cases where Canadians—and others—elected to ignore their country's indifference or active opposition and join foreign conflicts. The cases include participation in the Second Boer War (1899–1902), the Spanish Civil War (1936–1939), and the Vietnam War (1960s–1975) and conscription to two foreign outfits—the Kurdish *peshmerga* and the Israeli Defense Forces.

The Second Boer War (1899–1902)

Paardeberg. Mafeking. Doornkop. Leliefontein. Largely forgotten places in South Africa. But to Canadians living in the early years of the twentieth century, these were battlegrounds where Canadian men were fighting for Mother England.

In my hometown of London, Ontario, there is a museum dedicated to the Royal Canadian Regiment, fourth battalion. I remember visiting the museum as a high school history student and went back in late 2015. The obelisk marking the battles in those four cities—Paardeberg, Mafeking, Doornkop, Leliefontein—is still a central focus of the grounds, and there are detailed exhibits on the fighting inside. And yet why would a Canadian museum mark a battle fought thousands of kilometers and over a century away?

When war broke out between England and the Boer Republics in South Africa, many English Canadians wanted their country to support the empire since the conflict pitted British freedom, justice, and civilization against Boer "backwardness."[40] It is important to remember as well that the war began shortly after the Diamond Jubilee of Queen Victoria, a highpoint of the empire.

The government of Wilfrid Laurier did not want to commit Canadian troops, however. While English Canada was in favor of such action, French-speaking Canada and recent non-British immigrants were not. For them, it made no sense to fight in a war half a world away.[41] So Laurier compromised: he agreed to send a battalion of volunteers; Canada would pay to transport the men to South Africa, at which point Britain would assume their costs. In all, more than seven thousand volunteered. Two hundred sixty-seven of them never came home.[42]

In his contemporaneous book, *With the Royal Canadians* , war correspondent Stanley McKeown Brown describes the atmosphere in Canada in 1899:

There was scarcely a town or hamlet in Canada, and certainly no city that was not all bustle and excitement when, in October 1899, the call to arms came. Each separate community was ready with its representatives, anxious to put down on the roll books as many names as possible, and disappointed in many cases when more could not be sent. The latent loyalty to the motherland showed itself in spontaneous outbursts that made the whole Dominion respond with the blare of music and the clank of arms. The recruiting stations were literally besieged with men, flushed with the enthusiasm that the enlistment of soldiers for Africa had caused throughout the length and breadth of all Canada. Men of all classes came. The banker vied with the farmer for a place in the lines and followers of all professions competed in every way with regular soldiers to be among the first to offer their services. . . . What unbounded disappointment was felt by some of those who were rejected at the recruiting points can best be remembered when one recalls the several cases of suicide consequent on that rejection. [43]

According to the Canadian War Museum, "Canadians developed a profound sense of distinctiveness from their imperial counterparts that nourished feelings of national pride and a sense of independent military identity."[44] These feelings would of course be magnified in World War I.

The Spanish Civil War (1936–1939)

Just across from the Old City Hall in Ottawa (a stone's throw from the prime minister's residence) stands a monument tucked away under a tree. A barefoot figure is silhouetted in a wrought-iron frame, fist raised, standing to the side of a curved concrete step. On the step are a series of brass plates with lists of names—1,546 of them. Even a brief examination of the lists is interesting—revealing a wide variety of backgrounds: Anglo-Saxon, Slavic, Finnish . . . Jacob Loch, William Morrow, Aleksii Mironiuk, Tauno Stenberg, Jan Zemek, Vaino Ojala. Norman Bethune, the celebrated Canadian doctor who died in China in 1939 and even had an essay written about him by Mao Zedong, is also on the plaque. Some of the names have crosses beside them.

On the top of the concrete step is a phrase, in Spanish and English. It is a thank-you from Spanish poet Dolores Ibárruri to the 1,546 men:

Podéis partir con orgullo. Ya sois historia. Ya sois leyenda. Sois el ejemplo heróico de la democracía, de la solidaridad y de la univeralsalidad. No os ovidaremos y cuando el olivo de la paz florezca entrelazado con los laureles de la Victoria, volved! Amigos con todo el afecto y el reconocimiento de todo el pueblo español que hoy, como mañana grita y gritará "Vivan los héroes de la Brigada Internacional!"

You can go proudly. You are history. You are legend. You are the heroic example of democracy, solidarity, and universality. We shall not forget you. And when the olive tree of peace puts forth its leaves again, come back! All of you will find the love and gratitude of the whole Spanish people who now and in the future will cry out with all their hearts "Long live the heroes of the International Brigade!"

On another part of the monument it is written that the war was "(their) Promethean struggle for liberty, democracy and social justice." High words of praise indeed.

What is the purpose of this monument, erected in October 2001 with then-governor-general Adrienne Clarkson in attendance? It commemorates those Canadians who volunteered to fight on behalf of the Republic in the 1936–1939 Spanish Civil War—a war in which Canada played no official role. On the contrary, the government of the day passed legislation in 1937—the *Foreign Enlistment Act*—to prevent this kind of mobilization. The Canadians were organized into what was known as the Mackenzie-Papineau Battalion—the "Mac-Paps"—named after the leaders of the rebellions in Upper and Lower Canada in 1837. The Canadian brigade was part of the International Brigade, drawn from fifty-two nations.

The last surviving member of the Mac-Paps died in 2013. Jules Paivio left Sudbury for Spain at the age of nineteen and was captured in the spring of 1938 by Italians fighting with the Nationalists. Lined up to be shot, Paivio saw his life spared at the last instant, and he spent the rest of the war in a concentration camp. And his reason for joining the Mac-Paps? A desire to help the oppressed and confront the Fascists.[45]

So why would more than 1,500 Canadian men give up their lives to cross the Atlantic, against the wishes of their government, to fight in a war in a country most, if not all, had never seen? Before we examine their motivation, it is important to briefly review what the war was and why it broke out.

In February 1936, the Popular Front won the general election in Spain, following years of labor unrest and violent clashes between workers and the army. By spring there were street battles between the "left" (socialists, communists, and anarchists) and the "right" (monarchists, fascists, and the military). The right claimed that the governing left wanted to create a "Soviet Spain" and was alarmed at the spread of Marxism. On July 19, the right launched a coup, and war was on.

The Spanish Civil War saw its share of atrocities, as do all wars. States supporting the Nationalists (the right) saw the conflict as a theater in which to test new weapons and strategies of war. In one of the most infamous incidents, German planes strafed the Basque town of Guernica in April 1937. Most associate this atrocity with the Pablo Picasso work of the same name.

The left-oriented government appealed to the League of Nations for assistance, and a Non-Intervention Committee did deliberate, but to little effect. By late 1936 General Franco, earlier exiled by the government, was in control of the situation and Madrid had come under siege. Supported in large part by Italy and Germany, both of whom had helped bring Franco back, the Nationalists were by far the superior force.

The first of the International Brigades arrived in October 1936 and were welcomed by their hosts. In large part idealists, the soldiers of the brigades volunteered to stop the rise of fascism in Europe. All in all, more than thirty-five thousand foreigners fought in Spain: almost half were killed or wounded (out of a total war loss of a million). Two thousand eight hundred Americans volunteered in the Abraham Lincoln Brigade,[46] the first US volunteers leaving New York on Christmas Day 1936. One soldier, Bill Bailey, wrote in a letter to his mother,

> You see Mom, there are things that one must do in this life that are a little more than just living. In Spain there are thousands of mothers like yourself who never had a fair shake in life. They got together and elected a government that really gave meaning to their life. But a bunch of bullies decided to crush this wonderful thing. That's why I went to Spain, Mom, to help these poor people win this battle, then one day it would be easier for you and the mothers of the future. Don't let anyone mislead you by telling you that all this had something to do with Communism. The Hitlers and Mussolinis of this world are killing Spanish people who don't know the difference between Communism and rheumatism. And it's not to set up some Communist government either. The only thing the Communists did here was show the people how to fight and try to win what is rightfully theirs.[47]

African American Canute Frankson described his intentions as follows:

> I'm sure that by this time you are still waiting for a detailed explanation of what has this international struggle to do with my being here. Since this is a war between whites who for centuries have held us in slavery, and have heaped every kind of insult and abuse upon us, segregated and Jim-Crowed us; why I, a Negro who have fought through these years for the rights of my people, am here in Spain today? Because we are no longer an isolated minority group fighting hopelessly against an immense giant. Because, my dear, we have joined with, and become an active part of, a great progressive force, on whose shoulders rests the responsibility of saving human civilization from the planned destruction of a small group of degenerates gone mad in their lust for power. Because if we crush Fascism here we'll save our people in America, and in other parts of the world from the vicious persecution, wholesale imprisonment, and slaughter which the Jewish people suffered and are suffering under Hitler's Fascist heels.[48]

And as for the Mac-Paps, what drove so many of them—Canadians—to fight in Spain? The circumstances in Canada at the time played some role. The Depression was still ravaging the country, as neither conservative nor liberal factions seemed to know what to do to lift the nation from despair. Communists and leftists were raising awareness of the inequities of capitalism, and for some the war in Spain may have served as a surrogate for an uprising in Canada. The Canadian media were divided between support for the Republicans and the Nationalists. The Catholic Church and the military supported the latter, labor unions and socialists the former. For some, the war was nothing but a choice between two evils: communism and fascism. Most of the Canadians who went to Spain were more "anti-fascist" than anything else.[49] It was known simply as The Cause, or The Last Great Crusade.

Joseph Baruch Salsberg was the Communist Party of Canada's chief organizer among Ontario's trade unions.[50] Upon hearing of the outbreak of war in Spain, he told a colleague that "this is the decisive turning point in Europe, and therefore the world. The establishment of a fascist regime in Spain will strengthen the fascist forces in the very heart of Europe and thus endanger what it left of democratic Europe. Make no mistake about it."[51]

There were three main groups of volunteers in Canada: Anglos from British Columbia, Ukrainians from the prairie provinces, and Finns from Ontario.[52] Their average age was thirty-two (ranging from sixteen to fifty-seven).[53] Miners and lumberjacks made up 15 percent of the group;[54] 10 percent had criminal records;[55] many were recent immigrants to Canada.[56]

But as for why they chose to fight? There is no better source than their own words. Here are some personal testimonies from the volunteers:

- Nick Elendiuk: "I heard and read that the people of Spain had taken a stand and were fighting back against Franco and the Fascists, I immediately became very much interested. I figured any people that had the courage to do that deserved any help I could give them."[57]
- Frank Hadesbeck: "The pay was supposed to be good and conditions fairly good and one thing led to another. I blame most of it on the conditions here in Canada for me going over. I wanted to better myself and these people offered a way out."[58]
- Ed Shirley: "Was it because of ideals or money? Truthfully I couldn't answer. It was a mixture of both. I had nothing. And I had nothing to look forward to. I had ideals. It was a crazy mixed up thing."[59]
- Fred Kostyk: "There was nothing else to do around Winnipeg. No jobs. So like I said, it was hard times. I figured I might as well do something useful. So that's why I volunteered to go."[60]
- Jules Paivio (the longest-living Canadian soldier of the Spanish Civil War, mentioned above): "It was partly dissatisfaction with a lack of real purpose and this being an opportunity for a real purpose in life."[61]
- William Krysa (Ukrainian immigrant) drew a direct connection between the republican cause in Spain and the struggle of ethnic Ukrainians in Poland.[62]

- Hugo Lehtovirta (Finnish): "I made up my mind in the revolution in Finland back in 1918 that at the first opportunity I would fight to avenge the murder of my sisters and others."[63]
- German emigrant: "I knew the Fascists from Germany. When I lived in Germany and went to school, there was the Hitler Youth. And they were loud, quarrelsome, fighting, beating up people all the time. My hatred of them grew from then."[64]
- Isaac Schatz: "Being of Jewish origin, my hatred of fascism was so great as to compel me to leave a good home and fight the bastards."[65]
- Hugh Garner: "The one thing that keeps a fighting force together and makes them fight as a unit and make them brave as a unit is a crazy mixed up thing they call *esprit de corps*. Being afraid of the guy next to you, afraid that he will know you are a coward . . . that's what a fighting force is."[66]
- Anonymous: "I thought in my mind that it was something I should do. It wasn't good enough to just talk."[67]
- William Krehm: "I was 22. I was a young socialist of a drastic sort, with my head on fire. I was looking forward to the millennium that would replace the rather depressing reality of capitalism as it existed. I was quite informed about the seamy sides of communism and even the dangers of power. And here Spain offered a solution to both of these things. It was not only that it was anti-fascist. It was the beginnings of the socialist revolution, but also the social revolution that promised an alternative to Russia that did not have heavy-handed tyranny connected to it."[68]

The Royal Canadian Mounted Police was aware of the drive to recruit volunteers to go to Spain and had in place a number of informers with a view to penetrating the recruitment network.[69] The RCMP was particularly concerned about the involvement of the Communist Party of Canada.[70] With no clear instruction from the government, however, arrests were impossible. Even in the wake of the passing of the *Foreign Enlistment Act*, little direction was forthcoming. RCMP commissioner James Howden MacBrien appealed to the Minister of Justice for guidance. "It would be appreciated," MacBrien wrote, "if we could be advised as to whether you desire that the provisions of the *Foreign Enlistment Act* should be strictly enforced. . . . It is pointed out that the whole question of recruitment of volunteers for the Spanish Civil War is one which is cloaked with secrecy and unless secret informers are employed . . . it will be a very difficult—if not impossible—matter to secure convictions."[71] The government later told MacBrien that the department had reached no conclusion.[72]

When the war ended, the International Brigades—those that had not died in battle—came home. The Mackenzie-King government had sent Colonel Kelly of the Immigration Department to Spain to interview volunteers to determine who had a "right" to return. He allegedly reminded the men of their "criminal status" and refused many who could not clearly recount to him the circumstances of their arrival in Canada twenty years previously.[73] Kelly divided the Canadians into three categories: Canadians by birth, citizens who were either British-born or naturalized, and "aliens." He was convinced that spies were lurking among the third group.[74]

In February 1939, 272 volunteers disembarked in Halifax and boarded a train to Toronto. Their return had not been a sure thing. The RCMP had been adamant that the fighters were criminals and should not be allowed back into Canada. There was also a fear of communist ideology spreading at the hands of the Mac-Paps. Nevertheless, some of those soldiers did make it home, and the Halifax contingent was wildly welcomed at Toronto's Union Station by a crowd of ten thousand people.[75] There was no official Canadian representative, and the only government folks present were RCMP officers taking pictures and notes, searching for subversive elements.[76]

Shortly after their raucous welcome home, most of the soldiers were forgotten. Some reenlisted when World War II began, despite discouragement from the Communist Party of Canada, which saw the war as "imperialist."[77] Some prospective volunteers were rejected for military service because of their time in Spain; others were accepted.[78] Most went back to a normal life.

The RCMP continued to investigate some volunteers for years (some files were only closed in 1984). According to then-commissioner McBrien, "these youths are being sent to Spain largely for the sake of gaining experience in practical revolutionary work and will return to this country to form the nucleus of a training corps."[79] He feared that this would "result in the exclusion of a certain number of individuals who had learned the essentials of revolutionary warfare in Spain and who might, at a future date, apply this education to local circumstance in this country."[80]

The returnees were seen as "suspected communists and potential subversives."[81] The RCMP also objected to the creation of a veterans association in 1970, in part because of the influence of the Communist Party.[82]

In the end, no returnee engaged in activities upon his return to Canada that would constitute a threat to national security. The Mac-Paps had fought the good fight and gone back to their former lives. The fear of unrest and subversion was unfounded. Of course, it is easy to state this now with the benefit of hindsight. At the time, the influence of communism and socialism were seen as real threats in the West.

What can we draw from this small sample? First, the ethnic diversity of the Canadian volunteers comes across strongly. Second, the motivations vary with the individuals themselves. Some reasons were noble, others mundane. What does strike us, however, is the overall idealism and desire to fight for a just cause. Whether to defeat fascism or support a legal, democratic, besieged government, joining the Mac-Paps was simply the right thing to do.

Nevertheless, Canadians' first foray into a war that the government did not support was largely a nonevent on the home front.

The Vietnam War (1955–1975)

Few wars have left such a negative impression on society—in particular US society—as the Vietnam War. Waged by four American presidents, the Vietnam War is a synonym for failure and the limitations of power projection. The ignominious helicopter departure from the rooftop of the US embassy in Saigon (now Ho Chi Minh City) is an image as indelible as the young naked girl fleeing a napalm attack, Buddhists immolating themselves, and the Vietcong shot through the head by Saigon police.

Vietnam ripped America apart as the establishment squared off against the hippie antiwar movement. Controversies included the draft, the bombing of Cambodia, and the use of Agent Orange as a defoliant. The United States exited Vietnam in 1975 as a defeated nation, even as some were calling for an increase in troops to push for victory. The rest of the 1970s was a lost decade of sorts for the United States, with the oil crisis, high inflation, and a lowered sense of US strength. "Vietnam Syndrome"—a reluctance to engage in foreign wars—may even have influenced President Carter to not take direct action during the Iranian hostage crisis. And Carter's successor, Ronald Reagan, came to office after a campaign in which he promised that it was "morning time in America again"—a direct challenge to the Vietnam funk.

Almost sixty thousand American soldiers died in Vietnam. The aftermath of the war led to a mini-industry of films ranging from the ultrarealistic *Hamburger Hill*, *The Deer Hunter*, and *Apocalypse Now* to the satirical *Good Morning, Vietnam* as the United States struggled to make sense of two decades of war in the southeast Asian jungle. Returning veterans were often shunned: they had, after all, fought in a losing cause, unlike their World War II predecessors.

Why did the United States commit so much blood and treasure to a war halfway around the world? As usual, context is important. The post–World War II zeitgeist was one of a thirst for dominance, battled out between the United States and the Soviet Union, between democracy and communism. The two Cold War antagonists engaged in a number of proxy wars as each tried to influence third-world countries. Vietnam was a little different. Once a French colony, it had lapsed into an arena for ideological supremacy between North (communist) and South (colonial) Vietnam. Following the French departure, the United States, which had been sending military advisers to the region for years, adopted a much more direct posture as it sought to restrain

North Vietnamese—and hence communist—control in southeast Asia. The United States feared the so-called domino effect, whereby one communist takeover would threaten neighboring states and lead to regional upheaval. That in a nutshell is why the United States was so involved in what turned out to be a disastrous foreign-military affair.

Canada did not participate officially in the Vietnam War. It is true that Canada was part of the International Commission of Supervision and Control in Vietnam, a quasi-peacekeeping mission. But Canada did not support the US war or provide it any materiel or manpower. In fact, Canada became a haven for tens of thousands of draft dodgers (perhaps as many as one hundred fifty thousand).

What is less well known, however, is that several thousand Canadians volunteered to fight in Vietnam with the US Army. According to a former member of the Canadian Armed Forces, between twenty and forty thousand Canadians signed up to fight in Vietnam, and anywhere from five- to twelve thousand actually served.[83] One hundred seven Canadians died, and seven were listed as missing at the war's end in 1975. Like their US counterparts, Canadian returnees were largely ignored (their service was not acknowledged by the Royal Canadian Legion, and they were not allowed to participate in Remembrance Day ceremonies). Some were even targeted by antiwar protestors (the Vietnam War was never popular on both sides of the Canada–US border).

The question remains, Why did upward of thirty thousand Canadians seek to fight in a war to which Canada did not contribute officially? "There were a number of reasons Canadians served with American forces in the conflict," wrote the abovementioned former Canadian soldier. "Many of the Canadians who enlisted were in their early twenties, or late teens, and seeking adventure. Some joined out of a belief to fight communism, or for other political reasons. Others still hoped (that) joining the military might provide them with a trade or other job skills. Some were unable to pass the enlistment standards of the Canadian Armed Forces, but were accepted by the Americans. . . . Many simply wanted to experience honour and glory." Arthur Diabo, a Mohawk from Quebec, says "You're young and strong and you want to use that energy. And Vietnam was a good place to do that . . . for about two weeks. After that, you just tried to stay alive."[84]

Fred Gaffen, in his book *Unknown Warriors: Canadians in Vietnam*, provides a series of vignettes detailing the experiences of Canadians who willingly fought in Vietnam. He notes that the soldiers were from all social classes (primarily blue collar and the lower-middle class) and that the majority were in their late teens and early twenties. Some volunteered, some were drafted when their families relocated to the United States, and some were dual Canadian-American citizens. For some, enlisting in the US Army represented a career move, where skills could be acquired that could be used in the future. In addition, some believed that enlistment standards were lower in the US Army than in the Canadian Armed Forces. As in all wars, adventure was a major draw, while some wanted to escape the boredom of school or a civilian job. The notion of fighting communism was not a primary motivator. According to Joe Collard, president of Chapter 180 of the Vietnam Veterans of America in Sault Ste. Marie, Michigan, noted that he didn't "think that those who enlisted sat around discussing whether it was a just or unjust war; I think it was neighbours helping neighbours."[85]

Although the men whose stories are told in the book focus largely on their experiences once in Vietnam, there are snippets explaining their initial motivations for volunteering. Their accounts are given below.

- Richard Dextraze (son of General Jacques Dextraze, Canadian chief of Defence Staff from 1972 to 1977): "The Yanks are our friends and we have to do our bit to help them. Canada is not at war. . . . I want to do my share. . . . You [General Dextraze] fought in the last war for freedom and I'd like to go for a couple of years. When I come back I'll feel a better man. I'll feel I've contributed." His father added, "People say they were cranks, that they were stupid to go over there because it wasn't our war. But this war was to fight a common enemy."[86]
- Arne Sund had had "trouble with the law," and there was an open warrant for his arrest. He wanted to start a new life in a new environment and obtained a US visa and enlisted in the navy.[87]
- Dominic Bilotta of Niagara Falls, Ontario, "always wanted to be a Marine."[88]
- Dward Bowes of Dorchester, New Brunswick, tells the story of how, while in Ottawa in 1967, he came across anti-Vietnam protesters, was disgusted at the naiveté of self-righteous, self-appointed moral guardians and with their slogans of "Peace, Love and Dope," and traveled to Bangor, Maine, to enlist.[89]
- A Canadian Mohawk, Robert Johnson, volunteered partly to mature and become a man, partly for action and adventure, and partly to fight communism.[90]
- Dwight Anderson of Wadena, Saskatchewan, wanted to fight communism.[91]
- Eric Walsh of Ottawa was seeking adventure.[92]
- George Tissington, born in the UK and moved to Edmonton, Alberta, was motivated to enlist by draft dodgers and deserters.[93]
- Frank Kett, born in Detroit but raised in Ottawa, had a pregnant wife, had just been laid off by Canadian National Railways, and had few economic prospects and so enlisted.[94]

Returning Canadian Vietnam veterans faced challenges similar to their US counterparts. Not surprisingly, in a country that generally opposed the war, public opprobrium was high. Their service was not recognised by the Canadian military (all those dreams of acquiring skills and putting them to use back home were for nought). Benefits were hard to obtain, and many suffered PTSD or from the aftereffects of Agent Orange. None, however, were prosecuted under the 1937 *Foreign Enlistments Act*, despite government disdain for their actions.

Gaffen sums up the experience of the thousands of Canadian volunteers succinctly: "The Canadians who went to fight in Vietnam left quietly and returned the same way."[95]

In 1996, Tracey Arial self-published *I Volunteered: Canadian Vietnam Vets Remember*. Among the stories in her collection are a few Canadians reminisce about why they elected to enlist in the US Army.

- Mohawk Arthur Diabo from the Kahnawake reserve near Montreal noted, "You've got to remember back in 1966, '67 we were winning the war. . . . We could see what was going on on TV almost every night. We had no purpose in life to fill that gap between eighteen and twenty-one, so the marines were foremost on our mind." He added, "We have the traditional Indian spirit of the warrior. . . . As long as there are wars, there'll be Indian marines fighting in them."[96]
- Al Clause had been to Europe but wanted to see the rest of the world, and the marines looked like a good way to do it.[97]
- Richard Malboeuf was seventeen in 1968 and bored with his life. School was a drag, and there were no interesting jobs. He and his friends were looking for adventure, including taking cars for joyrides. When he saw the movie *The Green Beret*, starring John Wayne, he saw an opportunity to prove himself. Soldiers were heroes. But why Vietnam? "That's the only war we had."[98]

Not surprisingly, then, the Vietnam War remains as controversial in Canada as in the United States and the sacrifices of the men who volunteered unrecognised. What is striking about the reasons they had for going is that for the majority ideology played little part. Acquiring skills, seeking adventure, and even fleeing boredom prevailed. In the end, we are left with a group of young men doing what a lot of young men used to do: looking for an opportunity to prove themselves and have a good time doing it.

Fighting with the Kurds

The Kurds have to be one of the least-fortunate ethnic groups in history. Numbering somewhere in the vicinity of thirty million, this group is spread largely around the eastern portion of the Middle East, with concentrations in northwestern Iran, northern Iraq, eastern Turkey, and northeastern Syria, in addition to a substantial diaspora in western Europe and North America. They have often been called the world's largest homogenous group without a country to call their own.

This failure does not imply that the Kurds have not expended much effort to gain autonomy. Despite much optimism leading up to the Treaty of Sèvres in 1920 (essentially an accord between France and Britain, agreeing how to carve up the moribund Ottoman Empire, which had allied with Germany during World War I), an independent Kurdistan did not come about. Kurds became in essence citizens of the newly formed states of Iraq, Turkey, and Syria (Iran was already a long-standing independent nation). Turkey in particular has been unbending regarding Kurdish rights, refusing to allow Kurdish to be taught in schools and even dismissing ethnic Kurds as "mountain Turks." The drawn-out war with Kurdish militants in Turkey is a result of this inability to find common ground.

In Iraq, the Kurds have fared much better, albeit through tragedy. Toward the end of the first Gulf War,[99] Iraqi president Saddam Hussein unleashed his forces against the Kurds, whom he believed were allied to Iran. Perhaps the most infamous part of what the Iraqis termed Operation Anfal was the gassing of thousands of civilians in the village of Halabja.

Following the end of the second Gulf War, the United States and its allies imposed a no-fly zone in northern and southern Iraq to prevent similar atrocities. The Kurds built an autonomous mini-state with the protection of the United States. This statelet flourished economically, largely due to the significant oil deposits in its territory. But intragroup fighting, a constant problem among Kurds, remained, as did unresolved land claims, the most famous being the status of Kirkuk. The status quo continued throughout the third Gulf War, as the United States and its allies finally ousted Saddam Hussein from power.

Kurdish regions may be witnessing an increasing demand for independence and an unwillingness to settle for mere autonomy, especially among the youth. Recent progress in the ability of Kurds to run a proto-state and confidence that the near future may see a true homeland is driving this desire.[100]

The latest challenge to the hopes and aspirations of the Kurds is the rise of Islamic State. As IS began to make serious gains in eastern and northern Syria and northern and western Iraq, Kurdish territory came under threat. A variety of Kurdish forces became the best at slowing or stopping this advance. The outlawed PKK (the Kurdistan Worker's Party), as well as its armed wing, the YPG (People's Protection Units), successfully took back towns in both countries, and the Kurdish autonomous region served as a haven for Yazidis fleeing the barbarity of IS. Kurdish *peshmerga*—those who face death—have long had a reputation for prowess in battle. There is a certain aura of bravery surrounding Kurdish fighters, even the women, much to the chagrin of Turkey (never fond of Kurdish independence).[101]

Into this new battle came a handful of Westerners, including Canadians. Despite no official sanction—the Canadian government advised those wishing to fight IS to join the Canadian military instead—these "warriors" have found their way to Iraq and offered their services to Kurdish forces. There are also estimates that more than one hundred US citizens are fighting with the Kurds,[102] and as many as five hundred Western Europeans.[103] There is even a Hasidic Jew with the YPG.[104]

Why would Westerners volunteer to fight a war halfway around the world on behalf of a group whose language they do not speak and whose culture remains foreign to them? In addition, some of those who have come forward in their defense do not have military experience and hence may have been seen as a burden by their hosts (the Kurds have publicly welcomed the influx). Luckily, some of these soldiers have been interviewed by Western media and provided some insight into their motivation:

- Patrick Maxwell, a twenty-nine-year-old Iraq War veteran now selling real estate in Texas, never saw the enemy in his tours with the US Army and saw joining the Kurds as another chance to fight. "I may not be enlisted anymore, but I'm still a warrior. I figured if I could walk away from here and kill as many of the bad guys as I could, that would be a good thing." Maxwell added that he went back to Iraq because there was little keeping him in the United States.[105]
- Jordan Matson is a US citizen fighting in Iraq. He is upset that no one else has sent troops to help and is aghast at the genocide of the Yazidis. In his mind, "if my government wouldn't do anything about it, I would." He believes that he is defending the United States from IS, which intends harm to America. His family members were initially skeptical about his intentions but have come to support him.[106]
- Jesper Söder is a Swede fighting with the YPG. He justifies his move this way: "I felt the necessity to do something in the face of the massacres perpetrated by ISIS gangs against the people from other nations and faith groups. I would not be able to relieve my conscience by just donating a hundred kroners. Not everyone can join the YPG ranks but all can somehow contribute to the struggle. The Kurds welcomed me as a family member. It is not only Rojava and Syria but also the European countries that are facing a threat by the ISIS. I try to contribute to Kurds to stop ISIS there before it reaches here."[107]
- Windsor, Ontario, native John Gallagher was a former infantryman with the second battalion of the Princess Patricia's Canadian Light Infantry and who fought with the *peshmerga* for two months, describing the experience

as "good fun." He saw IS as an "incarnation of evil that must be fought." He had no time for "leftist pacifism and intellectualism."[108] He was killed in early November 2015 during a suicide attack carried out at night by IS.[109]

- Cody Bergerud is a twenty-six-year-old political philosophy major from Saltspring Island, British Columbia. He sees fighting IS alongside the Kurds as "a temporary phase in the long-term transformation of the Middle East, a small chapter in the grand narrative of the socialist struggle against the forces of capitalism and fascism." He is fascinated by Kurdistan's campaign to create a homeland and "had to come and find out if this is the case."[110]

- Brandon Glossop's adventure with the Kurds started as a joke. He and a few ex-military friends in Fort McMurray, Alberta, mused about quitting their jobs to fight IS. Glossop began taking the possibility more seriously after two IS–inspired terrorists killed two armed-forces personnel in Montreal and Ottawa in October 2014, and he finally made the decision to go over and fight when fellow Princess Patricia's Canadian Light Infantry veteran Damon Hillier left to fight. Glossop was incensed over IS's treatment of homosexuals as well as the call by Canadian jihadi John Maguire for attacks on Canada. As Glossop saw it, if Canadians were going to Syria to join ISIL, then they could fight on the other side as well.[111]

- Hanna Bohman, a former fashion model and salesperson, traveled to Iraq to join a women's brigade, known as the YPJ (Women's Protection Units). She claims that "no one event motivated me," but "seeing evil beyond evil," and as governments "weren't doing anything about it," she was impelled to go to Kurdistan. She had once considered joining the Canadian Armed Forces but didn't want to "sit around for years in Edmonton or Ottawa." Upon her return to Vancouver, she describes life back in Canada as "sucking air—I'm not doing anything that matters."[112] She volunteered over a year ago to fight IS in northern with YPJ. Upon joining up, "she only got four hours of training. But now, she says, foreign fighters are being trained for at least a month. 'Since September, new YPJ members spend around one month at the academy on language, ideology, politics, and history before joining the battlefronts.'" She said she's not afraid of being arrested either by Canadian authorities or the Kurdistan Regional Government, which "imprisons foreigners if they cross the border illegally for at least one month. 'Canada doesn't recommend [joining the Kurds in fight against ISIS], but there is nothing illegal about it.'" She is based in the city of Qamishli, in northeastern Syria, and claims there are approximately eighty foreign members of the Kurdish forces fighting IS in that region.[113]

- "Wali" got his nickname when he was a sniper with Canadian Forces during his tours in Afghanistan: "I feel like I must do something. If I can make a difference then I have to. [IS fighters] are like other fanatics but worse. Cutting heads off women and children, and no one is doing anything to defend them." Wali began to send dispatches from the front lines. In one, while speaking of refugee children, he wrote, "To think that in a few years that baby would have become an ISIL recruit, perhaps even an executioner, but he has been saved from that poisonous indoctrination. That is when I understood to what extent my work as a soldier has direct and palpable consequences on the lives of people. Nothing is hypothetical here. . . . As a soldier I was convinced and moved by the thought that it was worth it to die so that these people could live in peace."[114]

- Jill Rosenberg is an Israeli-Canadian who traveled to Kurdistan to "fight Islamic State alongside the Kurds to prevent genocide."[115] She had been convicted in 2009 in the United States for her role in a scam to trick American pensioners out of their money.[116]
- A Spanish fighter who goes by the alias "Paco Arcadio" felt a calling to combat "the fascism that ISIS represents" and to encourage "the advance of the region's proletariat."[117]
- UK civilian Macer Gifford described his decision to fight with the YPG thus: "The brutal rise of the so-called Islamic State took everybody by surprise. . . . Every day the news was dominated by another massacre or execution video. The image of Yazidi women—some as young as six—being paraded in market places and then sold into sexual slavery plumbed new depths of depravity. My horror soon gave way to anger. Anger at the Islamic State for committing the atrocities but also angry at my government for doing so little to stop it. I soon realised I didn't have to stand and watch the tragedy unfold. I decided to volunteer for the YPG and fight on the frontline against Isil."[118]
- Canadian army veteran Steve Krsnik noted that he "felt more countries should be doing something" and that his "skills were being wasted as a civilian." The terrorist attack on Parliament Hill by Michael Zehaf-Bibeau in October 2014 in which a "local boy" was killed, along with Corporal Nathan Cirillo, who at the time he was shot and killed was standing as honour guard by the National War Memorial, "sealed the deal" for Krsnik.[119]
- Sixty-seven-year-old Vancouver resident Zinar Garcia may be one of the oldest foreigners fighting alongside Kurdish forces. When asked why he joined, he said that "the Islamic State approaches as closely as is possible, in human form, pure evil. I'm not in any way political or in any way religious, but this is Spielberg evil."[120]

The Bellingcat report on US citizens fighting with the YPG found that Americans decided to join for the following reasons:

- Moral outrage or dismay
- Christianity
- Adventure or boredom
- Missing military camaraderie, missing combat, or trouble adapting after service and
- Displeasure with US policy. [121]

According to Jennifer Percy, who profiled several Americans fighting with the Kurds, among the reasons for volunteering were escaping life back home, old soldiers trying to fill a void, delusions of grandeur, solidarity, adventurism, fulfilling a childhood fantasy, or acting out some violent adolescent emotion. [122]

What of the possibility of legal sanction for those who fight with the Kurds? It is technically illegal under the *Foreign Enlistment Act* in Canada to engage in warfare with a foreign army. The Canadian government officially discourages its citizens from joining the Kurds, urging them to sign up with Canada's army instead (according to then–defence minister Jason Kenney, "We encourage Canadians who want to join the fight against genocidal terrorist organizations like ISIL to join the Canadian Armed Forces, who are having a real impact in degrading the capability of ISIL,"), although it does not appear to be paying too close attention to those that do. [123] And it is not just Canada that is struggling with this wave of "foreign fighters." Many countries are struggling with what to do with returnees.

Other reactions and measures vary from place to place:

- A Kurdish-Dane, Joanna Palani, may be charged with terrorist offenses after fighting with the KGK, formerly the PKK, a listed terrorist entity in the EU. Her case appears to straddle a legal gray zone, since the law forbidding Danish travel abroad was intended to target those joining terrorist groups such as Islamic State. Some have labeled her more a "hero rather than a traitor" to her country. [124]
- Brandon Glossop was unsure what to expect upon his return to Canada. The customs officer merely said, "Welcome home," shook his hand, and performed a perfunctory search of his luggage. [125]
- Hanna Bohman had a similar experience when she got back to Canada. "All they said to me was welcome home." When two weeks later an official from Canadian Security Intelligence Service contacted her, Bohman asked why it had taken them so long to contact her; in the end she concluded that the spy agency didn't seem concerned about her encounters with the PKK. The officer, she added, "wasn't worried about me." [126]
- In December 2015, Germany deported an Australian citizen who had traveled to Europe to take a break from fighting with YPG. [127]

- Former Canadian Armed Forces veteran Kenneth Chen was arrested by Iraqi authorities and held for forty-five days in 2015. Speculation as to why he had been detained ranged from rivalry between Iraqi and Syrian Kurds to Iraqi Kurdish government concerns over the flow of Westerners joining the YPG and transiting its territory.[128]
- A Dutch commando was arrested in January 2016 for his role in fighting with the YPG. It is alleged that he killed IS members.[129]

The aforementioned John Gallagher penned an essay before he left Canada in July 2015 to fight with the Kurds. Here are some excerpts from that piece concerning why he decided to go.

- "The cause of a free and independent Kurdistan is important enough to be worth fighting for all on its own."
- "I am prepared to give my life in the cause of averting the disaster we are stumbling toward as a civilization. A free Kurdistan would be good enough cause for any internationalist."
- "With some fortitude and guts, we can purge the sickness that's poisoning our society, and come together to defeat this ultimate evil."
- "Slavery, fascism and communism were all bad ideas which required costly sacrifice before they were finally destroyed. In our time, we have a new bad idea: theocracy."[130]

The overarching justification for fighting with Kurdish troops in Iraq appears to be a desire to help a people faced with what could be termed an existential threat to their existence. The Kurds have faced many foes over the centuries and yet remain a separate people who want a separate homeland. IS's threat to this hope, as well as the brutal atrocities IS has committed, have led many Westerners to leave their homes and assist the Kurds.

There has been an interesting debate about whether Canadians and others should be allowed to fight alongside Kurds. Some are worried about the effects of this war on Westerners. I learned in November 2015 that the newly created counter-radicalization center in Montreal was receiving phone calls from concerned parents, not out of a fear that their children were keen to join IS, but that they were bent on fighting for the Kurds. To these parents, to do so was in fact a form of radicalization. In January 2016, Canadian media reported that some of those who fought with groups that are listed terrorist entities could eventually face prosecution in Canada under antiterrorism laws.[131]

Joining the Israeli Defense Forces

Within days of its creation in 1948, the of the state of Israel was under attack by countries that did not accept the UN resolution carving out a country in the former British mandate territory of Palestine. The Israeli Defense Forces (IDF) were created at the same time and have had to defend the country in three major wars and a series of minor ones, not to mention against terrorist threats by groups such as Hezbollah, Hamas, and Palestinian Islamic Jihad, among others.

Tied of course to the state of Israel is the idea of *aliyah*, the return to the Jewish homeland. Millions have settled in Israel over the decades, and even for those who do not wish to live in the Jewish state there is a very strong pull to visit and connect with one's culture, history, and faith.

Conscription is universal in Israel (although ultraorthodox Haredim get waivers), and the IDF retains a very high level of respect and confidence among Israelis.[132] In its annual survey for 2015, the Israel Democracy Institute found that the military was the national institution with the highest level of trust among Israeli Jews.[133] An interesting subset of fighters seeking foreign battle is comprised of those who travel from abroad to fight with the IDF. There is even a name for it—the Nefesh B'Nefesh—the "lone-soldier program." Some estimates claim that there are as many as 2,500 such people (including several hundred Canadians) fighting with the IDF.[134] The IDF even has a Web page with instructions on how to join without taking out Israeli citizenship.[135] Volunteers probably see the David-versus-Goliath fight in Israel's struggle against its Arab enemies. Here are some of these foreign fighters' stories.

- Orli Broer was a student at McGill University when she decided to join the IDF. She claimed that she had an "inner feeling" and wanted to give back to Israel after having studied there for a year. "It's my home and I have to protect my home," said Broer, who now considers herself more Israeli than Canadian.[136]
- Shawn Hoffman is a sergeant with the IDF; he hails from Toronto. As he was finishing university and seeking options, he'd never thought a military career was in the cards. As the son of a Jewish mother, Hoffman had a right to *aliyah* and chose to emigrate. He recognized that his decision to enlist would not be taken well by his family—they thought he was "nuts." When challenged about why he did not join the Canadian military instead, he replied that the threat was not there and that his home country was not a "militaristic" nation.[137]
- A friend of Hoffman's described a "religious tug, a Zionist tug." This individual, whose grandparents were Holocaust survivors, sees serving in the IDF as an honor his grandparents could not receive.

Should Canadians be allowed to join the IDF? The answer is not simple, and I have heard arguments both for and against. This topic was often raised in meetings of the Cross-Cultural Roundtable, with some members stating that allowing Canadian citizens to travel to fight for Israel smacked of a double standard. There is a lot of criticism of the government for not prosecuting volunteers under the *Foreign Enlistments Act* and for treating Jewish volunteers differently than those who volunteer to fight for groups such as the Islamic State.

But there is a difference, of course. The IDF is a regular army of a nation-state that is member of the United Nations and ally of Canada; the Islamic State is a recognized terrorist group. To equate the two is wrong. And yet, to my mind, the critics have a valid point: It is illegal in Canada to enlist in a foreign army. Canadians may choose to do so, but they should be forced to renounce their Canadian citizenship. Someone who prefers the IDF over the Canadian military has clearly made a choice about which country they wish to be part of.

There is no question that Jewish identity plays the most important role in the commitment of non-Israelis to fight for the IDF. In the early years of the state, the threat from Israel's enemies was assuredly existential. It is less so now, but the tenacity and relentlessness of groups and some states will likely move many more to join the IDF.

DO RETURNING VETERANS POSE A THREAT
TO THEIR HOME COUNTRIES?

We have seen that, irrespective of the war at hand, individuals will respond to a variety of motivations and drivers in their decision to sign up to go to war. For each war, particular factors tied to the social and historical circumstances at that time contribute to why these people make the choices they do. We saw that patriotism, adventure, and a sense of duty were overwhelming drivers for Canadians in World War I. Ideological commitment and a desire to escape the Depression influenced the 1,500 or so Canadians and others in the Spanish Civil War. Twenty thousand–plus Canadians elected to go to Vietnam to get experience and a possible job; ideology appears to have played a smaller role. Those who fight with the Kurds and IDF see plucky armies amassed against real threats and want to help those forces protect and maintain their communities.

It seems safe to say that, for the most part, those who go to war—both "official" wars and wars of choice on the enlistee's part, where state sanction is lacking—do not present a significant danger upon returning home. We have not seen protracted campaigns of terrorist or other violence subsequent to any of the conflicts covered in this book. Even the RCMP's heightened

concern over the danger from surviving Canadian Spanish Civil War veterans never amounted to anything. And so it would seem that there is nothing
to worry about.

Or is there?

Aside from the burden on society stemming from the state of some returnees—psychological and physical injuries (both Canada and the United States
are seeing enormous costs arising from PTSD and serious wounds in Afghan—and for the US Iraq—war veterans, as well as a rise in suicides[138])—
can we conclude that these individuals never pose a danger to their fellow
citizens, at least from a terrorist perspective (remember that for terrorism to
take place, the violence must be inspired along ideological lines)?

While collected wisdom says no, there is one startling exception. Rather,
it would have been an exception had political outrage not forced the authors
of a famous (infamous?) report on returning US GIs to retract their warning.

I am referring naturally to a 2009 paper written by the US Department of
Homeland Security, *Rightwing Extremism: Current Economic and Political
Climate Fueling Resurgence in Radicalization and Recruitment*, which stated
that veterans of Afghanistan and Iraq may be susceptible to joining rightwing groups, which may lead to radicalization and violence. In the report,
DHS states that "the return of military veterans facing significant challenges
reintegrating into their communities could lead to the potential emergence of
terrorist groups or lone wolf extremists carrying out violent attacks."[139]

DHS was roundly criticized by, among others, the ACLU, Congress, the
American Legion, and House Leader John Boehner. In the end, the report
was withdrawn, the authors sacrificed on the altar of political correctness. An
honest assessment of threat was savaged in the interests of willful blindness
and ignorance.

Nevertheless, it remains true thus far that our governments, security-
intelligence agencies, and law enforcement do not need to devote precious
resources to monitor most soldiers upon completion of their tours abroad,
whether those tours are in wars we support or ones we don't.

SUMMARY

In this chapter we have seen a wide range of motivations and rationales
underpinning the decision to fight in a war. It seems to me that each war has
its particular push and pull factors. Canadians in the second Boer War were
largely drawn out of a desire to help Mother England, to which they felt a
very strong tie and from which many had emigrated to Canada. In World
War I, the same driver was prevalent, but so was a sense of adventure and a
yearning to try something more exciting than a life on the farm or in the
office. The Spanish Civil War may be the first where ideology had a major

role. True, many joined to escape the depths and depravity of the Depression, but there was a clear sense that fascism needed to be confronted and that the people of Spain needed help defending themselves against aggression.

For the Canadians who fought in Vietnam, adventure and thrill seem to dominate. There are not a lot of instances of ideological fervor (i.e., keeping communism in check), although fighting for a larger army where more opportunities for skill acquisition and advancement also loomed large. Westerners enlisting with the Kurds appear to be drawn by the "pluckiness" of the Kurds and the fact that they are in a struggle with a terrorist group whose actions are heinous in nature. Finally, foreigners who choose to join the IDF are clearly doing so largely because of their Jewishness and the belief that Israel faces an existential threat from its enemies.

So, while there are underlying themes and some commonality to these motivations, one element remains clear: The path to violent radicalization and extremism is an individual one. Backgrounds are of no use in determining why people choose to embrace violent ideologies. An extremist is as likely to be a highly educated, well-employed, "normal" married man with kids as he is to be from the wrong side of the tracks.

I believe the same goes for war enlistment in general. Volunteers can be the children of doctors, lawyers, or bankers or those of farmers, miners, and the unemployed. The decision to fight may have been nurtured over years or made on the spur of the moment. Some may see themselves fighting for a noble cause, while for others going to war may be just another job. I presume that some come to regret their choice while others may enlist several times.

And so certain questions remain: Do those who elect to join groups such as Al Qaeda and Islamic State do so for reasons similar to those whom we have just examined? Is it for adventure or a sense of purpose? What role does ideology play? Do they see themselves as part of a larger picture?

Again, it is important to note that I am not drawing moral or legal equivalence between regular armies or militias and terrorist groups such as IS. The latter are responsible for heinous crimes, and we should all do what we can to destroy this organization. Nevertheless, the questions surrounding *why* Westerners join is still a valid one.

We will look at the stories of Western fighters in the Islamic State in the next chapter.

NOTES

The first epigraph was cited in G. R. Stevens, *A City Goes to War: History of the Loyal Edmonton Regiment* (Brampton, Ont.: Charters, 1964), 8–9. The second epigraph is from Allen Abel, "Ghost Battle," *Canadian Geographic* 132, no. 1 (January–February 2012): 34–49, available online under an updated title, "Who Won the War?" http://www.canadiangeographic.ca/article/who-won-war.

1. Timothy Cook, *At the Sharp End: Canadians Fighting the Great War, 1914–1916* (Toronto: Viking Canada, 2007), 23.

2. Ibid., 21.

3. Ibid., 21.

4. Ibid., 23–24.

5. Ibid., 24.

6. Ibid., 25.

7. Ibid., 25.

8. Ibid., 26.

9. All quotations from Cook, *At the Sharp End*, 26.

10. Ibid., 27.

11. Ibid., 28.

12. Ibid., 28.

13. Ibid., 29.

14. Ibid., 30.

15. Ibid., 31.

16. The Canadian Letters and Images Project, "About Us," accessed throughout 2015, http://www.canadianletters.ca/content/about-us..

17. Jeffrey A. Keshen, "The War on Truth," *Canada's History* (August–September 2015): 52–56, available online at http://greatwaralbum.ca/Great-War-Album/About-the-Great-War/Unrest-on-the-homefront/The-War-on-Truth.

18. Alfred Herbert John Andrews, "Andrews, Alfred Herbert John Diary: 1914," The Canadian Letters and Images Project, accessed throughout 2015, http://www.canadianletters.ca/content/document-8444?position=0&list=9CBdN-t8kS-is_xjr5HGEFvqdhJ3f1olhEQ0SLuXLzQ.

19. William Beattie, "Cobourg World Letter: 1914 November 6th," The Canadian Letters and Images Project, accessed throughout 2015, http://www.canadianletters.ca/content/document-2926.

20. William Howard Curtis, "Curtis, William Howard, M.M. Letter: 1914 December 24th," The Canadian Letters and Images Project, accessed throughout 2015, http://www.canadianletters.ca/content/document-6777.

21. John "Jack" Davey, "Davey, John (Jack) Letter: 1914 August 16th," The Canadian Letters and Images Project, accessed throughout 2015, http://www.canadianletters.ca/content/document-11009.

22. Kenneth Walter Foster, "Foster, Kenneth Walter Memoir," The Canadian Letters and Images Project, accessed throughout 2015, http://www.canadianletters.ca/content/document-4021.

23. Alexander Matier, "Matier, Alexander Letter: 1918 January 8th," The Canadian Letters and Images Project, accessed throughout 2015, http://www.canadianletters.ca/content/document-2763.

24. Charles Henry Savage, "Savage, Charles Henry Memoir: 1936," The Canadian Letters and Images Project, accessed throughout 2015, http://www.canadianletters.ca/content/document-8359.

25. Amy J. Shaw, *Crisis of Conscious: Conscientious Objection in Canada during the First World War* (Vancouver: UBC Press, 2009), 3.

26. Ibid., 10.

27. Ibid., 13.

28. Ibid., 38–39.

29. Ibid., 38.

30. Ibid., 41.

31. Ibid., 41.

32. Ibid., 122.

33. Ibid., 132.

34. Full disclosure: I was an analyst in the Canadian-intelligence community at the time.

35. Tamara Lush, "9/11 Inspired Many Young Americans to Enlist in Military," *Seattle Times*, September 4, 2011, http://www.seattletimes.com/nation-world/9-11-inspired-many-young-americans-to-enlist-in-military/.

36. Ibid.

37. Ibid.

38. Lisa Daniel, "Recruiters Recall Patriotism of Post–9/11 America," U.S. Department of Defense: DoD News, September 8, 2011, http://archive.defense.gov/news/newsarticle.aspx?id= 65272.

39. Jessica Mendoza, "Why Millennials Want War against ISIS, but Don't Want to Serve,"*Christian Science Monitor*, December 12, 2015, http://www.csmonitor.com/USA/ Society/2015/1212/Why-Millennials-want-war-against-ISIS-but-don-t-want-to-serve.

40. Canadian War Museum, "Canada and the South African War, 1899–1902," accessed throughout 2015, http://www.warmuseum.ca/cwm/exhibitions/boer/boerwarhistory_e.shtml.

41. Ibid.

42. Ibid.

43. Stanley McKeown Brown, *With the Royal Canadians* (Toronto: The Publishers' Syndicate, 1900), 7–9.

44. Cameron Pulsifer, "Dispatches: For Queen and Country; Canadians and the South African War, 1899–1902," Canadian War Museum, accessed throughout 2015, http://www. warmuseum.ca/learn/dispatches/for-queen-and-country-canadians-and-the-south-african-war-1899-1902/#tabs.

45. Michael Petrou, "'You Are History. You Are Legend.' Canada's Last Spanish Civil War Vet Dies," *Maclean's*, September 11, 2013, http://www.macleans.ca/news/you-are-history-you-are-legend-canadas-last-spanish-civil-war-vet-dies/.

46. Abraham Lincoln Brigade Archives, "The Abraham Lincoln Brigade," accessed throughout 2015, http://www.alba-valb.org/.

47. Spartacus Educational, "Abraham Lincoln Battalion," accessed throughout 2015, http:// spartacus-educational.com/SPlincoln.htm.

48. Ibid.

49. Mark Zuelhke, *The Gallant Cause: Canadians in the Spanish Civil War, 1936–1939* (Mississauga, Ont.: John Wiley and Sons Canada, 1996), 14.

50. Ibid., 14.

51. Ibid., 15.

52. Mary Biggar Peck, *Red Moon Over Spain: Canadian Media Reaction to the Spanish Civil War, 1936–1939* (Ottawa: Steel Rail, 1988), 26.

53. Michael Petrou, *Renegades: Canadians in the Spanish Civil War* (Vancouver: UBC Press, 2008), 13.

54. Ibid., 14.

55. Ibid., 17.

56. Ibid., 22–23.

57. Ibid., 31.

58. Ibid., 31.

59. Ibid., 32.

60. Ibid., 32.

61. Ibid., 33.

62. Ibid., 37.

63. Ibid., 37.

64. Ibid., 37.

65. Ibid., 38.

66. Ibid., 48.

67. Ibid., 49.

68. Ibid., 149.

69. Ibid., 54.

70. Ibid., 172.

71. Ibid., 54–55.

72. Ibid., 54.

73. Ronald Liversedge, *Mac-Pap: Memoir of a Canadian in the Spanish Civil War*, ed. David York (Vancouver: New Star Books, 2013), 146.

74. Zuehlke, *The Gallant Cause*, 269.

75. Ibid., 283.

76. Ibid., 284.

77. Petrou, *Renegades*, 174.

78. Ibid., 175. One recruiting officer told Arne Knudsen upon learning of his Spanish Civil War experience, "Out! Out! Out! You're a Communist."

79. Ibid., 170.

80. Ibid., 171.

81. Geoff Nixon, "RCMP Accused of Spying on Spanish Civil War Vets," April 14, 2008, *Calgary Herald*, text available online at http://www.pressreader.com/canada/calgary-herald/20080414/281663955729857.

82. Petrou, *Renegades*, 179.

83. Canadian Military, "Vietnam: Canadians in the Vietnam War," http://canadianmilitary.page.tl/-Vietnam.htm.

84. Ibid.

85. Fred Gaffen, *Unknown Warriors: Canadians in Vietnam* (Toronto: Dundurn Press, 1990), 39.

86. Ibid., 39.

87. Ibid., 58–59.

88. Ibid., 102.

89. Ibid., 159.

90. Ibid., 163.

91. Ibid., 182.

92. Ibid., 195.

93. Ibid., 203.

94. Ibid., 229.

95. Ibid., 323.

96. Tracey Arial, *I Volunteered: Canadian Vietnam Vets Remember* (Winnipeg: Watson and Dryer, 1996), 16.

97. Ibid., 18.

98. Ibid., 18–19.

99. The first Gulf War was the 1980–1988 conflict between Iraq and Iran. The second was the US invasion in 1990 and 1991 following Saddam Hussein's annexation of Kuwait. The war to unseat Hussein (2003–) is the third Gulf War.

100. Dominique Soguel, "For Kurdish Youth in Turkey, Autonomy Is No Longer Enough," *Christian Science Monitor*, August 17, 2015, http://www.csmonitor.com/World/Middle-East/2015/0817/For-Kurdish-youth-in-Turkey-autonomy-is-no-longer-enough.

101. Mehmet Çelik, "Child Recruitment, Female Militants of PKK Idealized in Western Media," *Daily Sabah* (Istanbul), August 20, 2015, http://www.dailysabah.com/features/2015/08/20/child-recruitment-female-militants-of-pkk-idealized-in-western-media.

102. David Philipps and Thomas James Brennan, "Unsettled at Home, Veterans Volunteer to Fight ISIS," *New York Times*, March 11, 2015, http://www.nytimes.com/2015/03/12/us/disenchanted-by-civilian-life-veterans-volunteer-to-fight-isis.html.

103. Murat Kuseyri, "Around 500 Europeans Fighting in the Ranks of YPG," ANF (Firat News Agency), August 23, 2015, http://anfenglish.com/news/around-500-europeans-fighting-in-the-ranks-of-ypg.

104. Liron Nagler-Cohen, "Meet the Hasidic-Slogan-Tagging Jew Fighting in Syria," *Ynetnews* (Tel Aviv), August 31, 2015, http://www.ynetnews.com/articles/0,7340,L-4696101,00.html.

105. Adam Rawnsley, "Meet the Americans Flocking to Iraq and Syria to Fight the Islamic State," *Foreign Policy*, August 26, 2015, http://foreignpolicy.com/2015/08/26/meet-the-americans-flocking-to-iraq-and-syria-to-fight-the-islamic-state/.

106. Fox News, "Military Vet: Why I've Volunteered to Fight ISIS Abroad," February 19, 2015, http://video.foxnews.com/v/4070588282001/military-vet-why-ive-volunteered-to-fight-isis-abroad/? -sp=show-clips.

107. Murat Kuseyri, "Around 500 Europeans Fighting in the Ranks of YPG," ANF (Firat News Agency), August 23, 2015, http://anfenglish.com/news/around-500-europeans-fighting-in-the-ranks-of-ypg.""

108. Adnan R. Khan, "A Tale of Two Canadians, Fighting Islamic State," *Maclean's*, August 9, 2015, http://www.macleans.ca/news/world/a-tale-of-two-canadians-fighting-islamic-state/.

109. Stewart Bell, "Gunfire, Not Bomb, Killed Canadian," *National Post* (Toronto), November 9, 2015, available online at http://www.pressreader.com/canada/national-post-latest-edition/20151109/281492160199874.

110. Ibid.

111. Stewart Bell, "Canadians Who Travel Abroad to Fight ISIL Get Little Scrutiny Upon Return, Suggesting Canada Isn't Keen on Stopping Them," *National Post* (Toronto), June 1, 2015, http://news.nationalpost.com/news/canada/canadians-who-travelled-abroad-to-fight-isil-get-little-scrutiny-upon-return-suggesting-canada-isnt-keen-on-stopping-them.

112. Catherine Solyom, "Canadian Woman Returns from Fighting ISIS with the Kurds," *Montreal Gazette*, August 8, 2015, A3, http://montrealgazette.com/news/local-news/canadian-woman-returns-from-fighting-isis-with-the-kurds.

113. ARA News, "Canadian Fighter Joining Kurdish Female Units to Combat ISIS Northern Syria," April 6, 2016, http://aranews.net/2016/04/canadian-fighter-joining-kurdish-female-units-combat-isis-northern-syria/.

114. Catherine Solyom, "Capturing ISIL Up Close," *Montreal Gazette*, September 15, 2015, published online on September 14, 2015, as "Wali in Kurdistan: Dispatches from the Front," http://montrealgazette.com/news/local-news/wali-in-kurdistan-dispatches-from-the-front.

115. Ben Hartman, "Report: Israeli-Canadian Woman Who Went to Kurdistan to Fight ISIS Returns to Iraq to Work with Embattled Charity," *Jerusalem Post*, September 1, 2015,http://www.jpost.com/Middle-East/ISIS-Threat/Israeli-Canadian-woman-who-went-to-Kurdistan-to-fight-ISIS-returns-to-Iraq-to-work-with-embattled-charity-413866.

116. Eliran Aharon and Gil Ronen, "This Is the Woman Who 'Volunteered to Fight ISIS,'" December 11, 2014, Arutz Sheva (Israel National News), http://www.israelnationalnews.com/News/News.aspx/187359 -.VhHFQnpViko.

117. Frances Martel, "Spain's Communist Snipers Join 'Proletarian' Kurds to in Iraq Fight ISIS," Breitbart News Network, June 3, 2015, http://www.breitbart.com/national-security/2015/06/03/spains-communist-snipers-join-proletarian-kurds-in-iraq-to-fight-against-isis/.

118. Macer Gifford, "We Could Defeat Islamic State within a Year. I Know Because I Fought Them," *Telegraph* (London), September 17, 2015, http://www.telegraph.co.uk/news/worldnews/islamic-state/11866540/We-could-defeat-Islamic-State-within-a-year.-I-know-because-I-fought-them.html.

119. Stewart Bell, "Canadian Army Vet Arrested in Iraq," *National Post* (Toronto), December 14, 2015, published online on December 13, 2015, as "Canadian Veteran Who Travelled to Middle East to Fight ISIL Says He Was Arrested in Iraq and Held for 45 Days," http://news.nationalpost.com/news/canada/canadian-veteran-who-travelled-to-middle-east-to-fight-isil-says-he-was-arrested-in-iraq-and-held-for-45-days.

120. Cheryl Chan, "67-Year-Old Vancouver Man Who's Been 'a Logger, a Fisherman' Now Fighting ISIS with Kurdish Forces: Zinar Garcia Is Said to Be the Oldest Foreigner Fighting ISIS with Kurdish Forces," *Province* (Vancouver), updated December 22, 2015, http://www.theprovince.com/news/year+Vancouver+been+logger+fisherman+fighting+ISIS+with+Kurdish+forces/11608267/story.html.

121. "The Other Foreign Fighters: An Open-Source Investigation into American Volunteers Fighting the Islamic State in Iraq and Syria," Bellingcat (website), https://www.bellingcat.com/wp-content/uploads/2015/08/The-Other-Foreign-Fighters.pdf, cached article available at https://webcache.googleusercontent.com/search?q=cache:JQjByHmsUAMJ:https://www.bellingcat.com/wp-content/uploads/2015/08/The-Other-Foreign-Fighters.pdf+&cd=1&hl=en&ct=clnk&gl=us&client=safari.

122. Jennifer Percy, "Meet the American Vigilantes Who Are Fighting ISIS," *New York Times Magazine*, September 30, 2015, 39, http://www.nytimes.com/2015/10/04/magazine/meet-the-american-vigilantes-who-are-fighting-isis.html.

123. Stewart Bell, "Canadians Who Travel Abroad to fight ISIL Get Little Scrutiny Upon Return, Suggesting Canada Isn't Keen On Stopping Them," *National Post* (Toronto), June 1, 2015, http://news.nationalpost.com/news/canada/canadians-who-travelled-abroad-to-fight-isil-get-little-scrutiny-upon-return-suggesting-canada-isnt-keen-on-stopping-them.

124. Simon Bendsten and Allan Dansk Sørensen, "Kurder risikerer terrordom for at gå i krig mod Islamisk Stat," *Copenhagen Berlingske Tiden*, June 6, 2015, http://www.politiko.dk/nyheder/dansk-kurder-risikerer-terrordom-for-at-gaa-i-krig-mod-islamisk-stat.

125. Stewart Bell, "Canadians Who Travel Abroad to Fight ISIL Get Little Scrutiny Upon Return, Suggesting Canada Isn't Keen On Stopping Them," *National Post* (Toronto), June 1, 2015, http://news.nationalpost.com/news/canada/canadians-who-travelled-abroad-to-fight-isil-get-little-scrutiny-upon-return-suggesting-canada-isnt-keen-on-stopping-them.

126. Stewart Bell, "Young Kurdish Women Fighting ISIL and Also for Rights, Says Canadian Who Joined Them," *National Post*, August 28, 2015, http://news.nationalpost.com/news/world/young-kurdish-women-fighting-isil-and-also-for-rights-says-canadian-who-joined-them.

127. Agence France-Presse, "Germany Deports Man for Fighting against Isis," December 5, 2015, *Local* (Berlin), http://www.thelocal.de/20151205/germany-deports-australian-for-fighting-against-isis.

128. Stewart Bell, "Canadian Army Vet Arrested in Iraq," *National Post* (Toronto), December 14, 2015, published online on December 13, 2015, as "Canadian Veteran Who Travelled to Middle East to Fight ISIL Says He Was Arrested in Iraq and Held for 45 Days," http://news.nationalpost.com/news/canada/canadian-veteran-who-travelled-to-middle-east-to-fight-isil-says-he-was-arrested-in-iraq-and-held-for-45-days.

129. DutchNews.nl, "Former Dutch Soldier May Face Charges for Killing IS Jihadis," January 15, 2016, http://www.dutchnews.nl/news/archives/2016/01/83438-2/.

130. John Robert Gallagher, "'We Are All on the Front Lines': Canadian Reportedly Killed Fighting ISIL Wrote Essay about Why He Went to War," *National Post* (Toronto), November 5, 2015, http://news.nationalpost.com/news/world/israel-middle-east/we-are-all-on-the-front-lines-canadian-reportedly-killed-fighting-isil-wrote-essay-about-why-he-went-to-war.

131. Murray Brewster, "Canadian Volunteers Fighting with Kurds in Iraq Might Violate Anti-terror Law," *Globe and Mail* (Toronto), last updated January 28, 2016, http://www.theglobeandmail.com/news/national/canadian-volunteers-fighting-with-kurds-in-iraq-might-violate-anti-terror-law/article28426800/.

132. *The Economist*, "Locker Hurt," News, August 15, 2015, 43, http://www.economist.com/news/middle-east-and-africa/21660998-generals-blow-away-plan-cut-their-budgets-locker-hurt.

133. Isabel Kershner, "Israeli Veterans' Criticism of the Occupation Incites a Furor," *New York Times*, December 24, 2015, A6, online version published December 23, 2015, at http://www.nytimes.com/2015/12/24/world/middleeast/israeli-veterans-criticism-of-west-bank-occupation-incites-furor.html.

134. Katrina Clarke, "Dozens of Canadians Have Gone to Israel to Take Up Arms for the Jewish State," *National Post* (Toronto), July 23, 2014, last updated January 24, http://news.nationalpost.com/news/dozens-of-canadians-have-gone-to-israel-to-take-up-arms-for-the-jewish-state.

135. Israeli Defense Forces, "Volunteer Programs," accessed September 15, 2015, https://www.idfblog.com/about-the-idf/volunteer-programs/.

136. Katrina Clarke, "Dozens of Canadians Have Gone to Israel to Take Up Arms for the Jewish State," *National Post* (Toronto), July 23, 2014, last updated January 24, http://news.nationalpost.com/news/dozens-of-canadians-have-gone-to-israel-to-take-up-arms-for-the-jewish-state.

137. "16x9onglobal" (user name), "16x9 - Serving Your Country: Jewish Canadians joining the Israeli army," YouTube video, 6:02, April 30, 2012, https://www.youtube.com/watch?v=nN-MFGGNuqk.'"

138. Bruce Bower, "As Suicide Rates Rise, Researchers Separate Thoughts from Actions," *Science News* 189, no.1 (January 9, 2016), 22, https://www.sciencenews.org/article/suicide-rates-rise-researchers-separate-thoughts-actions.

139. U.S. Department of Homeland Security, Office of Intelligence and Analysis, *Rightwing Extremism: Current Economic and Political Climate Fueling Resurgence in Radicalization and Recruitment*, report (Washington, DC: U.S. Department of Homeland Security, 2009), made available through Federation of American Scientists at https://fas.org/irp/eprint/rightwing.pdf.

Chapter Four

Foreign Actors in Violent Jihad

When Damian Clairmont was seventeen he tried to commit suicide by drinking antifreeze. Although his attempt was unsuccessful, at the time doctors did not think he would survive, or, if he did, he would be reduced to a vegetative state. Clairmont surprised everyone, however, and pulled through. Two months or so after leaving hospital, he embraced Islam and believed his life had a purpose. Having lost time through his difficult period, he wanted to become more religious, even expressing interest in becoming an imam.

The war in Syria also grabbed Clairmont's attention. Angry at what the Assad regime was doing to women and children and frustrated at the West's unwillingness to "step up," he saw this conflict and his response to it as meaningful. When pressed by his mother about why he couldn't act in a similar way in Canada, Clairmont said that the country lacked a sense of faith and was full of distractions such as drugs, alcohol, and promiscuousness. On occasion he would challenge his mother's decision to have wine with dinner and would not eat at restaurants where female servers were immodestly dressed. He even talked about his desire to have more than one wife—an attitude his mother found strange, since Damian was from a liberal background and was now saying that women needed to be taken care of. At one point Clairmont raised the issue of "justified killing" with his mother, Christianne Boudreau. The two debated the topic and in the end agreed to disagree.

Clairmont told his mother that he wanted to study Arabic and Islam abroad. His initial choice was Saudi Arabia, but he switched to Egypt because it was more affordable. He left in late 2012 and ended up in Turkey. He maintained contact with his mother every two to three days in the beginning. By December he went offline for two months and then reestablished contact every two to three days. He told his mother he was on "vacation"—probably referring to his time with IS, for, in fact, he'd joined the terrorist organization—during which time she would not hear from him. Her last contact with him was via Facebook in August 2013; Christianne learned of her son's death in January 2014.

Damian's mother is convinced her son's decision to leave for Syria stemmed from his passion to do good. He had expressed a desire to join the military when he was younger and was keen on becoming a cook as well at one point.[1]

CHAPTER ABSTRACT

In this chapter we examine firsthand accounts of why Westerners have elected to leave their homes and join groups like Islamic State, Jabhat al-Nusra, and others. By the end, we will be able to determine if there are any patterns and whether their reasons share anything in common with those offered by volunteers in other, nonjihadi conflicts.

WHY COMPARE SOLDIERS TO TERRORISTS?

Some may be offended by the juxtaposition of Western soldiers who fought, and in some cases died, in just wars with Western citizens who became terrorists. As I noted in the introduction to this book, I am not equating the legitimacy or the morality of enlisting in the army with joining a terrorist group. Most would agree that there is a significant difference between the two.

When you look at the issue dispassionately, however, two things stand out: First, as already discussed, terrorist groups see themselves as armies and their members as soldiers, whether we agree with them or not. Second, if they view their actions in military terms, is it not worth examining whether the motivations they claim to act in support of are at all like those discussed in the previous chapter? I believe it is and that the reader may be surprised at these similarities (there are bound to be very important differences as well, and those too will prove interesting). We can continue to condemn acts of terrorism and terrorist groups but still subject them to study.

THE NATURE OF THE PHENOMENON

The current challenge of foreign fighters enmeshed with terrorist groups such as IS is without precedent. Figures keep shifting, but it is certain that tens of thousands have traveled to join, and fight with, such groups. For some countries (Canada and the United States, among others) the numbers are in the low hundreds. For others (Tunisia and Saudi Arabia, for example) the comparable figures are in the thousands. Nations such as the UK and France fall somewhere in the middle.

States and governments are struggling to deal with this flow. Rhetoric bordering on fear is all too common (especially in the 2016 American Republican presidential primaries but also during the 2015 Canadian federal election), and no one country appears to have figured out what to do with this. Air strikes against IS continue, and warnings of the reality of life in Syria (that is, don't believe IS propaganda that life with the group is Utopia) are everywhere, but still more and more Westerners are on the move. The November 2015 attacks in Paris, where some of the assailants had fought with IS in Syria, has only compounded the concern of blowback in the West.

So lots of Westerners are keen to go fight alongside IS. It is fair to ask why. Shouldn't the horror of the situation in Syria, not to mention the utterly inhumane brutality of IS (crucifixions, beheadings, immolations, throwing people off buildings), make a normal person flinch from associating themselves with the conflict? Don't prospective travelers think about what they are doing to their families? Sadly, no. They rationalize their decision to join and fight with the terrorist group, as we see later in this chapter.

While the wave of foreigners entering Syria and Iraq dwarfs previous conflicts, it is not unique. Several other so-called jihads have attracted outsiders. Let's have a look at a few.

HISTORICAL ANTECEDENTS

Perhaps the first major jihadist conflict to entice foreign fighters was the war in Afghanistan following the Soviet invasion in 1979. A lot has changed since then (although not as much as we would hope), so it is helpful to remind ourselves that the Cold War was still hot at the end of the 1970s. Proxy wars were simmering in parts of Africa and Asia as the United States and the USSR sought to maintain or extend spheres of influence. The Vietnam War had ended in the mid-1970s with an apparent Soviet client-state victory. As the decade came to an end, the USSR, ignoring the lessons of history, sent troops to Afghanistan to prop up a Communist ally. That decision would come to haunt the Soviet Union and, according to some, hasten its demise. For, just as Britain suffered a calamitous defeat in that country in 1842, the much-vaunted Soviet army limped home in 1989.

The invasion—a godless society occupying a Muslim nation—led to an international cry for Muslims to rise to the defense of their coreligionists. In response Abdullah Azzam famously issued his fatwa *Defense of the Muslim Lands*, and Osama Bin Laden became a somebody on the battlefields of Afghanistan (there is even an apocryphal story of the future Al Qaeda leader sleeping calmly during the battle for Jalalabad while war raged all around him).

According to Jason Burke, the number of foreign fighters, and their contribution to the war against the Soviet invaders, has been exaggerated. He cites twenty-five thousand in total, most of whom never fought but played supporting roles.[2]

I will not argue with Mr. Burke's figures, but I fear he underestimates the impact of the foreign contingent in Afghanistan. Their true actions may not be the most significant aspect of their presence. I suspect that being part of a ragtag army that defeated a superpower, their interactions with other jihadis from around the world, the material and ideology to which they were exposed while in theater, and their enhanced reputations (they went from talking the talk to walking the walk) should be considered when determining what threat they pose postconflict. And Afghan veterans went onto play roles elsewhere

Other conflicts attracted men with a desire to defend Islam and fight. Many "Afghan Arabs" left Asia for the Balkans and joined Bosnian Muslims in their internecine war with former Yugoslav Croats and Serbs. These veterans, together with others, may have numbered as high as four thousand.[3] Many stayed on in their adopted homeland and had families with locals, and some of these pose a threat to Bosnian, and greater Balkan, security today. It can also not be ruled out that some of these have moved on to the conflict in Syria—or have played a role in radicalizing the next generation, a theme we will return to at the end of this chapter.

Somalia has been a morass for decades, and a number of extremist groups have arisen over that time. It was not until the invasion by Ethiopian forces in mid-2006 that the never-ending war transformed into a call for jihad. This is not surprising, as the arrival of foreign troops, especially if they are not Muslim, is folded into the grand narrative that Islam is under attack and needs true Muslims to rise to its defense.

While figures are hard to come by, it is nevertheless a fact that there was a steady stream of foreigners traveling to Somalia after 2006, many of whom ended up with Al-Shabaab, the region's Al Qaeda affiliate. Included in this mix were Westerners, including Brits, Americans, and Canadians. Omar Hammami, the son of a Western mother and a Middle Eastern father, grew up in Alabama and became a leading figure in Al-Shabaab. Several Canadians are known to have traveled to join Al-Shabaab, some of whom died, including Mahad Ali Dhore, who was killed in a terrorist attack in Mogadishu in 2013.[4] The war in the Caucasus also drew foreigners: Canada's William Plotnikov was killed in Dagestan in 2012.

SCOPE OF THE PROBLEM

Now we come to the focus of this book: Syria and Iraq (where IS has territory and/or influence). There is no question that the sheer number of foreign fighters who have traveled to Syria or Iraq to join groups such as IS or Jabhat al-Nusra (Al Qaeda in Syria or in the Levant) is unprecedented. By the time this book is published, the figures cited here will be woefully inaccurate, but an examination of the situation as of November 2015 will give the reader a sense of both the scale and breadth of the problem. For it is not just the total number that shocks but also the wide variety of states from which fighters originate. It is not an exaggeration to state that we have never seen such an internationalization of violent jihad. Estimates of the total range from twenty- to thirty thousand, with approximately 3,500 from Western nations, although renowned Spanish researcher Fernando Reinares has stated that Western Europeans constitute at least 20 percent of the foreign-fighter contingent.[5] A study by the US–based Soufan Group in December 2015 claimed that thirty-one thousand foreigners from eighty-six nations had joined armed groups in Syria and Iraq.[6] Whatever the true figure, it dwarfs that of previous conflicts. IS as a whole is estimated to have anywhere from thirty- to one hundred thousand fighters, with a quarter of that total coming from abroad.[7]

Think tanks such as the UK's International Centre for the Study of Radicalisation and Political Violence (ICSR) have been monitoring the evolution of the foreign fighter problem in the Levant for years. The following chart is drawn both from its research as well as other open sources (e.g., the Soufan Group). Note that the table is not exhaustive but illustrative.

These figures are astonishing and, as of the time of writing, the flow does not seem to have ebbed. States will continue to deal with this phenomenon for years to come. ICSR's Peter Neumann has stated that the Syria conflict has generated more foreign fighters than Afghanistan, post-2003 Iraq, Somalia, Mali, and other fields of jihad combined.[8] In April 2016, the Netherlands-based International Centre for Counter-terrorism issued a detailed report on European foreign fighters, citing approximately four thousand individuals, with two-thirds originating in four countries (of France, Belgium, Germany, and the UK, Belgium has the highest number per capita).[9]

What I find astonishing is the fact that countries not historically "associated" with foreign fighters have seen their citizens leave for Syria or Iraq: upward of eighty-nine Trinidadians,[10] two hundred citizens of the Maldives (an archipelago in the Indian Ocean),[11] and even two students from Ghana.[12] And there are many more. I believe this points to the success IS has had getting its message out and painting a picture that appeals across a wide spectrum of societies.

Country	Number Believed to Have Joined Up
Indonesia[1]	500–700
Sweden[2]	300
Canada	100
United States	250
United Kingdom	500–760
Tunisia	1,500–6,000
France	1,000–1,700
Belgium	440
Spain	50–100
Germany	500–760
Saudi Arabia	1,500–2,500
Russia	800–7,000

1 "Indonesia: Authorities Struggle to Keep Tabs on ISIL Recruits" Channel News Asia 27, October 27, 2015 http://www.channelnewsasia.com/news/asiapacific/indonesia-found-out-isis/2221116.html.
2 "Pregnant Swedish Teen Freed from ISIS Captivity," The Local, October 29, 2015 http://www.thelocal.se/20151029/pregnant-swedish-teen-freed-from-isis-captivity.

WHO IS GOING?

I have long maintained that it is not possible to profile the kind of person who chooses to subscribe to violent ideologies and then moves on to commit acts of terrorism. There is simply too much variability in the backgrounds and characters of these individuals, whether we are looking at elements like education, employment, family background, marital status, criminal history, and so on, or internal characteristics like psychological state, personality type, mental illness, and on, and on. I have shown, using examples primarily from Canada, that those who went down the path to violent radicalization came from all walks of life and that it was impossible to zero in on one particular sector of society in the hope of limiting the search for the next terrorist.

As with radicalization, so with travel to conflict zones and joining terrorist groups abroad. The variation is tremendous, and it is worth listing a few examples from around the world to make this point clear.

- Salman Ashrafi, a Calgarian who carried out a suicide attack in Iraq in 2013, was a business analyst with oil companies Talisman and Exxon and a graduate of the University of Lethbridge.[13]

- "Jihadi John" (a.k.a. Mohammed Emwazi), a UK jihadi made famous through his brutal beheadings on behalf of IS, is a Kuwait-born computer-science graduate raised and educated in Britain and a former student at the University of Westminster.[14]
- Sally-Anne Jones is a forty-six-year-old Muslim convert from Chatham, Kent, who married an IS computer hacker.[15]
- At least twelve former members of the French military are among the estimated one thousand French citizens who've joined the Islamic State, including one highly trained special-forces commando radicalized while working as a security contractor in the Persian Gulf.[16]
- Samra Kesinovic is the daughter of middle-class Bosnian refugees in Austria and left for IS at the age of seventeen.[17]
- John Maguire grew up in a small town south of Ottawa, attended university, and later converted to Islam before leaving for Syria in December 2012.[18]
- Mohammed Ali Dirie, a convicted member of the Toronto 18, lost his father to violence in Somalia as a child, emigrated to Canada, got into drugs and gangs, served prison time for terrorism, and left to join Jabhat al-Nusra, only to die in 2013.
- Raphael Amar, son of a Catholic mother and Jewish father in France, studied computer science and was killed in late 2014.[19]
- Hisham Hussain Ahmed was an unaccompanied minor asylum seeker from Eritrea in 2003, raised by a foster family in Norway, and killed in October 2014.[20]
- Lucas Kinney is the twenty-six-year-old son of a British film director, a convert to Islam, and a former rock-band member. The "bright, normal teenager" became a leading figure with IS rival Jabhat al-Nusra.[21]
- María Cala Márquez is a "good Catholic girl" living in a pilgrimage town in Spain and now under arrest for trying to leave Madrid to join IS.[22]
- Upward of thirty German soldiers have left their country to join IS.[23]

This short list demonstrates clearly to my mind that those who have chosen the IS path come from a wide variety of backgrounds, some privileged and some less so. I repeat: as with radicalization to violence, so with foreign fighters—there is *no* profile.

MOTIVATIONS

In the earlier chapter on why people chose to go to war, we looked at a representative sample of fighters and drew conclusions based on that sampling. Here we work in a reverse manner. I have been able to identify a few broad themes based on my review of fighters' justifications for their decisions and my career as an intelligence analyst during which I had to draw broad conclusions based on massive data samples. We discuss each of these broad motivations here in brief, followed by quotations from individual fighters. Again, it is important to note that there is likely no exhaustive list of drivers and that each case should be examined individually. Furthermore, I acknowledge that relying on the offered rationale as reported by fighters is problematic. Some may be lying; others may have no real sense of why they chose to join IS. Nevertheless, it remains the best corpus of data we have on motivation, save interviews with actual fighters (which nevertheless suffer from the same shortcomings already cited).

I will not discuss certain motivations that have been proffered in recent months: search for identity, manliness, alienation, and so on. It is not that I do not believe that these may not be drivers for some but rather that it is very difficult to determine whether these motivations are at play. I am not a psychiatrist and am therefore not qualified to assess a person's psychological state or emotional needs. Nor have I seen comprehensive studies on the mental condition of foreign fighters (not surprisingly, they are difficult subjects to interview). In the end, a foreign fighter seeking meaning or who sees the war as an adventure is not likely to say so, as these reasons would be seen as mundane and not as heroic as others; after all, who wants to admit that they are trying to "find themselves"? As I am relying on the actual justifications these individuals provided, I can only use what is out there.

In addition, I am not sure the reasons just enumerated are helpful. Who doesn't experience a need to determine identity? We all have periods in which we are unsure who we are and what we want to do. For many people a sense of adventure is paramount. And for many men the confusing and changing landscape of gender roles may cause them to wonder just what being a man means today. I fear that resorting to these explanations does not get us very far. They certainly do not help those in authority narrow the population set that could be seen as more likely to become foreign fighters. As I have discussed before, these criteria will lead to many false positives and false negatives.

It is also important to note that groups such as IS—especially IS—are masters at getting their message out to the world and at painting the Caliphate as a utopia. Videos of families enjoying a fair—complete with cotton candy and Ferris wheels—as well as luxurious condos and swimming pools depict a normalcy that is attractive. The fact that the reality does not match the advertising is not emphasized. A researcher for Human Rights Watch described why twenty young men from a Dagestani village of two thousand have left for IS: "The flamboyant violence of the Islamic State for some of them is seen as an alternative to a corrupt, secular government."[24] People are flocking to join IS; they are not brainwashed or coerced.

"radicalism"?

Again, I prefer to see this section as theme-based and not individual-based. It has been my experience as an intelligence analyst that certain items rise to the top when you look at large data sets. This is true for violent radicalization, as I have demonstrated with my list of twelve indicators of radicalization.[25] In this chapter, I again return to the use of broad signs underlying why people join groups like IS.

In the following I discuss six motivations. The first four are generic in nature and can usually be found in any individual undergoing a process of violent radicalization. The last two are particularly germane to IS for reasons that will become clear.

Before continuing, it is important to reject the notion that those who join IS have been brainwashed or coerced. I am not sure what *brainwashed* would even mean in this case, and I fear it is often used without really putting much thought into it, as a throwaway, catchall term. Joining is a choice, and it is likely made consciously. As Canadian scholar Amarnath Amarasingam wrote, "Many of these youth did not seem to fit the stereotype we were peddling. They were not brainwashed or seduced. In fact, most were quite articulate and intelligent and believed in a cause they felt to be of utmost importance. They were true believers."[26]

THE *UMMAH* AT RISK

When we examined war in the previous chapter, we noted that on many occasions a sense of nationality, patriotism, or duty to one's country was often offered as a justification for joining the fight, both on a state as well as an individual level. It should not be surprising that governments seek to exploit these sentiments to encourage support for their decisions to fight. And as we saw in the section on conscientious objectors in the First World War, the disinclination to volunteer was frequently painted as unpatriotic.

In Islam, the notion of *ummah* can serve as a sense of global community. The concept stems from the Arabic consonantal root aleph-mim "mother," and while it can refer to a nation or state in general, it tends to be associated with the Islamic nation—that is, the collectivity of the world's Muslims, a community of believers. Interestingly, there is a belief that the world's different faiths broke up what was originally one *ummah*[27] (Judaism, Christianity, and Islam are described as the Abrahamic faiths that share a common prophetic tradition—that is, a community of humans.) As a former great civilization, the Muslim *ummah* has fallen, its influence waned. What began as a small community in western Arabia in the seventh century achieved, through conquest of arms as well as proselytization, the status of empire/Caliphate until the late nineteenth century. Even if the concept of *ummah* is an abstract one and bears little resemblance to current international polity, it does represent the ideal that the world's Muslims do belong to the same faith entity and that this entity transcends political and national bonds (in the Roman Catholic church prayers are said for the "universal" church—the word *catholic* comes from the Greek term for universal—and the end of the Nicene Creed speaks of "one holy, catholic, and apostolic church").

Terrorists see themselves as warriors for the idealized *ummah*. This follows from their conviction that they are the only "true" Muslims, seeking to return Islam to its glory days and rid the faith of its errors and innovations. Those who have joined IS will use the concept of the *ummah* in their justifications for fighting, as the following demonstrates:

- A Tajik member of IS, in a video praising the November 2015 attacks in Paris, said, "Allah permitting, we will enter your homes, O tyrants all over the world. Wait, for we the soldiers of the Islamic Caliphate, Allah permitting, will enter your homes and kill you in your homes, Allah permitting. You can do nothing, Allah willing. You have tanks, cars, weapons, and planes, but Allah is with us. Do not forget, O tyrants of the world, Allah permitting, the soldiers of the Caliphate . . . this is the *ummah* of Muhammad, Allah's peace and blessings be upon him."[28]
- A Russian-language *nasheed* from November 2015 threatened attacks and contained the following lines: "Soon, very soon / the blood will spill like an ocean / The *kafir* throats will tremble from the knives / The lions of the *ummah* have awoken. / They raised their swords, strengthening the *ummah* day after day."[29]
- In October 2015, an Indonesian member of IS urged his countrymen to join the group, enjoining them to "Prove your allegiance. Allah will reward you. If you are unable to make *hijrah*, then do jihad in your homeland. Remove partisan nature from your heart, stay away from divisions, seize the support of the *ummah*. Be honest in your intention! May Allah give you consolidation in your homeland so that it's easier for you to make *hijrah*."[30]

It is obviously in IS's interests to portray itself not only as the return of the Caliphate (see the following) but to position itself as fighting on behalf of the *ummah*. We see this in statements from the organization's leadership:

- In response to a newly created Saudi-led counterterrorism alliance, self-styled IS Caliph al-Baghdadi issued a statement in which he said that "the battle today is no longer a Crusader campaign alone, but it is the fight of all the nations of disbelief against the *ummah* of Islam. It is unprecedented in the history of our *ummah* that all of the world came against it in one battle, as it is happening today. It is the battle of all the disbelievers against all the Muslims, and every Muslim is involved in this war—involved in it by obeying the command of Allah upon him by fulfilling the obligation of jihad in the cause of Allah."[31]

- IS in Ninawa Province, Iraq, noted in December 2015 that "the Islamic *ummah* is the best *ummah* of peoples ever raised up from mankind, when it enjoins goodness, prohibits vice, and establishes the Shariah of the Lord of the Worlds." [32]

- IS Anbar Province eulogized a Jordanian suicide bomber in December 2015 with the words "Muhammad Mazen al-Dhalaein has departed the same as the heroes departed, defending the religion of Allah and giving up his pure blood cheaply to build the great monument of his *ummah*, contrary to others who spend their lives serving the tyrants."[33]

- The Algerian Province of IS issued a statement in October 2015 saying that "many people accuse the Islamic State of what is not in it. It is slandered by people of ignorance and even from those who believe they are knowledgeable, until some of these incorrect concepts were planted firmly in a wide swath of the Muslim peoples and of the mujahideen, believing these lies and falsehood. Amidst these difficult circumstances that the Muslim *ummah* is undergoing and what the State of the Islamic Caliphate is facing in terms of a vicious, barbaric Crusader war, it is our duty to defend it, because we are one structure, one body, and one *ummah*."[34]

- In its pledge of allegiance (*bay'a*) to IS, Nigeria-based Boko Haram said, "We pledged allegiance because the goodness of this *ummah*, concerning both its religious and worldly affairs, will not be achieved except with a leader who governs the people by Allah's law, forces the violators back to the truth, and wages war against those who are obstinately resistant and against those who obstruct the people from the religion of Allah."[35]

If IS can successfully claim that it is acting in the interests of the *ummah*, its reputation and draw will rise. What Muslim would not want to fight to support the universal community of believers? In a similar fashion, the Crusades were launched to protect Christians in the Holy Land, and the leader of the then Christian church, the pope, sought to rally his flock to action. It is worth underscoring that groups such as IS often refer to the West as "Crusaders" and see military action against Muslim-majority countries as an extension of the earlier Crusades. Appeal to a universal body of faith is a powerful tool, one that IS has used to its advantage.

HIJRAH/DISGUST WITH THE WEST

IS spends a lot of time talking about hijrah (migration). It even named the third issue of *Dabiq* (IS's magazine) after the concept—"The Call to Hijrah."

The group has succeeded in exploiting an event that occurred almost fourteen hundred years ago, in the early days of Islam, to call upon Muslims to abandon godless Western societies and travel to join up with the one, true Muslim nation—run by IS, of course.

The term *hijrah* originally referred to the departure of the Prophet Muhammad from his home in Mecca to the northern city of Yathrib (later named Medina in honor of Muhammad—from Madinat Al-Nabi, "the Prophet's city") in CE 622. Muhammad was fleeing his enemies and a probable assassination plot planned by those who were fed up with his message and how he challenged the status quo from which they derived much benefit. The Prophet tried to overturn long-held views and religious practices, and his doctrine of submission to Allah threatened vested interests. As a result, the leading figures in Meccan society decided that things would be better off without the "meddlesome priest." Warned of this attempt on his life, Muhammad succeeded in exiting Mecca with his closest followers.

The year 622 is significant for Muslims for several reasons: It marks year one of the Muslim calendar (*hijri*). It represents the beginning of the consolidation of the nascent Islamic community as Muhammad was able to gain further support, win some key battles against his enemies, and return in triumph to Mecca in 630. And it represented the desire of a religious sect to leave an environment of sin and vice and establish an ideal society where their deeply held beliefs could be practiced openly and safely.

Groups such as IS have frequently described the West as a den of sin and vice. Whether it is the consumption of alcohol, drug use, prostitution, homosexuality, or pornography, among other ills, the West is seen as a godless, corrupt world where religion has been sidelined. Of his time in the United States, Sayyid Qutb wrote in his memoir, *The America I Have Seen*, that

> the American girl is well acquainted with her body's seductive capacity. She knows it lies in the face, and in expressive eyes, and thirsty lips. She knows seductiveness lies in the round breasts, the full buttocks, and in the shapely thighs, sleek legs, and she shows all this and does not hide it. She knows it lies in clothes: in bright colors that awaken primal sensations, and in designs that reveal the temptations of the body—and in American girls these are sometimes live, screaming temptations! Then she adds to all this the fetching laugh, the naked looks, and the bold moves, and she does not ignore this for one moment or forget it! [36]

He went on to criticize the use of alcohol, the lack of spirituality, and racism in US society in similar fashion.

In response to this combination of unacceptable practices, extremist groups argue that Muslims cannot truly practice their faith in non-Muslim countries. Temptations are everywhere and provide opportunities for believers to stray from the one, true path. In addition, Muslims are prohibited—

according to the extremists—from carrying out their religious obligations (daily prayer, fasting during Ramadan, etc.) and are forced to obey laws that are in opposition to sharia (religious) law. Muslims also face daily discrimination for their appearance (e.g., hijabs, niqabs, and other religious clothing), as well as for their practices (daily prayer). In the eyes of many, the West is at a minimum Islamophobic and at a maximum openly at war with Islam.

As a result, Muslims in the West should leave their homelands and migrate to a land where sharia law applies and Muslims constitute the majority, so the logic goes. It is only under these circumstances that Muslims can practice freely and fulfill their obligations as dictated by Allah. And since IS has reestablished the long-abandoned Caliphate, it is incumbent upon Muslims to defend and build it. According to IS:

- A hadith (saying): "There will be hijrah after hijrah. The best people on earth will be those that keep to the land of Ibrahim's hijrah."[37]
- Citing Ibn Taymiyyah, Islamic scholar of the thirteenth century: "So the best of the people on the earth in the end of times will be those who keep to the land of Ibrahim's hijrah, which is Sham [Syria]."[38]
- From issue 3 of *Dabiq*, IS's magazine: "Living amongst the sinful kills the heart, never mind living amongst the *kuffar* [nonbeliever]! Their *kufr* [unbelief] initially leaves dashes and traces upon the heart that over time become engravings and carvings that are nearly impossible to remove. They can destroy the person's *fitra* [instinct] to a point of no return, so that his heart's doubts and desires entrap him fully."
- Also from issue 3 of *Dabiq*: "The crux of hijrah is to abandon sin and its people. . . . And so, the *zunāh* [fornicators/ adulterers], *lūtiyyah* [sodomites], abandoners of jihād, *ahlul-bida'* [people of religious innovations], alcoholics, are all harmful for the religion of Islam, and intermingling with them is also harmful. They do not assist in righteousness nor piety."

As Radio Free Europe/Radio Liberty reported on an issue of *Dabiq*, "The militant group's response was to warn Syrians that leaving IS–controlled lands is a 'dangerous major sin' that will result in 'one's children and grandchildren abandoning Islam for Christianity, atheism, or liberalism.' Even if Syrian refugee children in Europe do not become 'infidels,' they will be 'under the constant threat of fornication, sodomy, drugs, and alcohol,' *Dabiq* preaches. And those children who do not 'fall into sin' will still suffer, because they will forget how to speak Arabic, the language of the Koran and Islam."[39]

Individuals who have left the West to fight with IS often make reference to their hatred of Western society and the need to perform hijrah. The following examples demonstrate these feelings:

- A UK fighter: "I could feel my heart clinging to *dunya* [the material world]. Thoughts of my family, comfort, and so on started to spring into my chest, and I could feel the whispers of *Shaytan* [Satan] becoming more intense as things started to become a reality to me. This feeling gave me the motivation I needed as I knew my soul was clinging to nothing but desires and it was time to let go and move on."[40]
- An American fighter: "When I went back to Florida, it was no good [because of the *fitnah*, or "temptations"]. . . . We were striving for months so we could reach jihad in Syria."[41]
- "So if you can't make *hijrah* you sit, eat & sleep & tweet like cattle and watch your brothers getting slaughtered & sisters raped?"[42]
- "Who has called all Muslims, whether young or old, single or in families, to make hijrah to the state of Islam. A land that has established the shariah, in which a Muslim doesn't feel oppression when practicing [sic] their religion. In which a parent doesn't feel the worry of losing their child to the immorality of society. In which the sick and elderly do not wait in agony, tolerating the partiality of race or social class."[43]
- John Maguire, a Canadian, wrote: "Evil is very prominent in Canadian culture, homosexuality, fornication and adultery are generally accepted, drugs and alcohol are easily accessible and widely accepted as being 'normal,' women and men are often not properly covered, music is widespread in public places . . . one should sacrifice what he has in the West and make hijrah to a land of jihad."[44]
- Farah Shirdon, a Canadian: "This is a message to Canada and all the American *tawagheet* [tyrants]: We are coming and we will destroy you, with permission from Allah the Almighty. I made hijrah to this land for one reason alone, I left comfort for one reason alone—for Allah, Glorified and Exalted be He—and Allah willing, after Sham [Syria], after Iraq, after the [Arabian]Peninsula, we are going for you, Barack Obama."[45]

IS has successfully painted the Caliphate as a pure Muslim land and has used prophetic events (Muhammad's flight to Medina) to encourage Westerners to abandon sin and vice and migrate to the land of the righteous.

DESIRE TO HELP

The war in Syria has resulted, as of the end of November 2015, in two hundred thousand deaths and millions of refugees and internally displaced people. Europe is drowning under the refugee flow, and the neighboring countries of Lebanon, Jordan, and Turkey are dealing with fleeing Syrians of at least a magnitude of order greater. The conflict has seen the use of barrel bombs and chemical weapons as the Assad regime does not appear to care whether civilians are killed or not. The cruelty and slaughter effected by the Syrian government is horrendous.

What began as yet another chapter in the Arab Spring of 2011 has morphed into a humanitarian catastrophe. The international response has been mixed, and the West in particular has been blamed with ignoring the tragedy, even if that accusation is not entirely fair. The calls for assistance have echoed, and governments and NGOs have replied, sending money and supplies to those suffering in Syria.

Not surprisingly, a desire to help is often the first pull for those who eventually become foreign fighters. Muslims in the region and in the West see what is happening and the inadequate response and feel a need to assist their Muslim brothers and sisters. The fact that they are being killed by a fellow Muslim and not the apostate West (the usual suspect) could have been an obstacle to action: As we shall see, there is a way around this (call the regime un-Islamic).

It is important to note as well that not all foreign fighters leave with an initial intent to join a terrorist group such as IS. They may travel to partici-pate in humanitarian aid, only to see this aid as insufficient, or they may be recruited by terrorist groups once in theater. It is also important to remember that some individuals may cite their desire to perform charitable acts to deflect security-service and law-enforcement attention from their true intent. Abdel Lebon, a native of Brussels, would tell his mother that he was engaged in humanitarian work despite videos showing him with the IS flag.[46] There have also been many cases of individuals who claim to be traveling to study (Arabic or Islam) in order to hide their true intent. Damian Clairmont told his mother this story, as we saw at the start of this chapter. Indonesians keen to join IS told relatives that they were traveling on vacation or to Saudi Arabia to perform *umra* (minor pilgrimage).[47]

It is likely that in many cases anger at the situation in Syria constitutes a future foreign fighter's initial foray into the world of jihad. It is, after all, not hard to see why people can move from sincere concern to frustration and disappointment over the lack of effort leveraged to stop the atrocities to an acceptance that action is necessary. For the small number, relatively speak-ing, that choose to join extremist groups, violence is the only answer.

We can see this overarching need to help in the following excerpts:

- John Maguire tweeted in October 2012, "how can I sleep with what is happening in Syria."[48] He later traveled to and is believed to have died in Syria.
- According to the mother of a Dutch foreign fighter, images of "suffering Syrians" touched her son and his friend greatly. They crossed into Syria in November 2013; one has since returned.[49]

- Ifthekar Jaman of Portsmouth, UK, followed events in Syria from the beginning of the uprising in 2011 and moved from humanitarian motives to joining Jabhat al-Nusra.[50]
- According to an Australian report, the Assad regime is responsible for 75 percent of civilian deaths, and this level of atrocity will continue to be an important recruitment tool for terrorist groups.[51]
- From a Dutch foreign fighter: "I came here because it is my duty to do this. I am Muslim and know that the sisters of the *Ummah* are being put into jail and they're being raped, and the children are being killed by the Arab army. . . . I cannot just sit and eat and live with my wife and do nothing, just watch television and do nothing. I'm not that kind of person."[52]
- Abu Abdullah Al Muhajir: "There's something in Islam we call priority and we have to prioritize what we do. So we can't be going around picking olives when there's sisters and brothers inside prisons over here locked up for years and years and are being assaulted, and our mothers are being tortured and raped. How can we live with ourselves in the West, living a comfortable life, when all the brothers are inside these prisons and all the sisters are inside these prisons. Brothers have told us when they're garrisoned on points such as the Central Prison of Aleppo, that they can hear the screams of the sisters when they're getting raped."[53]
- A young Belgian man who died fighting in Syria in 2013 wrote to his mother after his departure, "Please mum, don't be angry. I came here to help Syrian people because nobody helps them."[54]

ANTI-SHIA/ANTI-ASSAD

Bashar al-Assad and his family belong to a small Islamic sect called the Alawites. The Alawite sect is a form of Shiism, to which approximately 10 percent of the world's Muslims belong. Animosity and hatred between Shia and Sunni—mostly directed by the latter against the former—has been going on for almost 1,400 years. There are many places where the two are engaged in mortal combat: Afghanistan, Yemen, Pakistan, and Iraq come to mind.

Within Syria, the Alawites constitute a minority—approximately 12 percent of the population—but have a stranglehold on power and have done so since the rise of Hafez al-Assad (father of the current president). As a minority, the Assads have ruled by oppressing others brutally, best seen in the Hama massacre in 1982 against the Muslim Brotherhood (Sunni Muslims). The Assads have retained power through the use of violence.

For Islamist extremists, who are Sunnis, the only good Shiite is a dead one. Sunni extremists see Shia as apostates and non-Muslim: They are referred to as *rafidain* (those who reject) or *murtaddin* (ones that turn their back on Islam). Neither term is positive, and these descriptors have been used to justify the killing of Shia. Literature and websites are replete with violent language and encouragement to eliminate the Shia.

As the first Shia government to face a formidable indigenous fighter movement, the Assad regime has found itself vilified. This is the first significant jihad in which the governing power is Shia (interestingly, now that the Shia also dominate the state in Iraq, IS has also turned its attention there). Anti-Assad imagery and incitement provide the justification for some to take up arms. As well, Shia communities elsewhere in the Islamic world have provided fodder for IS brutality. Here are a few examples from jihadi postings:

- In a statement marking a suicide attack in Iraq in July 2015, IS posted the following: "In a blessed operation for which Allah facilitated its causes, and as revenge for the weak ones from among the Sunni people, a knight from the knights of martyrdom, the martyrdom-seeker Abu Omar al-Lubnani, wrapped in his explosive belt, launched to immerse amidst a gathering of the Rafidha militia the League of the People of Falsehood, which is responsible for murdering the Sunni people in al-Tuz district. He invoked Allah and detonated his explosives to tear them into scattered parts. After the militias gathered to transfer the killed and wounded, a parked motorcycle was blown up. So the toll was sixty between killed and injured. We ask Allah to accept our brother in the bellies of the green birds [as a martyr] and reward him on behalf of the *Ummah* of Islam."[55]
- The West African branch of IS carried out a suicide bombing against a Shia mosque in northern Nigeria in November and issued the following statement: "In a blessed operation for which Allah facilitated its causes, the martyrdom-seeking brother Abu Suleiman al-Ansari—may Allah accept him—launched with his explosive belt towards a gathering of the polytheist Rafidha in the city of Kano, northern Nigeria. When our brother reached his target, he detonated his explosive belt amidst their gathering, which led to the killing of at least thirty Rafidha and injuring more than one-hundred, and unto Allah is all praise and gratitude. Allah permitting, our operations will continue to harvest the polytheist Rafidha until the land is cleansed of their filth."[56]
- Following a suicide attack on a Shia mosque in Baghdad, IS stated: "In a security operation for which Allah facilitated its causes, a soldier of the Caliphate, Abu Hassan al-Ansari—may Allah accept him—was able to detonate his explosive belt inside a temple of the polytheist Rafidha in the al-Rasheed sub-district. The blast resulted in the killing and wounding of more than 27 Rafidha, and unto Allah is al praise for His enablement and success."[57]

The anti-Shia hatred also inspires individuals in their acts of terrorism:

- In a posthumously released video from the Al Hjjāz province of IS, the suicide attacker at a mosque in Najran, Saudi Arabia, declared his hatred for Shiites: "My first message is a threat for the Ismaili Rafidhah [Shiites]: You will not have a foundation, Allah permitting. By Allah, who there is no god but He, we surely will take revenge for our mother 'Aisha and the pure Companions of our Prophet, may Allah be pleased with them all. You will not enjoy life in the Peninsula of the best one among creation. The Almighty said: 'O you who believe! Fight those of the disbelievers who are close to you, and let them find harshness in you; and know that Allah is with those who are Al-Muttaqun [the pious]' [At-Tawbah: 123]."[58]
- Canadian IS member Farah Shirdon tweeted in June 2014, "Beheading Shia is a beautiful thing."[59]
- "Jihadi John" (Mohammed Emwazi) converted from Shiism to Sunnism under the influence of the leader of Al Qaeda's Khorasan network.[60]

LURE OF THE CALIPHATE

The Caliphate is a political office that dates back to the time of the Prophet Muhammad. Upon his death, his successor (*khalif* in Arabic, caliph in English; *khilafa*—caliphate) was chosen to maintain and expand the nascent Muslim community. One form of the Caliphate or another was in existence until 1924, when it was abolished by Turkish president Ataturk in the wake of the dissolution of the Ottoman Empire. Extremists view that event as a nadir for Islam and Muslims.

No terrorist group has sought to reestablish the Caliphate until Omar al-Baghdadi did in June of 2014. The Taliban under Mullah Omar did create the Islamic Emirate of Afghanistan, and Omar himself was seen as the Commander of the Faithful (*Amir al Mu'min*), but he did not assume the mantle of caliph. Al Baghdadi's declaration was controversial in 2014 and remains so today. The vast majority of the world's Muslims do not recognize the validity of al-Baghdadi's claim. In December 2015, the Tehrik-e-Taliban Pakistan (TTP), a leading Pakistani militant group, rejected the Caliphate of al-Baghdadi's as it neither provided real justice nor governed the entire Islamic world.[61]

Nevertheless, the re-creation of the Caliphate is an important draw for several reasons: It speaks to facts on the ground; even if IS does not have complete control over its territory, much of which is uninhabitable desert, it still constitutes a "state." Many groups have called for the seizure of land and the establishment of a country from which the Caliphate will arise; IS has fast-forwarded right to the Caliphate. A state leads to governance and revenue generation, which IS appears to be doing very successfully, in part through the sale of oil and artifacts and the collection of taxes.

But perhaps the most important part of the appeal of the Caliphate is the symbolism of the declaration. Islam was at its height, both regionally and globally, under the Caliphate of the Abbasids from 750 to 1258. Islamic scholars and scientists advanced a host of fields, ranging from medicine to astronomy to optics. Many argue that Islam has never been higher. Thus, if IS can claim—credibly—to have re-created the polity under which Islam was at its apex, this will draw people in. IS knows this and has used its proclamation to its advantage in its propaganda. Here are a few excerpts from the first issue of IS's primary organ, the magazine *Dabiq*:

- "Glad tidings for the Muslim *ummah*."
- "A new era has arrived of might and dignity for Muslims."
- "The time has come for the *ummah* of Muhammad to wake up from its sleep, remove the garments of dishonor, and shake off the dust of humiliation and disgrace, for the era of lamenting and moaning has gone, and the dawn of honor has emerged anew."
- "Rush, O Muslims, to your state. Yes, it is your state. . . . The State is a state for all Muslims."
- "It is a state where the Arab and the non-Arab, the white man and black man, the easterner and westerner, are all brothers."
- It is a *Khilafah* [caliphate] that gathered the Caucasian, Indian, Chinese, Shami [Syrians], Iraqi, Yemeni, Egyptian, Maghribi [North African], American, French, German, and Australian."
- "Their blood mixed and became one, under a single flag and goal, in one pavilion, enjoying this blessing, the blessing of faithful brotherhood."
- "The Muslims have succeeded today, by the grace of Allah, in bringing the governance of Allah back to the land once again. It is the Caliphate."[62]

We see many references to the Caliphate by those who have elected to join IS:

- From an Indonesian fighter with IS: "My name is Abu Fikri, fifty-one years old, from Bekasi. I was just an ordinary person who didn't really know much about the religion, I don't have a background in formal shar'i education. I just joined some study forums which taught the Qur'an and the religion, like many people had done. . . . Then I heard the *Khilafah* declaration and its leader Shaykh Ibrahim Ibn 'Awwad al-Baghdadi. You have lived too long under this democratic system, inside your homelands. . . . All effort that you do there will result in stabilizing the taghut, the democracy of Pancasila. Join the *Khilafah*, make hijrah to the Islamic

State. No matter how small it is what you do here, it contributes to building and stabilizing the Islamic *Khilafah*."[63]

- From a fighter in West Africa: "The duty upon you all is to pledge allegiance to the Caliph, and this will vex the disbelievers and strengthen the mujahideen. Know that Islamic Shariah has forbidden dispersion and multitudes of allegiances after the selection of the Caliph."[64]

- An IS fighter: "We give advice to the youths and the brothers in all the lands. First, as it is obligatory, compulsory, and in compliance with the command of Allah, Glorified and Exalted be He, they must immigrate from the land of disbelief immediately. They must take the reasons into consideration, no matter what, to immigrate from the land of disbelief to the land of Islam, to the land of the Caliphate, to the Islamic State, where it has honor, happiness, and joy in this life and the hereafter."[65]

- Canadian John Maguire wrote on Facebook that opposing the Caliphate was "apostasy."[66]

- German extremist Denis Cuspert: "I praise God who made you a part of this caliphate [the name given by IS to the lands under its control] and made your province its province. . . . This is the grace of God, that he took you out of decline and chaos and gave you light, the light of the caliphate, the light of victory."[67] He also told Chechen fighters, "Dear brothers, this message is for the Chechen and Dagestani youth and the rest of the youth in Caucasus Province: O my mujahideen brothers, o youth, I urge you to join the caravan of the Caliphate, join Caucasus Province. Those who have not sworn, I urge you to pledge allegiance to the Emir of the Believers. Rush to jihad! Come and be a part of this Caliphate! This Caliphate was built by the grace of Allah and His blessings."[68]

- Canadian Farah Shirdon: "Run to the land of jihad brothers and help us in re-establishing the Islamic caliphate."[69]

- A former Dutch soldier, now a member of IS: "We sincerely love all our brothers and sisters in Islam and invite them to the lands of honor—the lands of the *Khilafah* and to the lands of Jihad."[70]

- A jailed terrorist in Baghdad told a reporter: "Islam is coming. What the Islamic State has achieved in the past year cannot be undone. The caliphate is a reality."[71]

Most Muslims hope for the restoration of the Caliphate one day.[72] For this same group, al-Baghdadi's Caliphate is not legitimate. And yet there is no question that for some the lure of the Caliphate is powerful.

APOCALYPSE

The Islamic State is the first terrorist group to make extensive use of millenarian and apocalyptic language and imagery in its propaganda and messaging. References to the end of days and the signs of the upcoming cosmic battle predate IS—in fact, they began in the early days of Islam—and can be found in the literature of other extremist groups, but it is IS that has brought this event to the fore and exploited. In fact, IS's premiere organ—the magazine *Dabiq*—is named after a place in northern Syria associated with this all-important war.

William McCants of the Brookings Institution has done a very good job explaining the essence of IS and Armageddon in his recent book *The ISIS Apocalypse: The History, Strategy, and Doomsday Vision of the Islamic State*, and I refer the reader to Mr. McCants's writing.[73] Suffice it to say, IS is singularly placed to take advantage of apocalyptic symbolism, due largely in part to the centrality of Syria in the millenarian literature. IS realized this and has devoted quite some time and energy to placing the Caliphate and its role on the historical stage at the center of its messages. Again, a few examples taken from *Dabiq* and other propaganda will illustrate IS's thinking and interpretation of this matter.

The vocabulary and imagery used when referring to these end-of-days events include the *Mahdi* (a figure who will appear to lead true Muslims in battle), *Issa* (Arabic for "Jesus," who will return and fight alongside the *Mahdi*), the *Dajjal* (an anti-Christ-like figure who represents evil and the enemy of Islam), and the Armies of Khorasan.

Some of this language is reflected in the testimonials of those who have traveled to join IS:

- A UK woman: "How can you not want to leave behind offspring who may by the will of Allah be a part of the great Islamic revival? Imagine raising a son and he participates in the Al Malahem? Or having a grandson who is a part of the army of the Mahdi?"[74]
- German extremist Denis Cuspert: "Here the crucial battle will happen, between Imam [Belief] and Kufr [disbelief], between Haqq [Truth] and Batil [falsehood], and you know the revelations, my dear brothers and sisters, and those who don't know, seek for the informations about Sham [Syria], seek for knowledge about 'Isa Ibn Al-Maryam,' about 'Mahdi' about the final battle which will take place here, the Battle between Truth and Falsehood, between Iman and Kufr, between Islam and the religions of the Kuffar, those who follow the Satan."[75]
- A Kosovar fighter: " By Allah, O brothers, we have experienced numerous blessings on this land. Many brothers saw the Messenger, Allah's peace and blessings be upon him, in visions, giving them glad tidings that the

situation is paving the way for the appearance of the Mahdi [Messiah]. By Allah, epics are coming. If you do not go to jihad today, then when?"[76]

- Farah Shirdon: "Shaam [Syria] will undergo an embargo as our Prophet stated [saw]. So for those who are shocked by the Turkish attempt to close the border don't be! The army of Dajjal is getting ready. This is the best time to make *Hijra* my brothers. Prepare for the great wars of Iman [Faith] vs. Kufr [Disbelief]."[77]

- From a jihad e-book: "We Muslims in the West will be fighting the neo-Nazi militias of Western countries and not their armies because their armies will be in *Dabiq*, Syria fighting the great Malhama [slaughter or Armageddon] against the Islamic State."[78]

It is difficult to assign priority to the call for cosmic warfare in the panoply of reasons why individuals in the West leave to fight with IS. There does, however, based on my experience as an intelligence analyst, appear to be a general awareness of the *Mahdi* and the ultimate battle. It is possible that if someone is seriously considering becoming a jihadi and engaging the enemy, with the possibility of martyrdom at the end, the thought that one's death could contribute to the ultimate victory of Islam over its enemies may add motivation. After all, if I am committed to dying *fi sabil Allah* (in the cause of Allah), what better place to do so than at the side of *Issa* and the *Mahdi* as they destroy Islam's foes? Not only are there rewards for martyrdom, but you would take your place among the true, heroic Muslims who answered the call and helped usher in an era of perfection. According to French professor of Middle East studies and author of *Apocalypse in Islam*, Jean-Pierre Filiu, "It's a very powerful and emotional narrative. It gives the potential recruit and the actual fighters the feeling that not only are they part of the elite, they are also part of the final battle."[79]

MISCELLANEOUS FACTORS

There are a few factors that have contributed to the high number of foreign fighters who have made their way to Syria and the Islamic State. I believe that these factors were not always present in previous conflicts that were, as a result, not as attractive for foreigners. Furthermore, it may be the combination of these factors that has led to the current boom in Syria and Iraq.

Ease of Access

Unlike jihads in Afghanistan and Somalia, the Syrian conflict is relatively easy to enter. Interested fighters can take cheap flights to major hubs (Istanbul, Cairo, or Beirut) and travel by land or commuter flight to the border with Syria. To further evade detection, aspiring jihadists can perform the hajj in

Mecca or fly to any European destination and travel over land through Turkey to Syria.

Social Media

It is no exaggeration to say that the conflict in Syria is the first to be played out over social media. Groups such as IS and Jabhat al-Nusra avail themselves of Twitter, Facebook, WhatsApp, and any number of platforms to distribute propaganda, provide updates on progress on the battlefield, and portray life in their territory as normal. In addition, the availability of Internet and cell-phone connections appeals to the largely young pool from which foreign fighters are drawn.

Instructions on How to Travel

Tied to the ubiquity of social media are the meticulous details provided those seeking to travel to the region. Aspirants are coached on how to buy tickets, which flights to avoid, whom to contact upon arrival in a transit zone, and what to bring. IS has taken the uncertainty out of joining a terrorist group.

RELIGION AS A MOTIVATOR

It is only really with IS (or AQ or Al-Shabaab or . . .) that we see religion as a dominant factor for foreign fighters. I am not suggesting that it is the only factor, or even always the overarching one (several fighters from the UK had a copy of *Islam for Dummies* with them when they left). But it does surface consistently in the videos, audio files, tweets, and other communications that these people create. To ignore it, therefore, would be a huge error in understanding why more than 3,500 Westerners have made the trip to the Levant.

None of this should be surprising, of course. IS and others such as Jabhat al-Nusra are, after all, Islamist extremist groups for which Islam has a paramount role. They express themselves in religious terms and see themselves as iconic Muslims—so much so that they kill Muslims they perceive as less valid than them. People inspired by these groups, then, would be drawn in part by the religious narrative they spin.

It would be interesting to compare the motivations associated with IS and similar groups to those of non-Islamist groups on the ground in Syria, such as the Free Syrian Army (FSA). We could put forward the hypothesis that members of the FSA join for nationalist or other rationales: People driven largely by religion would surely opt for IS, no?

It is important to understand motivation if we want to try to discourage the movement of our citizens to Syria. It is only by achieving that understanding that we can devise strategies to deal with those individuals in the hope of diverting them from the path to destruction—their own of that of others. This chapter is a small contribution in that direction.

As with radicalization and counter-radicalization, so with foreign fighters. Each case must be examined on its own merits and individualized solutions proffered. We can identify larger trends, but only in getting at the specific drivers of each individual can we hope to make progress.

WHY ARE SOME PEOPLE COMING BACK?

Despite the seemingly never-ending flow of fighters and the vast amounts of IS propaganda encouraging more to come, some of those who joined up and spent time in the Caliphate are returning—and telling their stories. This activity is risky, as disgruntled warriors are subject to execution for wanting to leave and expose themselves to retribution by publicly undermining the Islamic State. We will discuss the issue of using returnees as props in counterterrorism efforts in the next chapter.

PARALLELS WITH CHILD SOLDIERS?

The majority of Western Muslims who choose to fight in foreign wars are young (eighteen to thirty, although some are younger). There have been attempts, at times, to compare the recruitment and deployment of younger members to that of child soldiers, a scourge that we often associate with brutal wars in Africa but which is actually defined in such a way that it applies to the enlistment of any child (under the age of eighteen). So, are there parallels?

In my opinion, not really. Research into the reasons why children fight have found the following general factors:

- High rates of poverty
- Education (either lack of or opportunity for state/militias to recruit or indoctrinate)
- Employment (lack thereof)
- Influence of family and friends (i.e., it is normal or expected)
- Need to overturn an oppressive regime
- Leaders use ethnicity or nationalism to mobilize
- The peculiarities of adolescence:

  - Self-image
  - Search for identity
  - A sense of strength and power
  - Opportunity

- Acceptance of violence in one's culture or community[80]

The research also shows that not all children in these situations join and that context plays a huge role.

How do these factors play into the foreign-fighter pool? Not well. Aside from the presence of a desire to overthrow an oppressive regime and leaders' use of ideology, the parallels seem few and far between. True, there is a sense of identity search and self-image may play a role, but I see few lessons to learn from the child-soldier literature. Furthermore, there is a much greater incidence of coercion and force in many child-soldier situations than there is with foreign fighters. The latter are not coerced: They willingly choose to join.

SUMMARY

What then can we conclude about why thousands of Westerners elect to fight with groups like IS? Even with a small sample set, certain patterns emerge. Not dissimilar to those soldiers who fought in the Spanish Civil War and with the IDF, there are individuals who want to help an underdog (there is little question that IS is at a disadvantage with respect to the Russian- and Iranian-supplied Syrian army and air force). The notion of the *ummah* recalls the patriotism of Canadians post–World War I and Americans after 9/11. The long-simmering sectarian hatred between Sunni and Shia helps to explain some cases. And then there are the uniquely IS ideas of the reestablishment of the Caliphate and the cosmic battle at the end of time. There are surely other reasons. I cannot comment on the adventure or thrill aspect for IS fighters, as I did not measure it. The other motivations, however, are clearly unique to Islamist extremist groups.

The reader should be struck by the ordinariness of many of these justifications. They have been present throughout history and will likely exert pull in the future. As a result, the common notion that foreign fighters are volunteering for invalid reasons appears to be false. Yes, we are at war with IS and we need to come up with ways to stop foreign fighters from going to Syria, but we cannot reduce their motivations to mental illness or mere crazed religious fervor.

Even if not all aspiring fighters are religiously driven, the main narrative as constructed by IS is religious in nature. Discomfort at discussing this factor will serve us ill as we make decisions on responses. We need to get past the fear of talking about Islam when we talk about IS.

Before we turn to the main theme of this book—whether these foreign fighters pose a threat to the societies they left—we need to discuss the new phenomenon of females in IS.

NOTES

1. Christianne Boudreau in discussion with the author, August 2015.

2. Jason Burke, *Al Qaeda: Casting a Shadow of Terror* (New York: I. B. Tauris), 58.

3. Craig Pyes, Josh Meyer, and William C. Rempel, "Bosnia Seen as Hospitable Base and Sanctuary for Terrorists," *Los Angeles Times*, October 7, 2001, http://articles.latimes.com/2001/oct/07/news/mn-54505.

4. Stewart Bell, "Canadian Linked to Terrorist Group Was Killed in Suicide Attack in Somalia: Community Source," *National Post* (Toronto), April 15, 2013, http://news.nationalpost.com/news/canadian-linked-to-terrorist-group-was-killed-in-suicide-attack-in-somalia-community-source.

5. Fernando Reinares, "Fábricas de Terroristas," Real Instituto Elcano, October 27, 2015, http://www.realinstitutoelcano.org/wps/portal/web/rielcano_es/contenido?WCM_GLOBAL_CONTEXT=/elcano/elcano_es/zonas_es/terrorismo+internacional/reinares-fabricas-de-terroristas.

6. Lucy Westcott, "Report: Number of Foreign Fighters in Iraq and Syria Double to 31,000," *Newsweek*, December 7, 2015, http://www.newsweek.com/foreign-fighters-syria-and-iraq-double-31000-86-countries-report-402084.

7. *The Economist*, "Fighting Near and Far," Briefing, November 21, 2015, http://www.economist.com/news/briefing/21678847-islamic-state-may-be-lashing-out-abroad-because-it-has-been-weakened-nearer-home-it-will.

8. Daniel Byman, "What Do the Paris Attacks Tell Us about Foreign Fighters?" *Washington Post*, November 16, 2015, https://www.washingtonpost.com/news/monkey-cage/wp/2015/11/16/what-do-the-paris-attacks-tell-us-about-foreign-fighters/.

9. International Centre for Counter-terrorism (ICCT), "The Foreign Fighters Phenomenon in the European Union: Profiles, Threats and Policies." ICCT research paper. The Hague: ICCT, 2016. https://www.icct.nl/wp-content/uploads/2016/03/ICCT-Report_Foreign-Fighters-Phenomenon-in-the-EU_1-April-2016_including-AnnexesLinks.pdf.

10. *Latin American Herald Tribune* (Caracas), "Trinidad Creates Hotline for Tips on Would-Be Jihadists," December 3, 2015, http://www.laht.com/article.asp?ArticleId=2401239&CategoryId=14092.

11. Oliver Wright, "Islamic State: The Maldives—A Recruiting Paradise for Jihadists," *Independent* (London), September 13, 2014, http://www.independent.co.uk/news/world/asia/islamic-state-the-maldives-a-recruiting-paradise-for-jihadists-9731574.html.

12. Lydia Tomkiw, "ISIS in Africa: Islamic State Recruits 2 Ghana Students, Targets African Universities," *International Business Times* (New York), August 28, 2015, http://www.ibtimes.com/isis-africa-islamic-state-recruits-2-ghana-students-targets-african-universities-2073572.

13. Stewart Bell, "Iraq Suicide Bomber Was Once a Calgary Business Analyst Who 'Seemed like a Regular Guy,'" *National Post* (Toronto), June 4, 2014, http://news.nationalpost.com/news/canada/calgary-business-analyst-seemed-like-a-regular-guy-before-he-became-a-suicide-bomber-in-iraq.

14. Associated Press, "Mohammed Emwazi Photo Shows 'Jihadi John' as University Student," February 28, 2015, CBC News, http://www.cbc.ca/news/world/mohammed-emwazi-photo-shows-jihadi-john-as-university-student-1.2977027.

15. Rowena Mason, "Four Britons Fighting with Islamic State Sanctioned by UN," *Guardian* (London), September 28, 2015, http://www.theguardian.com/world/2015/sep/28/four-britons-fighting-isis-put-on-un-sanctions-list.

16. Mitchell Prothero, "Former Members of France's Military Have Joined Islamic State," *McClatchy DC*, February 4, 2015, http://www.mcclatchydc.com/news/nation-world/world/article24779653.html.

17. Allan Hall, "One of the Teenage Austrian 'Poster Girls' Who Ran Away to Join ISIS Has Been Killed in the Conflict Says UN," *Daily Mail*, December 18, 2014, http://www.dailymail.co.uk/news/article-2879272/One-teenage-Austrian-poster-girls-ran-away-join-ISIS-killed-conflict-says.html.

18. Andrew Duffy and Meghan Hurley, "From JMag to Jihad John: The Radicalization of John Maguire," *Ottawa Citizen*, February 7, 2015, http://ottawacitizen.com/news/local-news/from-jmag-to-jihad-john-the-radicalization-of-john-maguire.

19. Jewish Telegraphic Agency, "French Islam Convert with Jewish Father Dies Fighting with ISIS in Syria," November 12, 2014, found online at http://www.haaretz.com/jewish-world/jewish-world-news/1.626127.

20. Ola Haram and Kadafi Zaman, "Two Norwegian ISIS Fighters Killed in Syria," TV2 (Norway), November 18, 2014, http://www.tv2.no/2014/11/18/nyheter/6248152, and found online in English translation at http://eastafro.com/2014/11/19/two-norwegian-isis-fighters-killed-in-syria.

21. Tom Wyke and Neil Sears, "EXCLUSIVE: British Son of Hollywood Movie Director, 26, Is Revealed as Bloodthirsty Star of Al-Qaeda Propaganda Videos After Converting from Catholicism and Smuggling Himself to Syria," *Daily Mail*, updated October 19, 2015, http://www.dailymail.co.uk/news/article-3278441/Revealed-British-son-Indiana-Jones-movie-director-al-Qaeda-jihadi-poster-boy-bent-terror.html.

22. Fiona Govan, "Judge Questions 'Good Catholic Girl' Who Converted into a 'Bride of ISIS,'" *Local* (Madrid), October 21, 2015, http://www.thelocal.es/20151021/judge-questions-good-catholic-girl-who-converted-into-a-bride-of-isis.

23. *Local* (Berlin), "German Soldiers 'May Have Joined ISIS in Syria,'" April 12, 2016, Deutsche Presse-Agentur and *Local* (Berlin), http://www.thelocal.de/20160412/german-soldiers-may-have-joined-isis-in-syria.

24. Andrew Roth, "The Russian Village That Sent 20 Men to Wage Jihad in Syria," *Washington Post*, October 27, 2015, https://www.washingtonpost.com/world/europe/the-russian-village-that-sent-20-men-to-wage-war-in-syria/2015/10/27/7cfd158a-7444-11e5-ba14-318f8e87a2fc_story.html.

25. The twelve indicators of radicalism are (1) a sudden increase in intolerant religiosity, (2) the rejection of different interpretations of Islam, (3) the rejection of non-Muslims, (4) the rejection of Western ways, (5) the rejection of Western policies (domestic, military, foreign, social, etc.), (6) associations with like-minded people, (7) an obsession with jihadi websites, (8) an obsession with the narrative, (9) a desire to travel to conflict zones, (10) an obsession with jihad, (11) an obsession with martyrdom, and (12) an obsession with end of time. For a complete discussion of this topic, see my previous book, *The Threat from Within: Recognizing Al Qaeda–Inspired Radicalization and Terrorism in the West* (Rowman & Littlefield, 2016).

26. Amarnath Amarasingam, "What Twitter Really Means for Islamic State Supporters," War on the Rocks (website), December 30, 2015, http://warontherocks.com/2015/12/what-twitter-really-means-for-islamic-state-supporters/.

27. Anthony Black, *The History of Islamic Political Thought* (New York: Routledge, 2011), 13.

28. SITE Intelligence Group, "Belgian, Algerian and Tajik IS Fighters in Deir al-Zour Promote Paris Attacks, Call Upon Lone Wolves," November 23, 2015, https://news.siteintelgroup.com/Jihadist-News/belgian-algerian-and-tajik-is-fighters-in-deir-al-zour-promote-paris-attacks-call-upon-lone-wolves.html (subscription required).

29. SITE Intelligence Group, "IS Releases Russian Video Chant Threatening Attacks in Russia," November 12, 2015, https://news.siteintelgroup.com/Jihadist-News/is-releases-russian-video-chant-threatening-attacks-in-russia.html (subscription required).

30. SITE Intelligence Group, "Indonesian IS Fighter Calls on Muslims to Travel to Join IS, Attack at Home," October 17, 2015, https://news.siteintelgroup.com/Jihadist-News/indonesian-is-fighter-calls-on-muslims-to-travel-to-join-is-attack-at-home.html (subscription required).

31. SITE Intelligence Group, "IS Leader Abu Bakr al-Baghdadi Criticizes Saudi-Led Islamic Military Alliance, Threatens Enemy States," December 26, 2015, https://news.siteintelgroup.com/Multimedia/is-leader-abu-bakr-al-baghdadi-criticizes-saudi-led-islamic-military-alliance-threatens-enemy-states.html (subscription required).

32. SITE Intelligence Group, "IS' Ninawa Province Releases Video of Fighters Training with Tanks, Amphibious Military Vehicles," December 11, 2015, https://news.siteintelgroup.com/Jihadist-News/is-ninawa-province-releases-video-of-fighters-training-with-tanks-amphibious-military-vehicles.html (subscription required).

33. SITE Intelligence Group, "IS Video Focuses on Suicide Bomber Son of Jordanian MP," December 6, 2015, https://news.siteintelgroup.com/Jihadist-News/is-video-focuses-on-suicide-bomber-son-of-jordanian-mp.html (subscription required).

34. SITE Intelligence Group, "IS' Algeria Province Releases Audio Promoting group, Predicting Russian Failure in Syria," October 21, 2015, https://news.siteintelgroup.com/Jihadist-News/is-algeria-province-releases-audio-promoting-group-predicting-russian-failure-in-syria.html (subscription required).

35. Islamic State of Iraq and the Levant, "Shari'ah Alone Will Rule Africa," *Dabiq*, no. 8 (March 30, 2015): 15.

36. Sayyid Qutb, "The America I Have Seen," 1949, available online at http://www.kalamullah.com/Books/The America I have seen.pdf.

37. Islamic State of Iraq and the Levant, "A Call to Hijrah," *Dabiq*, no. 3 (September 10, 2014): 10.

38. Ibid.

39. Joanna Paraszczuk, "How Islamic State Use the Iconic Photo of Drowned Syrian Child to Warn Against Leaving Its 'Caliphate,'" Radio Free Europe/Radio Liberty, September 10, 2015, http://www.rferl.org/content/islamic-state-aylan-kurdi-syria-propaganda-/27237850.html.

40. Ibid., 34.

41. Ibid., 41.

42. SITE Intelligence Group, "Jihadi Fighters on Twitter Call for Donations, Lone Wolf Attacks," August 17, 2015, https://news.siteintelgroup.com/Western-Jihadist-Forum-Digest/jihadi-fighters-on-twitter-call-for-donations-lone-wolf-attacks.html (subscription required).

43. SITE Intelligence Group, "IS Fighter Distributes Message from UK Family of 12 on Immigrating to Caliphate," July 3, 2015, https://ent.siteintelgroup.com/Chatter/is-fighter-distributes-message-from-uk-family-of-12-on-immigrating-to-caliphate.html (subscription required).

44. Stewart Bell, "Extremist Named John Maguire: Ottawa Student Likely Joined ISIS after Converting to Islam and Moving to Syria," *National Post* (Toronto), August 25, 2014, last updated January 24, http://news.nationalpost.com/news/canada/extremist-named-john-maguire-ottawa-student-likely-joined-isis-after-converting-to-islam-and-moving-to-syria.

45. Rita Katz, "From Teenage Colorado Girls to Islamic State Recruits: A Case Study in Radicalization via Social Media," *Insite Blog on Terrorism and Extremism*, [December 2014], http://news.siteintelgroup.com/blog/index.php/submissions/21-jihad/4445-from-teenage-colorado-girls-to-islamic-state-recruits-a-case-study-in-radicalization-via-social-media.

46. Katrin Kuntz and Gregor Peter Schmitz, "The Belgium Question: Why Is a Small Country Producing So Many Jihadists?" *Spiegel Online*, January 27, 2015, http://www.spiegel.de/international/world/belgium-muslim-youth-turning-toward-jihad-in-large-numbers-a-1015045.html.

47. *Channel NewsAsia*, "Indonesia Found Out ISIS Militants Were Citizens Only After Their Deaths," October 27, 2015, http://www.channelnewsasia.com/news/asiapacific/indonesia-found-out-isis/2221116.html.

48. Stewart Bell, "Extremist Named John Maguire: Ottawa Student Likely Joined ISIS after Converting to Islam and Moving to Syria," *National Post* (Toronto), August 25, 2014, last updated January 24, http://news.nationalpost.com/news/canada/extremist-named-john-maguire-ottawa-student-likely-joined-isis-after-converting-to-islam-and-moving-to-syria.

49. Samar Batrawi and Ilona Chmoun, "Dutch Foreign Fighters Continue to Travel to Syria," *CTC Sentinel* 7, no. 7 (July 2014): 11–14, available online at https://www.ctc.usma.edu/posts/dutch-foreign-fighters-continue-to-travel-to-syria.

50. Shiraz Maher, "From Portsmouth to Kobane: The British Jihadis Fighting for ISIS," *New Statesman*, November 6, 2014, http://www.newstatesman.com/2014/10/portsmouth-kobane.

51. Sophie McNeill, "Islamic State Will Thrive while President Assad's Atrocities Go Unpunished, Middle East Correspondent Reports," *ABC News*, August 23, 2015, http://www.abc.net.au/news/2015-08-23/assads-atrocities-go-unpunished-but-isis-to-thrive/6716788.

52. SITE Intelligence Group, "'Al Muhajirun' Video Promotes Role of Foreign Fighters in Syria, Calls Muslims to Come for Jihad," July 17, 2015, https://news.siteintelgroup.com/Jihadist-News/al-muhajirun-video-promotes-role-of-foreign-fighters-in-syria-calls-muslims-to-come-for-jihad.html (subscription required)

53. Ibid.

54. Nina Lamparski, with Olivia Rondonuwu, Agence France-Presse, "Muslim Mothers Fight 'Toxic' Merchants of Terror," March 31, 2016, Yahoo! News, https://www.yahoo.com/news/muslim-mothers-fight-toxic-merchants-terror-062454826.html.

55. SITE Intelligence Group, "IS Claims Suicide Attack on Shia Militants in Kirkuk," July 25, 2015, https://news.siteintelgroup.com/Jihadist-News/is-claims-suicide-attack-on-shia-militants-in-kirkuk.html (subscription required).

56. SITE Intelligence Group, "IS' West Africa Province Claims Suicide Bombing on Shi'ites in Nigeria," November 28, 2015, https://ent.siteintelgroup.com/Statements/is-west-africa-province-claims-suicide-bombing-on-shi-ites-in-nigeria.html (subscription required).

57. SITE Intelligence Group, "IS Claims Suicide Bombing at Shi'ite Mosque in Southern Baghdad," November 20, 2015, https://news.siteintelgroup.com/Jihadist-News/is-claims-suicide-bombing-at-shi-ite-mosque-in-southern-baghdad.html (subscription required).

58. SITE Intelligence Group, "Najran Mosque Suicide Bomber Threatens Shi'ites, Saudi Soldiers in Posthumous IS Audio," October 27, 2015, https://news.siteintelgroup.com/Jihadist-News/najran-mosque-suicide-bomber-threatens-shi-ites-saudi-soldiers-in-posthumous-is-audio.html (subscription required).

59. Katrina Clarke, "Farah Mohamed Shirdon, Calgary ISIS Fighter Reportedly Killed in Iraq, Was 'Dead Inside' Long Ago, Friend Says," *National Post* (Toronto), August 15, 2014, last updated January 24, http://news.nationalpost.com/news/canada/calgary-islamist-who-fought-with-isis-is-dead-reports-say.

60. Robert Tait, "Jihadi John Radicalised after Meeting Al-Qaeda Chief, Kuwaiti Sources Say," *Telegraph* (London), March 1, 2015, http://www.telegraph.co.uk/news/11442904/Jihadi-John-radicalized-after-meeing-al-Qaeda-chief-Kuwaiti-sources-say.html.

61. *Khaama Press* (Kabul), "Pakistani Taliban Call Caliphate of Al-Baghdadi as 'Un-Islamic,'" December 20, 2015, http://www.khaama.com/pakistani-taliban-call-caliphate-of-al-baghdadi-as-un-islamic-4405.

62. SITE Intelligence Group, "IS' Ninawa Province Beheads, Shoots to Death Spies in Grisly Video," October 20, 2015, https://news.siteintelgroup.com/Jihadist-News/is-ninawa-province-beheads-shoots-to-death-spies-in-grisly-video.html (subscription required).

63. SITE Intelligence Group, "Indonesian IS Fighter Calls on Muslims to Travel to Join IS, Attack at Home," October 17, 2015, https://news.siteintelgroup.com/Jihadist-News/indonesian-is-fighter-calls-on-muslims-to-travel-to-join-is-attack-at-home.html (subscription required).

64. SITE Intelligence Group, "Fighter in IS' West Africa Province Urges Shabaab to Pledge to Baghdadi," October 14, 2015, https://news.siteintelgroup.com/Jihadist-News/fighter-in-is-west-africa-province-urges-shabaab-to-pledge-to-baghdadi.html (subscription required).

65. SITE Intelligence Group, "IS Fighters in Video Warn Migrants about Living in Europe, Must Not Leave 'Caliphate,'" September 17, 2015, https://news.siteintelgroup.com/Jihadist-News/is-fighters-in-video-warn-migrants-about-living-in-europe-say-they-must-not-leave-caliphate.html (subscription required).

66. Stewart Bell, "Extremist Named John Maguire: Ottawa Student Likely Joined ISIS after Converting to Islam and Moving to Syria," *National Post* (Toronto), August 25, 2014, last updated January 24, http://news.nationalpost.com/news/canada/extremist-named-john-maguire-ottawa-student-likely-joined-isis-after-converting-to-islam-and-moving-to-syria.

67. Joanna Paraszczuk, "German Ex-Rapper Deso Dogg 'Stars' in Russian IS Recruitment Video," Radio Free Europe/Radio Liberty, August 7, 2015, http://www.rferl.org/content/islamic-state-ex-germen-rapper-in-russian-recruitment-video/27176362.html.

68. SITE Intelligence Group, "German Fighter Denis Cuspert Congratulates 'Caucasus Province' in IS Video," August 5, 2015, https://news.siteintelgroup.com/Jihadist-News/german-fighter-denis-cuspert-congratulates-caucasus-province-in-is-video.html (subscription required).

69. Stewart Bell, "New Details about Canadian Jihadist Farah Shirdon Reveal Militant Ideology behind ISIS," *National Post* (Toronto), October 7, 2014, http://news.nationalpost.com/news/canada/new-details-about-canadian-jihadist-farah-shirdon-reveal-militant-ideology-behind-isis.

70. SITE Intelligence Group, "IS Fighter Reaches Out to Muslims in Militaries, Claims Dutch Soldier Recently Joined IS," September 4, 2015, https://news.siteintelgroup.com/Western-Jihadist-Forum-Digest/is-fighter-reaches-out-to-muslims-in-militaries-claims-dutch-soldier-recently-joined-is.html (subscription required).

71. Martin Chulov, "No Regrets, No Remorse: Isis Mastermind Who Sent Out 15 Suicide Bombers," *Guardian* (London), August 31, 2015, https://www.theguardian.com/world/2015/aug/31/isis-mastermind-15-suicide-bombers-baghdad-islamic-state.

72. Sami Moubayed, "What an Alternative Islamic State Looks Like," *Telegraph* (London), September 23, 2015, http://www.telegraph.co.uk/news/worldnews/islamic-state/11884532/Many-Muslims-do-want-a-Caliphate-just-not-this-one.html.

73. William McCants, *The ISIS Apocalypse: The History, Strategy, and Doomsday Vision of the Islamic State* (New York: St. Martin's Press, 2015).

74. SITE Intelligence Group, "British Woman Describes Life of Female Emigrants in Syria," April 21, 2014, https://news.siteintelgroup.com/Western-Jihadist-Forum-Digest/british-woman-describes-life-of-female-emigrants-in-syria.html (subscription required).

75. SITE Intelligence Group, "German Rapper Turned Jihadist Ruben Cuspert (Deso Dogg) Pledges to ISIL," April 11, 2014, https://news.siteintelgroup.com/Jihadist-News/german-rapper-turned-jihadist-ruben-cuspert-deso-dogg-pledges-to-isil.html (subscription required).

76. SITE Intelligence Group, "Kosovo Fighter Promotes Jihad in Syria in ISIL Video," October 14, 2013, https://news.siteintelgroup.com/Jihadist-News/kosovo-fighter-promotes-jihad-in-syria-in-isil-video.html (subscription required).

77. SITE Intelligence Group, "Prominent IS Recruiters Call for Continued Migration via Turkey, Condemn Others Expressing Doubt," July 29, 2015, https://news.siteintelgroup.com/Western-Jihadist-Forum-Digest/prominent-is-recruiters-call-for-continued-migration-via-turkey-condemn-others-expressing-doubt.html (subscription required).

78. SITE Intelligence Group, "Jihad E-book Suggests Muslims in the West Form Gangs as Step towards Jihad, Seizing Rome," July 6, 2015, https://news.siteintelgroup.com/Jihadist-News/jihadi-e-book-suggests-muslims-in-the-west-form-gangs-as-step-towards-jihad-seizing-rome.html (subscription required).

79. Rukmini Callimachi, "U.S. Seeks to Avoid Ground War Welcomed by Islamic State," *New York Times*, December 7, 2015, http://www.nytimes.com/2015/12/08/world/middleeast/us-strategy-seeks-to-avoid-isis-prophecy.html.

80. Rachel Brett and Irma Specht, *Young Soldiers: Why They Choose to Fight* (Boulder, CO: Lynne Rienner, 2004).

Chapter Five

Women and Jihad

To women everywhere, especially those who care about the *ummah*, may you be aware that the *ummah* of Muhammad (pbuh), which would not rise without your help, do not disgrace the caliphate, but serve it even if it is by one word, may your sons be the bricks and mortar in the tower of majesty and minarets of the State of Islam.

—Al Khanassaa Brigade manifesto

CHAPTER ABSTRACT

The deployment of women in combat positions is controversial in the West as well as for Islamist extremist groups. While some groups have long used female operatives, the number of women traveling to join IS is unprecedented. The reasons are in part analogous to those of men, with slight differences.

WOMEN IN BATTLE

It is safe to say that warfare is a man's game. While Greek legends of the prowess of Amazon warriors provide an interesting exception, it is nevertheless true that the overwhelming majority of those who fight and die on battlefields are men. It is also true that women bear the lion's share of war's destructive aftermath: rape and sexual abuse, having to lead fatherless families, forced to flee as refugees, and so on. If you asked women across history if war is worth waging, I am fairly certain you would get a resounding no as an answer. There are also allegations that females in the military face alarming rates of sexual assault.

Nevertheless, women do sign up for the military. The reasons for doing so are probably similar to those for men: career opportunities, nationalism, a desire to serve one's country. There has also been a spirited debate in Canada and the United States about whether women should be placed in combat roles, with pluses and minuses on both sides. War is no longer just for the boys, it seems.

WOMEN IN TERRORIST GROUPS

As in the military, most members of terrorist groups tend to be male. Again, this is not surprising. There are, nevertheless, some interesting exceptions. The Liberation Tigers of Tamil Eelam were particularly known for their use of women as suicide bombers. Some Chechen extremist groups also employed female operatives known as Black Widows. But the presence of females as frontline terrorists remains rare.

In my experience as an intelligence analyst, women served as support for their terrorist partners. Their contributions ranged from ideological acquiescence to what their husbands or brothers were involved in to actual promotion of violence. The wife of one of the leaders of the 2006 Toronto 18 cell was a keen fan of her husband's violent extremism.

Other women have actually carried out, or planned to carry out, terrorist attacks. These include the following:

- Roshanara Choudhry was a gifted university student in London, England, before she radicalized and stabbed her local MP with a knife in May 2010.
- The San Bernardino terrorists of December 2015 included a Pakistani immigrant to the United States, Tashfeen Malik, who together with her husband killed fourteen people and wounded many more before being shot dead by police.
- Muriel Degauque was a Belgian convert to Islam who blew herself up north of Baghdad in 2005, killing five police officers.
- Authorities in southern France arrested a couple in late December 2015 and charged them with planning a terrorist act. The woman, a twenty-three-year-old convert to Islam and mother of a two-year-old, had in her possession a fake pregnant belly that had been hollowed out: Police fear that it could have been used to store explosives.[1]

Nevertheless, female operatives appear to be the exception and not the rule to date.

WOMEN AND WAR IN ISLAM

There is not a great deal written about the role of women in warfare throughout Islamic history since the issue was of no consequence: Men were responsible for battle. On the other hand, there is a great deal of jurisprudence concerning how to treat women (and children) in war. Women cannot be targeted for killing. Women captured as slaves in war can be treated as sexual partners.

When it comes to terrorist groups, however, the exchange of views has proved interesting. The wife of then-Al Qaeda second-in-command Ayman al-Zawahiri wrote an essay to the "Muslim sisters" in which she entreated women to support jihad and their mujahid husbands and family members. Children should be raised to love jihad, and women should encourage their male relatives to defend Muslim lands and take back those areas occupied by Islam's enemies. Women should also support jihad financially and aid those families whose mujahideen are captured or injured.

Umaymah Hasan Ahmad Muhammad Hasan[2] also spoke of whether or not jihad was *fard 'ayn* for women. She noted that, while all Muslims are obliged to fight, it is "not easy" for a woman, as she needs a *mahram* (male relative) to accompany her when she travels. A better role is one of support, although Hasan did praise those women who carried out suicide attacks in Palestine, Chechnya, and Iraq.[3]

A female member of the Islamic Movement of Uzbekistan, Umm Safiyya, renounced her German citizenship in 2011 and released a message titled "Unity and Justice and Freedom" in which she eulogized her husband and called on Muslim women to join her in jihad. Here are some excerpts from her posting:

- "What is worse than being together with your children, unarmed and destitute, humiliated and scorned, and living under the enemy of Islam and under their disbelieving laws?"
- "Why did we go to jihad? In order to completely deny disbelief and tyranny."
- Regarding women's roles in jihad, "We as women live far from the places of fighting. We live in places that are already conquered and safe. We dedicate ourselves to our Islamic duties . . . and to educate our children and our future mujahideen."
- "Many of the sisters volunteered to bake bread, cookies, and cakes and send them to the fighters in the trenches. On the other hand, some give up something and donate their weekly allowances to the mujahideen."
- "As the sisters here volunteer for *I'daad* [military training] for women to participate and provide for the war, they also reap, Allah willing, the huge reward of *Ribat* [the voluntary defense of Islam]."[4]

Chechen fighters from the Islamic Emirate of the Caucasus provided the following advice to Muslim women participating in jihad in 2010:

- Increase your faith.
- Bring your children up in Islam, and teach them about jihad.
- Collect money for the mujahideen.
- Help in the "territory of jihad as much as possible."[5]

A UK IS fighter and recruiter addressed an essay to women in the West in December 2015 in which he noted that "Some sisters feel sorrowful and others may feel a sense of hopelessness due to them believing they cannot assist the Mujāhidīn in this war. No doubt fighting is for the men of this *Ummah*, however sisters can play a vital role in this war. Not only should a sister be doing sincere *du'ā* [prayer of supplication] for the Mujāhidīn and encouraging their male relatives to fight jihad, they should also be contributing financially to this war."[6] It is interesting to note that IS did allow for women to engage in jihad as long as there is a fatwa authorizing it when the situation of the *ummah* has become "desperate."[7]

What is common in all these sets of recommendations is the focus on family, children, and support. There is no general call to take up arms in warfare. In addition, the numbers of women who are close to areas of jihad are relatively modest.

WOMEN AND IS

We are seeing a sea change with the advent of IS, however. The conflict in Syria and the concomitant rise in the Islamic State has been accompanied by a remarkable phenomenon not seen in earlier jihads: a large number of Western females (and whole families, including ones with very young children) are traveling to join up. The wars in Afghanistan, Somalia, and elsewhere did not see serious female participation, and violent radicalization in the West remains largely a male game (yes, there are cases of females, some of whom took on active roles in theater, but these remain the exception and not the rule).

While numbers are hard to come by, as they are for foreign fighters in general, we do have some figures at hand. The Institute for Strategic Dialogue (ISD), a UK think tank, estimates that over five hundred of the three thousand–plus Western foreign fighters are women.[8] As many as a quarter of French fighters are women.[9] By March 2015, the number of calls received at a toll-free French hotline for radicalization that reported potential candidates for jihad showed that women surpassed men.[10] Reports from the UK show that the percentage of females leaving to join IS is rising, with fifty-six individuals in 2015 alone.[11] Research carried out by French sociologist Farhad Khosrokhavar has demonstrated that French women outstrip men. Among the reasons is what he calls an "antifeminist postfeminism"—the desire to be with a jihadi who exhibits traditional male values. He also found that women were as attracted to violence as their male counterparts. [12]

Given the stories of rape and sexual abuse, not to mention Islamist extremist misogyny in general, it is fair to ask what the attraction is for Western women. While there has been some debate in extremist circles over the last few years about whether women can participate in jihad—some say that as jihad is *fard 'ayn* a woman does not need permission to fight, while others say a *mahram* (male guardian) is needed and that women are best suited for background roles. It is thus not the safest or most glamorous environment for females, yet they are flocking to Syria. Why?

Here are a few testimonies:

- For twenty-nine-year-old Heather Coffman of Glen Allen, Virginia, it was the feeling of belonging to a supportive circle of Muslims online who were engaged in a noble struggle for the sake of Allah despite overwhelming international opposition. [13]
- Sally Jones of Kent, in England, was hoping to become the first IS female suicide bomber in 2015. [14]

In 2014 alone, the following US females sought, successfully or not, to join IS:

- Two Colorado teenage sisters and their female schoolmate were intercepted at Frankfurt Airport en route to Turkey while intending to reach IS.
- Shannon Conley pleaded guilty to conspiracy to provide material support to IS after she was caught boarding a flight from Denver to Turkey, with ultimate plans to join the group in Syria.

In 2015 US–linked women aligned with the Islamic State included the following:

- Pennsylvania-based Keonna Thomas was charged with attempting to provide material support to IS as she tried to board a plane from Philadelphia to Barcelona, with subsequent plans to reach Syria by bus.
- Two New York–based roommates, Noelle Velentzas and Asia Siddiqui, were arrested on conspiracy to use explosives in an IS–inspired terrorist attack. Siddiqui purchased propane gas tanks for use in the attacks and had a step-by-step guide to use them.
- Mississippi-based Jaelyn Delshaun Young and her husband, Muhammad Oda Dakhlalla, were charged with conspiracy and attempting to provide material support to IS.
- Three women based in the US Midwest—Sedina Unkic Hodzic, Mediha Medy Salkicevic, and Jasminka Ramic—were arrested as part of a larger

cabal that conspired and provided material support to IS–aligned terrorists.

- Heather Coffman pleaded guilty to lying to authorities in relation to assisting a foreign national to join IS.
- Other US women were successful in reaching the so-called Caliphate,
such as Hoda Muthana, formerly from Alabama. [15]

A British woman who converted to Islam and moved to Syria to join
Jabhat al-Nusra stated that she "couldn't bring myself to live any longer
amidst my enemies." She continued,

> So many sisters . . . have lost their Religion trying to integrate with society, a
> society rid of blessings, a society built on the blood of the innocent, a society
> at war with Islam and the Muslims. . . . Besides, I prefer to live amongst the
> Muslims and die amongst the Muslims, swelling their ranks . . . indeed I prefer
> my money and efforts go towards the Muslims . . . so how many of us can say
> for certain that we are not contributing to the spilling of Muslim blood and the
> usurping of Muslim wealth and land with our own taxes? [16]

An interesting case in Canada ended happily. Three girls of Somali heri-
tage in Toronto—two sisters and a friend, ranging in age from fifteen to
eighteen—left suddenly late in 2014. They flew to Cairo and on to Istanbul
with the intention of joining IS. Thanks to cooperation between law enforcement, the families, and the Somali community, Turkish authorities were engaged and detained the girls before sending them back to their home country. [17]

According to Dean Alexander, director of the Homeland Security Research Program at Western Illinois University, among the narratives used by
IS to lure Western females are leaving the decadence and apostasy of the
home country, where Muslims are unwelcome; joining the jihad and being
empowered by living in a true Muslim land (the Caliphate); and contributing
to the cause by marrying an IS fighter and parenting the next generation of
warriors. In addition, life in the Caliphate is painted as more exciting, meaningful, and better than life in the West. [18]

IS stresses the role women have in raising the next generation of mujahideen: "teaching those under your custody to hate the cross and its people
[i.e., Christians], for this is the first step in making a Mujahid generation." [19]
Women should also fight the "ideological war" by abstaining from the life-
styles of the "crusaders." [20]

Luckily, excellent research has been carried out in recent months on this
new phenomenon. In the ISD paper *Becoming Mulan*, the following reasons
were offered by Western women:

- A desire to ease the oppression of Muslims

- Seeking an alternative society
- Contributing to the building of the Caliphate
- *Fard 'ayn*
- Romance and marriage and
- Sisterhood and camaraderie.[21]

A researcher at ISD, Erin Saltman, told Jihadology.net in July 2014 that many women join IS for two main reasons: the utopian lure of the Caliphate and the decentralized messaging employed by IS (using, among other platforms, Twitter, WhatsApp, Facebook, Tumblr, AskFM, and blog posts), which allows for greater participation and a more fluid back-and-forth.[22] In Saltman's opinion, some of the push factors for women mirror those for men: identity crisis, a feeling of isolation, the persecution of the Muslim community in the West, and anger at the lack of reaction to the atrocities in Syria. Pull factors include a sense of religious duty, building a better world, belonging, sisterhood, romanticization, and even the presentation of male fighters as "eye candy." There are no profiles as far as age and country of origin are concerned and no solid numbers of how many are in Syria. Interestingly, in Saltman's estimation, few defect to the West (one-tenth the rate of males).

At times the reasons proffered mirror those of their male counterparts. Some are clearly angry at what the Assad regime is doing to its own people in Syria. Others are against the West in general and the coalition fighting IS in particular. A common overarching theme is the treatment accorded Muslims in countries where they constitute the minority. There are even instances where women are intrigued by the violence in Syria: One woman, upon repeated viewings of a beheading video, demanded more.[23]

University of Western Ontario professor Laura Huey has collected data on Twitter accounts of women who have joined IS, Jabhat al-Nusra, and Al-Shabaab. She has found that women play several roles within these groups:

- "Fan girls" are not very ideologically committed but great at spreading propaganda.
- "Baqiyah" (remaining) members see themselves as supporting their brothers and sisters.
- Recruiters serve as contact points, providing information, and emotional and other support to females seeking to migrate to Syria to join IS.
- Migrants are the success stories that IS can use to promote its brand and society.
- Mothers of the Caliphate prove that a functioning polity exists and are bearers of the next generation of jihadists.[24]

A 2015 paper by the Quilliam Foundation, "Caliphettes: Women and the Appeal of Islamic State," suggests that IS has successfully adapted its messaging to women by making four "promises":

- Empowerment: by joining IS women can escape marginalization and oppression
- Deliverance: resolving the grievances women have with Dar al-Kufr
- Participation: in the state offered by IS
- Piety: IS is divinely sanctioned, and all Muslims must join it.[25]

A Virginian university student known as "Umm Jihad" stated in early 2015 that she misses nothing of her former life in the West and believed it was her obligation as a Muslim to join IS. She could not wait for her husband to become a martyr, viewing the death as a "celebration."[26]

Many of the reasons cited by women in support of their decision to join IS mirror those identified by men. It remains uncertain whether this is due to male influence or is reflective of independent rationalization.

THE KHANSSAA BRIGADE

In the summer of 2014, shortly after the seizure of the Syrian city of Raqqa, IS created an all-female cohort known as the Khansaa Brigade. Part morals police, part education squad, it is the duty of this brigade to enforce Islamic norms and punish transgressors. Given the strictures against the mingling of the sexes in Islam, it makes perfect sense to have a female team deal with other females. In a twist on Islamic modesty, anti–IS individuals were enveloping themselves in female garb, able to pass through checkpoints, since male guards were reluctant to search what they believed to be women. Women in the brigade are trained and armed, and some have taken their responsibilities overly seriously and brutally, detaining women for violations of which the detainees may be completely ignorant.[27] Punishments meted out include sixty lashes for trying to escape and forty lashes for improper attire.[28] The brigade's January 2015 manifesto sought to undermine "Western civilisation," notions of gender equality (women are "inherently sedentary" according to IS), and provide impetus and encouragement for other Western women to join IS.[29]

SUMMARY

The unprecedented rise in females seeking to travel to join IS is an interesting phenomenon and one that needs more analysis. It is unlikely, however, that this trend will continue to rise. A few factors stand in the way:

- Islam is, generally speaking, a conservative faith that places constraints on the freedom of movement for women. The need for a male companion (a *mahram*) is often raised.
- Terrorist groups are even more conservative, bordering on intolerant fundamentalism and misogyny, and are loath to allow females to assume greater roles.
- Violence and extremism have historically been more appealing to men than to women.

Nevertheless, the large number of women in IS will have implications for measures and programs to deal with those who survive, or defect from, the organization. Levels of sexual and emotional abuse will be high. Women will have young children that must be accommodated and treated. It is also uncertain whether existing counter- and deradicalization programs will have to be adjusted to fit the unique problems women with extremist groups present.

NOTES

In the epigraph, *PBUH* stands for "peace be upon him."

1. François Barrere, "Les policiers de la SDAT ont-ils découvert une kamikaze à Montpellier?" *Midi-Libre*, December 23, 2015, http://www.midilibre.fr/2015/12/22/une-kamikaze-a-montpellier,1261464.php.

2. SITE Intelligence Group, "Female IMU Member Lauds Women's Role in Jihad," October 26, 2011, https://news.siteintelgroup.com/Jihadist-News/female-imu-member-lauds-womens-role-in-jihad.html (subscription required).

3. Umaymah Hasan Ahmad Muhammad Hasan, "A Message to Muslim Sisters," Al Fajr Media Center, December 16, 2009.

4. SITE Intelligence Group, "Female IMU Member Lauds Women's Role in Jihad," October 26, 2015, https://ent.siteintelgroup.com/Jihadist-News/female-imu-member-lauds-womens-role-in-jihad.html (subscription required).

5. SITE Intelligence Group, "Chechen Fighters Address Muslim Women in Jihad," March 25, 2010, https://ent.siteintelgroup.com/Jihadist-News/site-intel-group-3-25-10-chechen-fighters-muslim-women-jihad.html (subscription required).

6. SITE Intelligence Group, "IS Recruiter Requests Financial Support From Women Outside of Syria," December 23, 2015, https://news.siteintelgroup.com/Western-Jihadist-Forum-Digest/is-recruiter-requests-financial-support-from-women-outside-of-syria.html (subscription required).

7. Al-Khanssaa Brigade, "Women of the Islamic State: A Manifesto on Women by the Al-Khanssaa Brigade," translation of the original text into English and analysis by Charlie Winter, Quilliam Foundation, February 2015, https://www.quilliamfoundation.org/wp/wp-content/uploads/publications/free/women-of-the-islamic-state3.pdf.

8. Caroline Hoyle, Alexandra Bradford, and Ross Frenett, "Becoming Mulan? Female Western Migrants to ISIS" (London: Institute for Strategic Dialogue, 2015), http://www.strategicdialogue.org/wp-content/uploads/2016/02/ISDJ2969_Becoming_Mulan_01.15_WEB.pdf.

9. Harriet Sherwood, Sandra Laville, Kim Willsher, Ben Knight, Maddy French, and Lauren Gambino, "Schoolgirl Jihadis: The Female Jihadists Leaving Home to Join ISIS Fighters," *Guardian* (London), September 29, 2014, http://www.theguardian.com/world/2014/sep/29/schoolgirl-jihadis-female-islamists-leaving-home-join-isis-iraq-syria.

10. D. N., Antoine Heulard, and Sarah-Lou Cohen-Bacri, "Départs pour le jihad: Plus de filles que de garçons en mars," BFM TV, April 15, 2015, http://www.bfmtv.com/societe/departs-pour-le-jihad-plus-de-filles-que-de-garcons-en-mars-877612.html.

11. Richard Ford, "Number of Girls Travelling to Syria Jumps," *Times* (London), January 12, 2016, http://www.thetimes.co.uk/tto/news/uk/article4663194.ece.

12. Agence France-Presse, "More French Girls Lured by Islamic State than Boys: Source," Channel News Asia, March 11, 2016, http://www.channelnewsasia.com/news/world/more-french-girls-lured/2591880.html.

13. Harriet Sherwood, Sandra Laville, Kim Willsher, Ben Knight, Maddy French, and Lauren Gambino, "Schoolgirl Jihadis: The Female Jihadists Leaving Home to Join ISIS Fighters," *Guardian* (London), September 29, 2014, http://www.theguardian.com/world/2014/sep/29/schoolgirl-jihadis-female-islamists-leaving-home-join-isis-iraq-syria.

14. Agamoni Ghosh, "ISIS: British Jihadist Sally Jones Plans to Be First Western Female Suicide Bomber in Syria," *International Business Times* (New York), November 30, 2015, http://www.ibtimes.co.uk/british-jihadist-sally-jones-may-blow-herself-become-isis-first-female-suicide-bomber-1531070.

15. Dean Alexander, "Islamic State's Lure to Foreign Women," Opinion, *Jerusalem Post*, December 20, 2015, http://www.jpost.com/Opinion/Islamic-States-lure-to-foreign-women-437896.

16. MEMRI, "In New Jabhat Al-Nusra English Magazine, British Woman Shares Story of Her Emigration to Syria," July 6, 2015, http://www.memrijttm.org/in-new-al-qaeda-affiliate-jabhat-al-nusras-english-magazine-british-woman-shares-story-of-her-emigration-to-syria.html.

17. Michelle Shephard, "Islamic State Militants Luring Western Women as Wives," *Toronto Star*, October 17, 2014, https://www.thestar.com/news/world/2014/10/17/islamic_state_militants_luring_western_women_as_wives.html.

18. Dean Alexander, "Islamic State's Lure to Foreign Women," Opinion, *Jerusalem Post*, December 20, 2015, http://www.jpost.com/Opinion/Islamic-States-lure-to-foreign-women-437896.

19. Mallory Shelbourne, "Islamic State's Female Jihadists Use Social Media to Lure Women Recruits," *The Long War Journal*, February 27, 2015, http://www.longwarjournal.org/archives/2015/02/islamic-state-female-recruits-use-social-media-to-lure-recruits.php.

20. Ibid.

21. Hoyle, Bradford, and Frenett, "Becoming Mulan?"

22. Karl Morand, "Jihadology Podcast: The Western Women of ISIS with Erin Saltman," Jihadology, July 14, 2015, http://jihadology.net/2015/07/14/jihadology-podcast-the-western-women-of-isis-with-erin-saltman/.

23. *The Economist*, "Caliphate Calling," News, February 28, 2015, http://www.economist.com/news/international/21645206-how-islamic-state-appeals-women-caliphate-calling.

24. Laura Huey in discussion with the author, June 2015.

25. Haras Rafiq and Nikita Malik, "Caliphettes: Women and the Appeal of Islamic State," foreword by Baroness Sandip Verma (London: Quilliam Foundation, 2015), https://www.quilliamfoundation.org/wp/wp-content/uploads/publications/free/caliphettes-women-and-the-appeal-of-is.pdf.

26. Michelle Shephard, "Why It's Wrong to Underestimate the Islamic State's Female Recruits," *Toronto Star*, March 29, 2015, https://www.thestar.com/news/world/2015/03/28/why-its-wrong-to-underestimate-the-islamic-states-female-recruits.html.

27. Kathy Gilsinan, "The ISIS Crackdown on Women, by Women," *The Atlantic*, July 25, 2014, http://www.theatlantic.com/international/archive/2014/07/the-women-of-isis/375047/.

28. Louella-Mae Eleftheriou-Smith, "Escaped ISIS Wives Describe Life in the All-Female al-Khansa Brigade Who Punish Women with 40 Lashes for Wearing Wrong Clothes," *Independent* (London), April 20, 2015, http://www.independent.co.uk/news/world/middle-east/escaped-isis-wives-describe-life-in-the-all-female-al-khansa-brigade-who-punish-women-with-40-lashes-10190317.html.

29. Al-Khanssaa Brigade, "Women of the Islamic State: A Manifesto on Women by the Al-Khanssaa Brigade," translation of the original text into English and analysis by Charlie Winter,

Quilliam Foundation, February 2015, https://www.quilliamfoundation.org/wp/wp-content/uploads/publications/free/women-of-the-islamic-state3.pdf.

Chapter Six

Returning Foreign Fighters and the Threat They Pose

CHAPTER ABSTRACT

Now that we have examined why otherwise normal Westerners elect to fight
with terrorist groups like IS, we need to ask whether those that return are
threats to our security or as harmless as the vast majority of normal veterans.
Unlike the vast majority of Westerners who fought in unsanctioned wars
over the last century who do not appear to pose significant danger to their
homelands, I will argue that IS foreign fighters do pose a threat in three
different ways: before they go, while they are in conflict zones, and when
they return. We will discuss each phase separately.

WHAT DO WE KNOW?

A number of scholars have examined the threat from returning foreign fighters, including Norwegian academic Thomas Hegghammer and American David Malet. In his 2013 paper "Should I Stay or Should I Go? Explaining
Variation in Western Jihadists' Choice between Domestic and Foreign Fighting," Hegghammer found that at most one in nine foreign fighters returns to
his country and carries out a terrorist attack. His data, covering plots in the
West from 1990 to 2010, suggests that the presence of a veteran extremist in
a terrorist cell increases the chances of a successful attack.[1] This makes sense
intuitively if we factor in the training received abroad, as well as battle
experience, increased exposure to violent ideology, and special skill sets that
may be more difficult to acquire in one's homeland.

One in nine (let's say 10 percent as a ballpark figure) is a comforting figure on the one hand. As Hegghammer states, "far from all foreign fighters are domestic fighters-in-the-making."[2] These findings should allay fears that all, or even a large percentage of, the thousands of foreigners in IS will pose a clear and present danger upon their return. Hegghammer's study is historical and predates the rise of IS, and in a later study, "Assessing the Islamic State's Commitment to Attacking the West," he concluded that those inspired by IS posed a greater menace than those who had fought and returned.[3] Again, the study was written before the events in Paris of November 2015.

I have no reason to distrust Hegghammer, who is recognized as one of the world's true experts on terrorism. If the numbers are as low as 10 percent, that is indeed good. But one important caveat remains: It is impossible to determine which one in nine represents the greatest threat. There is certainly no model I am aware of that allows security and law-enforcement agencies to narrow in on a particular individual of concern and prioritize their investigations on that basis. Hence, these agencies are forced to look at *all* returnees to ensure that an attack does not take place. This requirement has important implications for these organizations—a topic I will return to in chapter 7.

Canadian scholar Amarnath Amarasingam has classified returnees into three broad categories: "operational" returnees, who are tasked with carrying out attacks in their homelands; those who are disengaged but still tied to the broader jihadist cause; and disillusioned individuals who found that the Caliphate was not as advertised. Amarasingam cautions against treating all with the same approach.[4] While I do not disagree with him, as I noted in the previous paragraph, determining who is who remains a challenge. True disillusionment may be obvious, as will operational returnees, but what do we do with the disengaged? After all, a disengaged person who does not deradicalize can easily reengage in the right circumstances. Unfortunately there are no easy answers.

THE THREAT BEFORE TRAVEL

How can I talk about the threat from foreign fighters *before* they travel? Is that not a non sequitur? Not at all. Many people are obsessed with foreign conflicts and express a desire to travel to join up with groups like IS. In fact, this obsession is one of the signs of violent radicalization that I have spoken of at length.

The problem is that not all those who want to travel succeed in doing so, for reasons that will become clearer in the next chapter. While they remain in situ, prospective foreign fighters constitute a worrisome influence on others: In other words, they can act as radicalizers. Recall that these individuals do

— NO

not travel to become violent radicals: That process happens before they leave
(yes, their radicalization can deepen once with IS, but IS does not begin the
process). Hence, they are in an environment that provided the seed for their
radicalization, and they can pass their ideology on to others.

No,

In the worst-case scenario, aspiring foreign fighters, when faced with the
impossibility of leaving (for a variety of reasons: state intervention, lack of
resources, lack of commitment, etc.) may in the end turn their attention to
their own country and elect to plan a terrorist attack on home soil.   *— possible .*

We in Canada are unfortunately all too familiar with this possibility. The
two terrorist attacks that occurred two days apart in October 2014 were
executed by two Canadians whose hopes to leave the country were frustrated.
Martin Couture-Rouleau was keen to fight in Syria: When his passport was
delayed, he targeted two Canadian Armed Forces personnel outside Montreal
and ran them over, killing Warrant Officer Patrice Vincent. Within forty-
eight hours, Michael Zehaf-Bibeau, who had attempted to leave to fight in
Libya (he had Libyan citizenship) but had had his passport application sty-
mied by the Libyan embassy in Ottawa, shot and killed Corporal Nathan
Cirillo at the National War Memorial before trying to storm Parliament,
where he was killed. Both men were discovered to have been inspired by IS.   *?*

Aside from actual plots, agencies such as CSIS and the RCMP are forced
to dedicate vast amounts of resources to investigate wannabe foreign fighters, as we shall see.

THE THREAT DURING TRAVEL

Those that succeed in gaining access to IS, either through the use of fraudu-
lent documentation, "broken" travel patterns, tacking a trip to Syria onto
otherwise legitimate travel (hajj, education, etc.), or through deception and
avoidance of law-enforcement and security-intelligence agencies (after
which they boast and taunt such agencies on social media) pose a different
kind of threat. No country wants its citizens to join terrorist organizations.
And no country wants its citizens to plan or participate in terrorist attacks
abroad.   *— foreign fighting*   *?*

Staying with Canada for the moment, a number of citizens have taken part
in terrorist acts abroad after having left the country to join extremist groups:

- Abdul Rahman Jabarah of St. Catharines, Ontario, was killed in 2003 in
  Saudi Arabia. He had played a role in a terrorist attack in Riyadh earlier
  that year.
- Xristos Katsiroubas and Ali Medlej of London, Ontario, helped Al Qaeda
  in the Islamic Maghreb kill more than forty foreign gas workers at a plant
  in Amenas, Algeria, in January 2013.

- Toronto native Mahad Dhore died in a suicide attack in Mogadishu, Somalia, in April 2013.

In addition to the acquisition of skills that could enhance their ability to carry out lethal action, the stage where these individuals are abroad is a critical one.

Those still fighting with IS have also encouraged others to carry out attacks in the West. A German IS extremist exhorted his "beloved brothers" to "follow this convoy before it is too late, and be with your brothers and support them. If you do not support them with your immigration and your coming to jihad, then support them in Germany. Attack the infidels in their homes, kill them where you know of them. If you cannot kill them, then there can be nothing less than showing your repudiation of them."[5] It is thus clear that foreign fighters can inspire others while in situ. The expanding use of social media tells the story of their exploits, their heroism, and their defense of Islam and serves as role model and example to emulate.

AFTER THEY RETURN

Assuming that only 10 percent of returnees (based on Hegghammer's data) are likely to proceed to plan and execute an attack once returned to their homeland, does this imply that the rest are of no concern? Not at all. There are a number of activities returnees can engage in, some less worrisome and some very dangerous indeed.

Nothing

For some, their experience with IS may lead to a realization that their choice was a bad one, and they return with no desire to repeat their error. This is undoubtedly a good outcome and would be the preferred result, as we shall see.

Returning as "Broken Men"

A certain percentage of those that somehow succeed in leaving IS and finding their way home may pose challenges for the host country's health system. Some may return with serious injuries that will warrant expensive and lengthy medical care. Others may be severely psychologically scarred by their experiences abroad and require help dealing with their recent past. In both cases, their countries of citizenship may have no choice but to treat them, despite public pressure to punish them for their decisions to join terrorist groups. ≠ foreign fighting.

Acting as Radicalizers

Years ago I met with somebody who told me something very important and very ominous. We were discussing radicalization in Canada and how and where it was occurring. He looked at me and said that Canada should pay particular attention to those who had fought abroad in foreign conflicts. These people, he added, were "like flowers, and the kids in their milieu are like bees, hovering around, learning and absorbing from the flower."

This of course makes sense. Returning fighters are examples of those who have walked the walk and not merely talked the talk. They have street cred and can take advantage of their travel experiences to influence others. The veracity of what they actually did abroad is not really important—in fact, based on my experience, it is often exaggerated or even invented. What does matter is their ability to tell stories to an impressionable audience.

People in this position will often encourage others to emulate them and take up the torch themselves. They can provide contact information, useful tips on how to travel to the conflict zone, and advice on how to avoid security-intelligence and law-enforcement agencies. I have seen such an individual in action (see the introduction to the next chapter), and I must confess that the performance was impressive and potentially very effective.

I also recall a situation in a Canadian city where one individual, radicalized in Canada, left not once but twice to fight in two separate conflicts (unsuccessfully, it ensued, as he was arrested by local authorities on both occasions). Upon his return from the first attempt he radicalized two men in his social circle, one of whom later left to fight abroad (again, without success). This protégé returned and began to radicalize a group of at least a half dozen men, most of whom subsequently left for Syria. At least three of that group died fighting. Should any of the others survive and make their way back to Canada, there is a good chance they too will pass on their experiences and enhanced ideological commitment to others.

Making Preparations to Leave Again

A few of those who have fought with IS are actually serial travelers. They return to their homelands for a variety of reasons (medical care, raising money, spreading the word, etc.) and eventually return to the front. I am aware of a few cases in Canada, but in light of the distances involved, planning to travel on multiple occasions is a little more problematic than in countries much closer to the action. I have heard of cases in Europe where fighters will go to Syria for a few days every once in a while, return, and set out again, in what has been called "jihadi tourism."

Executing Terrorist Acts at Home

As Hegghammer has noted, there is a very real risk of foreign fighters carrying out acts of terrorism upon their return, even if the figure is "only" 10 percent. Again, according to Hegghammer, the attacks perpetrated by those who have experience abroad tend to be more lethal than those executed by homegrown terrorists. We have seen quite a few attacks of late by these returnees:

- The horrendous attacks in Paris in November 2015 were carried out by western Europeans (largely French and Belgian citizens) who had fought with IS.
- Mohammed Merah, the French citizen who killed seven in a spree in southern France in March 2012, had been with Al Qaeda in Afghanistan and Pakistan.
- The *Charlie Hebdo* attacks in January 2015 were carried out by at least one individual who had fought in Yemen with Al Qaeda in the Arabian Peninsula.
- The May 2014 terrorist who carried out an attack on a Jewish museum in Brussels, Mehdi Nemmouche, had fought with IS.
- The wife of suspected Paris 2015 attack mastermind Salim Benghalem told French authorities that her husband would only come back to France to carry out an attack.[6]
- A German citizen arrested after returning from fighting in Syria told authorities that IS was recruiting Germans to carry out attacks in their homeland.[7]

> all terrorist organisations ≠ foreign fighters.

SUMMARY

This cohort—the IS veterans—poses a distinct problem for one simple reason: They have joined and spent time with a terrorist group. ✓

I have no intention of launching into the "what is terrorism" debate. I am sure that there are many good and interesting books available on that topic. So let us accept for the purposes of this book that IS is a terrorist entity and that it is thus different than other organizations (the IDF, the YPG, etc.) that are not. Does this make a difference?

Clearly it does. Terrorist groups are entities that resort to acts of violence along purely ideological grounds. Yes, we can debate what ideology is in the same way we agonize over what terrorism is, but what seems obvious to me is that an individual who radicalizes along a particular violent ideology— here IS or AQ—and elects to join that group, fight, kill, and perhaps torture the perceived enemy, represents a different problem.

↳ civilians?

Indeed, returning soldiers do suffer similar hardship and come back psychologically damaged. In Canada, a number of armed-forces personnel have returned from Canada's mission in Afghanistan and committed suicide.

But those who elected to fight with a group like IS developed a hatred for their native land, through their radicalization process, and took that hatred with them when they left to join IS. That hatred was further nurtured and deepened "over there," and for a percentage that hatred is lifelong. Some will return to Canada and other Western countries with their rage intact. Unlike "ordinary" soldiers, radicalized foreign fighters did not go to a war condoned or even tolerated by their host nations. They are not feted by their governments or their citizenry. Their sacrifices are not recognized. There are no memorials built in their honor.

Furthermore, they see their homelands as the enemies of Islam, participants in the "war on Islam." This distinction is critical, and it is for this reason that the "foreign-fighter phenomenon" is of such concern to Western governments, even if only 10 percent eventually carry out acts of terrorism upon return. This has no parallel, to my knowledge, with other foreign-fighter waves.

So, what can we do about this threat? We turn to what measures are being taken in the next chapter.

NOTES

1. Thomas Hegghammer, "Should I Stay or Should I Go? Explaining Variation in Western Jihadists' Choice between Domestic and Foreign Fighting," *American Political Science Review*, February 2013, doi:10.1017/S0003055412000615, text available online at http://hegghammer.com/_files/Hegghammer_-_Should_I_stay_or_should_I_go.pdf.

2. Ibid.

3. Thomas Hegghammer and Peter Nesser, "Assessing the Islamic State's Commitment to Attacking the West," *Perspectives on Terrorism* 9, no. 4 (2015), http://www.terrorismanalysts.com/pt/index.php/pot/article/view/440/html.

4. Amarnath Amarasingam, "Three Kinds of People Return Home after Joining the Islamic State—And They Must All Be Treated Differently," *Vice News*, December 3, 2015, https://news.vice.com/article/three-kinds-of-people-return-home-after-joining-the-islamic-state-and-they-must-all-be-treated-differently.

5. SITE Intelligence Group, "Austrian Fighter Mohamed Mahmoud Calls for Lone-Wolf Attacks in Austria, Germany in IS Video," August 15, 2015, https://news.siteintelgroup.com/Jihadist-News/austrian-fighter-mohamed-mahmoud-calls-for-lone-wolf-attacks-in-austria-germany-in-is-video.html (subscription required).

6. Willy Le Devin, "Salim Benghalem m'a dit que s'il revenait, c'était pour faire un attentat," *Libération*, November 30, 2015, http://www.liberation.fr/france/2015/11/30/salim-benghalem-m-a-dit-que-s-il-revenait-c-etait-pour-faire-un-attentat_1417319.

7. Hubert Gude and Wolf Wiedmann-Schmidt, "Back from the Caliphate: Returnee Says IS Recruiting for Terror Attacks in Germany," *Spiegel Online*, December 16, 2015, http://www.spiegel.de/international/world/german-jihadist-returns-from-syria-and-gives-testimony-a-1067764.html.

Chapter Seven

Evaluating and Countering the Threat Posed by Returning Fighters

THE RADICALIZER

In the spring of 2014, I participated in an outreach event with my colleagues at Public Safety Canada in a Muslim community in a Canadian city. These events were designed to engage Canadians on issues related to national security and have been carried out across the country. In this particular session, matters surrounding radicalization and violent extremism were discussed and attendees were asked their views on how to deal with these phenomena. Part of the evening consisted of reading aloud a narrative based loosely on a true Canadian story of a person who had radicalized and continued on to an unfortunate end (incarceration, death, or membership in a terrorist group). This initiative had been used on several occasions prior to this instance and had received a very positive response.

This night was to be different, however. Shortly after the narrative was read, a young man offered that the story was not credible and that no one in that community would engage in such actions. He further questioned why the Canadian government was concerned about such matters and that we were not welcome. Despite challenges and displeasure by the rest of the assembled group, he continued to argue that we were wasting our time and did not know what we were talking about.

I later learned that this young man was in fact a returnee: He had traveled to Syria to join a terrorist group. His presence back in Canada was due to unknown circumstances, but it was clear that he saw the outreach session as a way to thumb his nose at the government and, more importantly in my view, share his opinions with other Muslims. In fact, two men also present at the event appeared to be interested in his extremist mind-set. It is my opinion that he was recruiting these individuals to perhaps follow in his footsteps.

The most alarming aspect of this young man's appearance was the boldness with which he proclaimed his ideas and the tenacity with which he dismissed any argument put forward by attendees (in fact, tempers flared, and a fight almost broke out at one point). And this in spite of the presence of an RCMP officer (who regularly participated in the Public Safety Canada program).

This incident points to a worrisome consequence of the foreign-fighter problem: Individuals who have fought and returned home can act as radicalizers of others. Their experiences and accomplishments (they have in fact walked the walk and not merely talked the talk) accords them credibility and influence.

or terrorist?

CHAPTER ABSTRACT

In this chapter we look at what governments and societies are doing to confront the issue of foreign fighters, more specifically those seeking to join terrorist groups in Iraq and Syria, at the three points discussed in the previous chapter: before, during, and after travel. We examine the options and explore the pluses and minuses of each approach.

IMPORTANT NOTE

Nowhere in this chapter do I discuss military action. I am not a military expert and have no qualifications to argue the pluses and minuses of air strikes, drone strikes, or ground forces. It is probable that these have a role to play in the struggle against IS, of which foreign fighters, including Westerners, play an important function, but I leave that debate to true specialists.

I also mirror the approach used in the last chapter. In other words, I discuss what measures can be applied before foreign fighters leave, while they are abroad, and once they return. It becomes clear that some of the same measures can be implemented at each stage of the foreign-fighter phenomenon.

HIGH-RISK TRAVELER (HRT) PROGRAM

In Canada the Royal Canadian Mounted Police created a special high-risk individual (HRI—formerly known as high-risk travelers—HRT) team to deal with the historically unprecedented number of Canadians leaving to join groups such as IS. The RCMP works with its domestic partners—the Canadian Security Intelligence Service (CSIS), the Canada Border Services Agency (CBSA), local law enforcement at the provincial and municipal levels, and others to identify these individuals. Measures range from investigation, arrest, and prosecution to passport seizure in an effort to prevent extremists from boarding planes.[1]

The RCMP approach for dealing with foreign fighters "focuses on coordinating interdepartmental actions based on *reasonable grounds to suspect* that an individual, or group of individuals, intends to leave Canada to participate in a foreign conflict."[2] As the RCMP notes, the issue is not a new one and goes back to the Mackenzie King government's *Foreign Enlistment Act* legislation (recall the earlier discussion in the section on the Spanish Civil War in chapter 3). It is interesting to note that in these instances the RCMP has stated that it requires "reasonable grounds to suspect": in normal police work, a higher threshold, reasonable grounds to believe, is necessary. Travel for these purposes is a crime as detailed in section 83.01 of the Canadian Criminal Code. There does not appear to be similar legislation in the United States, unless a citizen fights against his or her own country, an action that constitutes treason.[3]

BEFORE TRAVEL

As we noted in the previous chapter, potential foreign fighters do pose a threat to their societies on a number of levels. Consequently, in the period leading up to departure for a conflict zone, a series of measures can be put in place to reduce the numbers of people who successfully leave to join terrorist groups. One step is legislation and policy that states that it is forbidden to leave a country to hook up with a terrorist group. Several countries have adopted such practices:

- In October 2015, eighteen EU nations signed an additional protocol to the Convention on the Prevention of Terrorism to prevent EU citizens from traveling to join groups such as IS. The protocol outlaws traveling abroad for the purpose of terrorism, receiving training for terrorism, and the financing, organization, and facilitation of such journeys.[4]
- In early October 2015, French lawmakers adopted a draft law requiring minors to have permission from their parents or legal guardians before leaving the country in a bid to curb departures for jihad in Iraq or Syria. France had also set up a hotline for people to call to report suspicions of violent radicalization.[5]
- In Canada it is an offense to travel to join a terrorist group, as it is in the United States.

- In early December 2015, the major political parties in Sweden agreed to a series of antiterrorism measures, including the criminalization of traveling to commit terrorism abroad.[6]

EARLY INTERVENTION/COUNTER-RADICALIZATION

NO

Individuals bent on leaving Canada and other Western countries are most often radicalized before departure. They may become further radicalized once in theater, but the seeds of violent ideology are already planted well before they show up in Syria or other conflict zones. Radicalization to violence poses a potential threat in and of itself. Our responses to violent radicalization range from early identification and intervention to investigation, arrest, and incarceration (after trial).

It must be emphasized, though, that in most cases those on the verge of purchasing airline tickets and leave to join groups outside the country are likely not good candidates for early intervention. These individuals are well *NO* down the pathway to violent radicalization. We believe instinctively that the longer one is on that path, the less likely intervention and counseling is appropriate. In all likelihood it is now a matter for investigation. *Children?*

Another initiative that has been tried is the establishment of telephone hotlines to receive information from the public worried about violent radicalization or travel for terrorist purposes. Information provided by families, friends, and others can be channeled either to intervention centers or to law enforcement and security intelligence for action:

- The government of Trinidad and Tobago has decided to be part of a hotline developed by a Trinidadian Muslim. Tips will be passed on to the National Security Ministry.[7]
- A "deradicalization" center in Montreal has been getting many phone calls from parents worried that their children want to leave Canada to fight, even in cases where the end destination is to fight with the Kurds against IS.[8]
- In its first day of operation, a Spanish "antijihadist" hotline received twenty-nine calls from the public worth investigating. People can anonymously leave messages specifying activity that may indicate radicalization.[9]

INVESTIGATION AND MONITORING

If law-enforcement and security agencies collect information on an individual keen to travel to join a terrorist group, the agencies have the option to investigate that person, since their intent poses a threat to national security or

what about FSA?

to the security of another country. Based on my experience with CSIS, this measure is used fairly frequently.

It is important to note, however, that investigations are expensive ventures. A major counterterrorism investigation can run into the millions of dollars. Human resources are also labor intensive: human-source and agent recruiting and handling, communications monitoring under court warrant (even more difficult if multiple languages are involved and technologically challenging if the subject uses hard to exploit methods), and physical surveillance. I have been told that to watch one person takes on average of forty people full time.[10] Multiply that figure by a hundred individuals of interest, and we are quickly up to thousands of officers. It is hard to maintain that coverage the longer the investigation continues.

It is unclear how long even the best law-enforcement and security services can continue the highest level of operations on a given individual, and this is of course magnified when multiple cases are prioritized simultaneously. There is a lot of talk of "intelligence failure" when an attack occurs. I realize that my past colors my views, but I find the accusations suffer from a lack of context. Investigating dozens of individuals in a constantly changing environment is not easy. When you realize, for example, that French authorities (or UK authorities, for that matter) have ten thousand people potentially engaged in violent activities, it is no wonder that the odd attack is successful. I find that people are all too quick to blame police and intelligence when things go wrong but then are equally quick to refuse giving those agencies more powers or resources to keep up with the threat level.

Regardless of the capacity and professionalism of law-enforcement and security agencies, some people will evade detection and successfully exit the country (and in many cases they boast of their exploits at avoiding the feds and sometimes cite divine intervention—"Allah blinded them to my intent"). The best services cannot detect everyone. And groups such as IS are getting better at providing would-be travelers with practical advice on how to fool authorities (travel routes, how to escape suspicion and detection, etc.). One tactic used is known as "broken travel": going to intermediary locations (Europe, Saudi Arabia for the hajj) that when taken at face value do not raise red flags. Extremists are also adept at avoiding "no-fly lists" by choosing flights that do not cross the airspace of the country where they are listed. There are many examples from many countries of individuals who successfully evaded detection and ended up in Syria, whether they were the subjects of active investigations or were under the radar:

- Windsor, Canada, resident Mohammed El Shaer evaded Canadian authorities in March 2015 to travel to Turkey, where he taunted officials, writing, "Allah's plan has beaten your fragile entire nation's plan. May Allah guide you to the truth or destroy you."[11]

- Another Windsor native, Ahmad Waseem, returned to Canada after having been wounded in Syria, only to leave again for the conflict zone, probably on a false passport.[12]
- Cardiff, Wales, medical student Nasser Muthana left the UK in 2014 and is believed to have participated in beheading Syrian soldiers.[13]
- Siddhartha Dhar, a London resident suspected of appearing in an IS video in which five people were murdered, was able to leave the UK despite having been arrested on six occasions (the government did not confiscate his passport).[14]
- Five UK residents linked to the banned extremist group Al-Muhajiroun were able to depart for Syria and Pakistan, where some subsequently were killed in drone strikes, despite having no passports and being placed on a watch list.[15]

ARREST/PEACE BOND

When authorities have enough information that meets the evidentiary-standard test, they can move in to arrest those seeking to travel abroad. Note that an offense has been committed under the criminal code even though the individual has not actually "done" anything. Several countries, including Canada, have made it illegal to attempt to leave the country with the intent to join a terrorist group. Here are a few recent cases where this tool has been leveraged: *← what about ESA or hvds?*

- Mohamed Hersi was arrested in May 2011 as he tried to leave Toronto to travel to Somalia to join Al-Shabaab. He was found guilty in 2014 and sentenced to ten years in prison.[16]
- Spanish authorities arrested a man of Moroccan origin in Pamplona, Spain, and charged him with seeking to leave the country to join IS.[17] He had come to the attention of the Guardia Civil after showing clear signs of radicalization.[18]
- On some occasions those who have left to fight with IS have been charged in absentia. In September 2015, the Royal Canadian Mounted Police charged Farah Shirdon with several counts under section 83 of the Canadian Criminal Code, including leaving Canada to join a terrorist group and instructing someone to carry out a terrorist act on behalf of IS.[19] The RCMP noted that rumors of Shirdon's death had proven false. Shirdon is famous for a video in which he burned his Canadian passport and for an interview with Vice in which he threatened Canada and the United States.[20]
- Norway is considering legislation to both prevent travel for terrorist purposes as well as to facilitate charges on returnees.[21]

- A Montreal teen convicted on two terrorism-related charges for attempting to join up with Islamic State militants was handed a three-year sentence on April 7, 2016. The boy, now sixteen, was found guilty in December 2015 on two charges: committing a robbery in association with a terror organization and planning to leave Canada to participate in the activities of a terrorist group abroad. The case stems from an October 2014 convenience store robbery by the teen, then fifteen, who had hatched a plan to go to Syria to help IS.[22]

Canada has also used a measure known as a peace bond in several cases where individuals were identified to be supportive of terrorist activity (usually online propaganda) or at risk of traveling abroad to join groups such as IS. According to data from the Public Prosecution Service of Canada, peace bonds have been issued nine times since 2014 to "limit and/or monitor the movements of people suspected of plotting terrorist attacks."[23] In June 2015, the RCMP sought a peace bond against Winnipeg, Manitoba, resident Aaron Driver for fear he would contribute to the activity of a terrorist group (in this case, IS).[24] In October 2014, a youth in Thunder Bay, Ontario, was originally issued a peace bond for "threatening and passport offences" but was later charged and sentenced.[25]

A peace bond is a preventative tool and does not constitute the laying of a charge under the Canadian Criminal Code. While there is no presumption of innocence there is neither a reasonable standard of evidence that could lead to charges. Conditions for those under this type of peace bond include the surrender of all electronic-communications devices; a promise to stay off the Internet; confiscation of materials that promote terrorism, violence, or extremist ideology; ending contact with named individuals; and an agreement to live with a trustworthy individual (often a parent, as many of those subject to peace bonds are youths). Not surprisingly, given the onerous conditions placed on people who have not been charged with a criminal offense, the tool is seen by some as a serious restriction on Charter-protected freedoms.

Authorities in Minnesota have proposed an interesting hybrid plan. They are considering the adoption of pretrial release and probation programs that will combine "traditional" supervision and counseling. The theory is that in some cases local religious and community members would assume responsibility for the individual and attempt to convince them that they are on the wrong path and have adopted an invalid version of Islam. Officials acknowledge, however, that there is little experience with this method and little academic study.[26]

BANNING TRAVEL TO CONFLICT ZONES

When I arrived in Australia in February 2016 to attend a conference organized by the Canadian High Commission on radicalization, I encountered a sign at Sydney airport warning that if I had recently been to Syria or Iraq my admittance to Australia would be prohibited. That government is one of few countries that have made it an offense to merely travel to conflict zones where terrorist groups are active. The law states that exceptions will be made for "legitimate" purposes—that is, journalism, aid work, and, presumably, official Australian governmental work. The Danish government considered a similar act in April 2016, proposing a six-year sentence for those who left for a conflict zone where a "terrorist organisation" was one of the belligerents.[27]

The challenges to such legal action are obvious: How to determine who goes to Syria for what reason. Information and intelligence gathering is difficult enough in that area of the world, and it will be interesting to see how future court cases unfold. In addition, do these laws provide wannabe jihadis with ready-made alibis? Will future travelers in Australia and Denmark evade detection by resorting to claims that they have justified exceptions for travel? What happens to those who do leave for valid reasons but change their minds once on the ground and fight for a terrorist group?

PASSPORT SEIZURE

In several cases, authorities have elected to seize or cancel passports to prevent individuals from leaving the country. This measure is taken carefully, as many see holding a passport and having freedom of movement as a human right (actually, passport issuance is a privilege, not a right). Carrying out this method solves an immediate threat—the individual cannot leave to join a terrorist group (unless they steal or alter an existing passport or own a second passport on account of dual nationality). As we have seen, however, preventing travel may lead the extremist to displace their extremist intent toward their native land: This is exactly what happened in Canada in October 2014 when two wannabe jihadists were frustrated in their plans to join groups abroad:

- Authorities in East Jutland, Denmark, confiscated the passports of three people suspected of preparing to leave Denmark to fight in the Syrian civil war in August 2015.[28]
- In a similar measure the Danish Immigration Service revoked the residence permit of a foreign fighter, marking the first time that a 2015 law was used to rescind an individual's legal residency in Denmark. The law also gives police the right to confiscate passports and impose travel bans

on Danish citizens suspected of planning to travel to Syria or Iraq to fight.[29]

- Indonesian authorities were considering as of late 2015 to revoke the passports of foreign fighters.[30]
- Belgian authorities were debating the issue in late 2014, unsure whether the move to revoke travel documentation would lead to an attack similar to the one on Parliament Hill in Ottawa in 2014.[31]
- In early 2016 the Norwegian Justice Minister proposed allowing authorities to confiscate or refuse to issue passports to people the government believed to be potential foreign fighters. According to the minister, "It is important to have effective tools for preventing people from travelling to conflict areas, both to prohibit the very serious crimes that are committed in these areas and because people who return can post a serious threat to Norway and Norwegian interests."[32]
- The Indonesian government announced in January 2016 that it would revoke the passports of those on a wanted list of suspected ties to IS.[33]

DOING NOTHING?

On occasion you will come across those that say "Let them go—they'll probably get killed anyway and solve the problem for us!" This attitude is not valid for at least the following reasons:

- They might not get killed and return more capable of carrying out an attack at home.
- They may carry out an attack and kill innocent civilians.
- They may carry out an attack in an allied country.
- They may return as "rock stars" and help to radicalize a whole new generation.

The bottom line is that no country should knowingly allow its citizens to leave with the intent of carrying out terrorist action. We should not "export terrorism" in order to rid ourselves of a problem. We need to deal with our own dirty laundry at home.

The decision to prevent travel or to stand aside is not an easy one. As a senior UK counterterrorism official stated in December 2015, "This illustrates the dilemma we face. Those that want to carry out a terrorist attack may then carry it out here. Stopping people travelling is a risk, but it's a risk we take account of."[34]

AFTER TRAVEL

Citizenship Revocation

In the midst of the 2015 Canadian federal-election campaign, the governing Conservative government announced that it was taking steps to revoke the citizenship of convicted terrorists in Canada, although it was unclear what implications this move would entail. There were voices calling for similar steps to be taken against foreign fighters with IS. After the Liberals won a majority, they quickly put a hold on this measure in Canadian courts.

Part of me feels that this is just displacing, and not solving, the problem. If we deport a terrorist to the country where they hold other citizenship (assuming that the other country agrees to take the individual—cases in Canada show that this can be convoluted), aren't we just giving our problem to someone else? What if that country practices torture or has no decent countering-violent-extremism programming? What's to stop that individual from reengaging?

Furthermore, and I don't think that this aspect has been discussed nearly enough, it seems that the individuals subject to possible citizenship revocation and deportation were actually radicalized in the West. Getting rid of them does not address the environment and the players where the radicalization occurred. In a sense, we own them. So, how does offing our problem make things better? Does it act as a deterrent? Those whose citizenship was revoked could just as easily return on false documentation. Legislation along these lines strikes me as vindictive and knee-jerk.

Another weakness in citizenship revocation is its limited application. States cannot render an individual stateless; hence a person can have their citizenship removed only if they have another one to fall back on. In the absence of dual citizenship, governments cannot use this tool. By doing so they in effect create two tiers of citizenship and apply laws discriminately against one section of society. This strikes me as counter to the democratic systems we have built in the West.

Nevertheless, a number of countries have indicated that they will enact legislation to remove citizenship from terrorists:

- In December 2015, Australia passed a law to remove citizenship from those under four criteria: engaging in terrorist acts, providing or receiving training in preparation for a terrorist act, directing activities of a terrorist organisation, and recruiting or financing terrorists or terrorism; fighting in the service of a declared terrorist group; being convicted of a terrorism offense and sentenced to at least six years' jail; or being convicted of terrorism in the previous decade—retrospective measures allowing citizenship to be revoked for convicted terrorists in jail. [35]

- In October 2015, France announced plans to strip citizenship from five terrorists in its counterterrorism struggle.[36] This promise, repeated after the November 2015 attacks in Paris, was rescinded the following December when politicians decided it would be too divisive,[37] only to be reinstated a day later.[38] It would be applied to dual citizens convicted of terrorism offenses. The move led to accusations that France was pandering to the far right and was following in the footsteps of the World War II–era Vichy regime that stripped Jews of their French citizenship.[39] The planned measure remained controversial as of January 2016.[40] At the end of March 2016 the government finally announced it would not implement the measure.[41]
- Other countries considering such measures include Russia, Israel, Belgium, and Norway.[42]
- Other countries take away benefits and freeze bank accounts.[43]

Investigate and Monitor

The same challenges and restrictions that authorities face in investigating extremists before they leave are present once they leave. There is perhaps an added sense of urgency since these individuals may return with additional skills and in some cases instructions to carry out an attack in their home countries.

It has to be emphasized that investigating foreign fighters is far from simple. Gathering intelligence in a dangerous and constantly changing war zone like Syria and Iraq is difficult. Running human sources or agents into the area exposes human lives to a very high possibility of death. Signals intelligence (SIGINT) has traditionally fared better, but the increasing awareness by the bad guys that their calls and tweets are being monitored as well as the rise in the use of encryption has made this collection method harder. It is thus far from obvious that we can determine in most cases that returnees have engaged in activities while abroad to the extent where an investigation is warranted. Our security and law-enforcement agencies are busy enough dealing with the home-based threat. They are not in a position to investigate everyone to the same high standard.

Arrest/Trial/Conviction

If states have enough information on the activities of individuals who have traveled abroad to join groups like IS and return to their homelands, and this information is strong enough to pass the threshold of court examination, they can arrest and charge returnees. The challenges behind gathering evidence in a war zone should not be underestimated. Furthermore, the transition from intelligence to evidence is not always easy. Two cases in Scandinavia highlight these difficulties. Two sets of accused in Finland and Sweden have been arrested on charges of abetting killings in Iraq and Syria, the former by beheading. The contact of witnesses and the uncertainty whether the crimes committed constitute war crimes, terrorism, or some other offense subject to national law complicate matters.[44]

A number of countries have attempted, nevertheless, to lay charges for crimes committed by persons affiliated with IS:

- The Belgian prime minister, in the wake of the terrorist attacks in Paris and a rise in threat level to his country, stated in late November 2015 that foreign-fighter returnees "belong in prison."[45]
- In November 2015, a twenty-four-year-old Chechen man who had applied for asylum when he arrived in Austria in 2010 was sentenced to five years in prison for fighting with IS. According to Austrian investigators, the man spent several months in 2013 fighting alongside Islamic extremists struggling to overthrow the government of Syria.[46]
- The Swedish government arrested an Iraqi Swede in November 2015 over fears that he had returned to carry out an attack in his adopted country.[47]
- In October 2015, Canadian authorities arrested Mohammed El Shaer for the third time upon his return from Syria. El Shaer had been on the RCMP's high-risk-travelers list.[48]
- In February 2015, Norwegian authorities arrested a man who had been wounded while fighting in Syria.[49]
- In June of 2014, Germany arrested a French national suspected of returning to Europe after fighting with IS.[50]
- An Australian nurse who said he was "forced" to work for IS was arrested by authorities in July 2015 at Sydney airport.[51]
- In November 2015, Sweden charged two members of IS with murdering two people in Syria in 2013. The case was built largely on video and photographic evidence.[52]
- That same month, Estonian authorities charged two men with aiding a third to leave Estonia and join IS.[53]
- In October 2015, Spain jailed eleven members of a gang that recruited and helped send fighters to Syria.[54]
- In December 2015, Germany sentenced two returning IS fighters to short prison terms despite reports that they had come back "disillusioned."[55]
- One hundred forty-five "militants" have been detained in Malaysia since 2013. Authorities arrested a nineteen-year-old in early December 2015 and charged him with belonging to the Al Qaeda–linked Jund al-Aqsa cell.[56]
- Danish officials charged a man with joining IS in Syria in December 2015, a first under Danish law.[57]

- Sweden sentenced two terrorists to life in prison in December 2015 for having slit the throats of two men in Syria in 2013. [58]
- In December 2015, Swiss authorities announced that they would investigate the head of the multimedia department of the Islamic Central Council, Naim Cherni, on accusations of violating a ban on promoting Islamist extremist groups. Cherni apparently had traveled to Syria the previous October where he met with the leader of Jabhat al-Nusra and other extremists. Upon his return he created a forty-minute propaganda video in Arabic with German subtitles. [59]
- In January 2015, a court in France sentenced two French jihadists who had traveled to Syria to six and ten years in prison, the latter in absentia. The latter was last known to be working in IS's police unit and assisting with the recruitment of foreign fighters. [60] Seven more were scheduled to go to trial in 2016. [61]
- Bosnian officials arrested a man in January 2016 whom they believed had fought for IS from November 2014 to June 2015. The government had passed a law in 2014 to stiffen the penalties for foreign fighters. [62]
- In March 2016, a German court handed down a four and a half year sentence to a man who had served in IS's secret police. [63]
- Also in March 2016, an Austrian court sentenced a Bosnian citizen to eight years in prison for his role in recruiting on behalf of IS. [64]
- The Georgian government sentenced a man to fourteen years in prison for recruiting people on behalf of IS. [65]
- In March 2016, the Swiss government stated that it wanted to impose a minimum ten-year sentence on those that travel abroad to join terrorist groups. [66]

These measures are viable but expensive, as court cases in the West can last months and cost millions of dollars. Furthermore, once convicted, extremists are sent to prison where, at least in most countries, there is no standard effective program to deal with their ideology. In addition, research and experience both show that terrorists can use prisons to radicalize other inmates.

Use of Returnees in Antiradicalization Programs

There has been a lot of talk in recent years of using "former" terrorists to speak out against their ex-colleagues and denounce the narratives and goals of extremist groups. Programs such as these are akin to Scared Straight efforts, where at-risk youth are brought to prisons so they can see life on the "inside" and have convicted inmates give them a reality check on what a life of crime is like (interestingly, the US Justice Department cautions against these programs and believes that not only are they ineffective, they may actually be harmful[67]).

There is no question that those who lived and fought with IS have, more than anyone else (analysts, intelligence officers, academics, etc.), a tremendous amount of knowledge of the group and its ideology. This knowledge should be exploited by security and law enforcement as it could give them an advantage in their continuing campaign to fight the group. It is also noteworthy that some people are becoming disillusioned with IS as its actions undermine the terrorist organization's contention that it has created a utopian society for all Muslims.

Furthermore, "formers" have been critical of official government efforts to undermine the IS message. They believe that the United States and other states need to change their strategy to include the following measures:

- Let others do the talking: "A young person who's seriously considering committing murder in the name of Islam would never pay attention to a tweet or a video from the U.S. government, no matter how expertly crafted."[68]
- Present an alternative worldview.
- Don't shoot yourself in the foot (i.e., don't try to defend policies indefensible to your audience or take measures that seem contradictory—like asking people to turn away from IS while simultaneously announcing troop deployments).
- Step up production values and volume.
- Attack the snake from the head (i.e., go after IS leadership).[69]

The ICSR has identified four main topics that seem to crop up in the reasons why fighters abandoned IS[70]:

- Infighting: IS appears to be more interested in fighting other Sunni groups than the Assad regime.
- Brutality and atrocity: IS uses barbaric measures against people.
- IS is corrupt and un-Islamic.
- Life in the Islamic State is harsh and disappointing.

Some French fighters who maintained contact with their families and friends while fighting with IS complained about the conditions (lack of hygiene and the crowded sleeping conditions), and some deserted soon after arriving.[71]

Terrorism scholar Anne Speckhard noted that some of those who had left IS were confused about how the group could sell oil to the Assad regime or make deals with other groups, saw IS members as hypocritical (some were smokers yet punished ordinary citizens who smoked), and grew disgusted at the stream of executions and cruelty.[72]

A Canadian youth who cut his ties with both IS and Jabhat al-Nusra told a Quebec reporter in early 2016 that there are no limits to the "stupidity" of IS and that the group and its leader have created a false Caliphate that cannot even protect the people under its leadership. IS, he claimed, was about to "drown" in the absence of science and Islamic knowledge. [73]

A number of former terrorists in Indonesia have pledged their allegiance to the government in order to help prevent terrorism, specifically with respect to the growing support of IS, which is reported to have been channeling funds to groups in the region. One former terrorist, Imron Baihaqi, is not seeking compensation for his help, as he merely wants an Indonesia untainted by the "inhumane actions of IS." [74]

What better people to use to not only discredit IS but to help convince those who may see the group as a viable destination (for reasons we discussed in the last chapter) to change their minds before it is too late? This option seems like a powerful tool that governments and civil society can use in the fight against radicalization and recruitment. There are, however, a few aspects to bear in mind:

• Not everyone who listens to a defector will be moved by their story. Some individuals are too far radicalized to be affected by what they would label "lies" by a traitor to a great cause.
• Not all defectors will want to go public with their experiences for fear of backlash (ranging from public opprobrium to possible arrest for having left the West to join a terrorist group). Some years ago, when I worked as an advisor to Public Safety Canada, I helped the UK think tank the Institute for Strategic Dialogue develop a series of films (called *Extreme Dialogue*) to help in counter-radicalization work in Canada. I attempted to locate former terrorists who would be willing to tell their stories on film and was in extensive talks with one. In the end, this person declined to participate. He paraphrased his story this way: "I am about to get married, I have a good job, life is going well. If I agree to do this, everyone will remember who I was and what I was. I can't afford to do that now." While I was disappointed, I understood this young man's viewpoint. I am certain there are others like him.
• Are defectors "true" defectors? We have to ensure that people claiming to be disillusioned with terrorism are not simply using this line to get back and reengage in terrorism back home. I do not want to overemphasize this likelihood, but it must be a consideration.
• The threat of retribution remains. IS is known to have killed those seeking to leave its state. Those who succeed in doing so are marked men and women. Their safety would have to be ensured before they would agree to expose themselves publicly. IS will do everything to prevent them from maligning the Caliphate. A stark reminder of this was the beating death of an Austrian young woman who had traveled to Syria but later sought to escape back to the West. [75]

Thus, by all means examine the possibility of using "formers" to help our efforts, but do it carefully.

REHABILITATION/DERADICALIZATION

When we talk of deradicalization programs we are usually referring to attempts to convince convicted terrorists of the error of their ways in the hopes of facilitating their return to everyday society. In a sense, then, this is a form of rehabilitation for terrorists. I have long argued that classic traditional rehabilitation programs designed for traditional criminal behavior is inadequate for terrorism insofar as terrorists are not similar to other criminals. Nonetheless, a number of countries have opted to create and administer such programs. The best known are those in Saudi Arabia and Singapore. Whether or not these efforts are successful remains to be seen, since most of them have not been in operation that long.

One Western country that has tried to fold returning foreign fighters into a broader deradicalization program is Denmark.[76] Although the program in the city of Aarhus has a prevention focus, it has begun to work with returning foreign fighters as well. Individuals are referred by anyone in the community, and participants (participation is voluntary) are offered counseling and mentorship once a risk assessment has been completed. Assistance is also provided for finding work, education, or housing. The program is run by the social services of Aarhus with police assistance. Of the thirty Aarhus residents who have fought in Iraq or Syria, seventeen have returned, and two-thirds of those are back at work or in school. It should be noted though that a dedicated exit program for returnees has yet to have any participants.

In the wake of the November 2015 Paris attacks, the French government has chosen to accelerate the establishment of deradicalization centers, both for returning fighters and for those still on the pathway to violent radicalization.[77] This move represents a change in French philosophy toward terrorism, insofar as traditionally only hard measures were implemented. French officials acknowledge that many questions remain as to how they can best establish procedures in these centers.

Sidney Jones, director of Jakarta-based Institute for Policy Analysis of Conflict, has strongly suggested that Indonesia work on a deradicalization program for returning IS supporters. She suggests that at least half of those deported back to Indonesia from Turkey are women and children, thus supporting the findings that a disproportionate number of foreign IS members are not male. Jones thinks that women who successfully go through the program could serve as "barriers" to help prevent further radicalization in their families.[78]

There is no question, as we have seen, that a certain percentage of foreign fighters will return disillusioned and sickened by what they saw. We have to also bear in mind that they will likely be traumatized to an extent and that this will have implications for whatever deradicalization or rehabilitation program is established in their homelands.

SUMMARY

There is no quick and easy solution to the problem of what to do with returning foreign fighters. As with radicalization to violence, each case must be examined individually to determine, where possible, what the intentions of the returnees are. This is not an easy task; those with violent intent will not openly declare.

Early intervention strategies are gaining momentum. While it is far from clear what role they play—if any—in those driven to fight abroad, they are nevertheless relatively inexpensive and may under the best of circumstances convince some of the ill-considered nature of their interest.

Law-enforcement and security agencies have a crucial part to play in identifying and neutralizing those who seek to do us harm. These organizations have a fairly good record and will need the resources to effectively protect us.

We in the West have just begun to develop and implement deradicalization and terrorist-rehabilitation strategies. As a result, it will take time to determine what works and what doesn't. Assessing true success rates will require years of data, and it will be necessary to not ascribe victory prematurely.

On the other hand, if historical trends continue, we know that relatively few returning foreign fighters will present a danger to national security. So, even if we do not have the ability to dedicate significant resources to figure out which ones do, we are confident that we will not be faced with an unmanageable menace to our societies.

NOTES

1. Colin Freeze and Carrie Tait, "RCMP Using New Measures to Stop 'High-Risk Travellers,'" *Globe and Mail* (Toronto), September 19, 2015, http://www.theglobeandmail.com/news/national/rcmp-using-new-measures-to-stop-high-risk-travellers/article20712700/.

2. Royal Canadian Mounted Police Federal Policing, "Foreign Fighters: Preventing the Security Threat in Canada and Abroad," February 2014. Emphasis added.

3. Joshua E. Keating, "Is It Legal for Americans to Fight in Another Country's Army?" *Foreign Policy*, September 2, 2011, http://foreignpolicy.com/2011/09/02/is-it-legal-for-americans-to-fight-in-another-countrys-army/.

4. Caroline Bishop, "Swiss Sign up to Stop Travel for Terrorism," *Local* (Stockholm), October 23, 2015, http://www.thelocal.ch/20151023/swiss-sign-up-to-stop-travel-for-terrorism.

5. Agence France-Presse, "France Adopts Bill to Keep Minors from Jihad," *Local* (Paris), October 9, 2015, http://www.thelocal.fr/20151009/france-adopts-bill-to-keep-minors-from-jihad.

6. Sveriges Radio, "Parties Present Anti-terror Deal," December 10, 2015, http://sverigesradio.se/sida/artikel.aspx?programid=2054&artikel=6323087.

7. *Latin American Herald Tribune* (Caracas), "Trinidad Creates Hotline for Tips on Would-Be Jihadists," December 3, 2015, http://www.laht.com/article.asp?ArticleId=2401239&CategoryId=14092.

8. CBC News, "Quebecers Wanting to Join Fight Against ISIS on the Rise, Expert Says," November 16, 2015, http://www.cbc.ca/beta/news/canada/montreal/wali-effect-anti-isis-recruitment-anti-radicalization-centre-quebec-montreal-kurds-1.3320980.

9. Jessica Jones, "Spanish Anti-jihadist Hotline Turns Up 29 'Suspects' in First 24 Hours," *Local* (Madrid), December 7, 2015, http://www.thelocal.es/20151207/spain-to-investigate-29-people-after-one-day-of-stop-radicalism-campaign.

10. According to *The Economist*, the number of people it takes to follow someone "around the clock" ranges from twenty to sixty. "Jihad at the Heart of Europe," Briefing, November 21, 2015, http://www.economist.com/news/briefing/21678840-brussels-not-just-europes-political-and-military-capitalit-also-centre-its.

11. Stewart Bell, "Windsor Man Who 'Got the Last Laugh' and Slipped Past No-Fly List into Turkey Now Back in Canadian Court," *National Post* (Toronto), October 16, 2015, http://news.nationalpost.com/news/canada/windsor-man-who-got-the-last-laugh-and-slipped-past-no-fly-list-into-turkey-now-back-in-canadian-court.

12. CBC News, with Adrienne Arsenault, "Ahmad Waseem, Jihadi in Syria, Ignored Family's Pleas to Stay in Canada," July 28, 2014, http://www.cbc.ca/news/canada/ahmad-waseem-jihadi-in-syria-ignored-family-s-pleas-to-stay-in-canada-1.2720169.

13. Levi Winchester, "Latest Briton Believed to Have Beheaded in the Name of IS—But Who Is Nasser Muthana?" *Daily Express* (London), November 17, 2014, http://www.express.co.uk/news/world/536444/Islamic-State-beheadings-Who-is-Nasser-Muthana.

14. Tom Whitehead, Gordon Rayner, and David Barrett, "Mounting Questions for Police and Home Officer after Terror Suspect Was Not Spotted Missing for Six Weeks," *Telegraph* (London), January 5, 2016, http://www.telegraph.co.uk/news/worldnews/islamic-state/12082474/Suspect-for-new-Jihadi-John-was-arrested-six-times-but-still-able-to-leave-UK.html.

15. Cahal Milmo, "UK Allows Five Islamists Linked to Same Extremist Group as 'New Jihadi John' Suspect Siddhartha Dhar to Slip Out of Country," *Independent* (London), January 7, 2016, http://www.independent.co.uk/news/uk/home-news/uk-islamists-jihadi-john-isis-siddhartha-dhar-abu-rumaysah-leave-a6799656.html.

16. CBC News, "Mohamed Hesri sentenced to 10 years for attempting to join Al--Shabad," July 24.2014.

17. Stewart Bell, "Peace Bonds Increasingly a Tool Against Terror as Officials 'Punish' Canadians Who 'May' Commit Crimes," *National Post* (Toronto), December 22, 2015, http://news.nationalpost.com/news/canada/peace-bonds-increasingly-a-weapon-in-fight-against-terror-as-officials-punish-canadians-who-may-commit-crimes.

18. Jessica Jones, "Moroccan Arrested in Pamplona for Planning to Join Isis and Go to Syria," *Local* (Madrid), December 1, 2015, http://www.thelocal.es/20151201/man-arrested-in-pamplona-for-planning-to-join-isis-in-syria.

19. Royal Canadian Mounted Police, "RCMP Alberta INSET Lays Terrorism Charges against Farah Shirdon," September 24, 2015, http://www.rcmp-grc.gc.ca/en/news/2015/24/rcmp-alberta-inset-lays-terrorism-charges-against-farah-shirdon.

20. Ben Makuch, "A Chat with the Canadian ISIS Member Who Burned His Passport on YouTube," Vice.com, June 23, 2014, http://motherboard.vice.com/read/a-chat-with-the-canadian-isis-member-who-burned-his-passport-on-youtube.

21. *Local* (Stockholm), "New Norway Law to Stop Citizens Fighting for ISIS," December 22, 2015, http://www.thelocal.no/20151222/new-law-proposals-aim-to-prevent-norwegians-from-fighting-in-syria.

22. Sidhartha Banerjee, the Canadian Press, "Montreal Teen in Terror Case Gets Three-Year Sentence," *Toronto Sun*, April 6, 2016, http://www.torontosun.com/2016/04/06/montreal-teen-in-terror-case-gets-three-year-sentence.

23. Stewart Bell, "Peace Bonds Increasingly a Tool against Terror as Officials 'Punish' Canadians Who 'May' Commit Crimes," *National Post* (Toronto), December 22, 2015, http://news.nationalpost.com/news/canada/peace-bonds-increasingly-a-weapon-in-fight-against-terror-as-officials-punish-canadians-who-may-commit-crimes.

24. CBC News, "RCMP Seek Peace Bond against ISIS Supporter in Winnipeg," June 5, 2015, http://www.cbc.ca/beta/news/canada/manitoba/rcmp-seek-peace-bond-against-isis-supporter-in-winnipeg-1.3102515.

25. Stewart Bell, "Peace Bonds Increasingly a Tool Against Terror as Officials 'Punish' Canadians Who 'May' Commit Crimes," *National Post* (Toronto), December 22, 2015, http://news.nationalpost.com/news/canada/peace-bonds-increasingly-a-weapon-in-fight-against-terror-as-officials-punish-canadians-who-may-commit-crimes.

26. Mila Koumpilova, "Minnesota Officials Envision Probation Program for People Facing Terrorism Charges," *Star Tribune* (Minneapolis), January 9, 2016, http://www.startribune.com/minnesota-officials-envision-a-probation-program-for-people-facing-terror-charges/364754521/.

27. Agence France-Presse, *Local* (Stockholm), "Denmark Seeks Syria Travel Ban after Arrests," *Local* (Stockholm), April 8, 2016, http://www.thelocal.dk/20160408/denmark-seeks-syria-travel-ban-after-arrests.

28. *Local* (Stockholm), "Police Seize Passports of 'Foreign Fighters,'" August 28, 2015, http://www.thelocal.dk/20150828/danish-police-seize-passports-syria-foreign-fighter.

29. *Local* (Stockholm), "'Syria Fighter' Loses Danish Residence Permit," September 1, 2015, http://www.thelocal.dk/20150901/denmark-strips-syria-fighter-residence-permit.

30. Wahyudi Soeriaatmadja, "Jakarta May Revoke Passports of ISIS Members," *Singapore Straits Times*, December 23, 2015, http://www.straitstimes.com/asia/se-asia/jakarta-may-revoke-passports-of-isis-members.

31. Marjan Justaert, "Bonte voert druk op in aanpak jonge jihadisten," *De Standaard* (Brussels), November 18, 2014, http://www.standaard.be/cnt/dmf20141117_01380781 (subscription required).

32. *Local* (Stockholm), "Norway Wants to Confiscate Foreign Fighters' Passports," January 20, 2016, http://www.thelocal.no/20160120/norway-wants-to-confiscate-foreign-fighters-passports.

33. Antara News, "Govt to Revoke Passports of Those Wanted Over Terrorism," January 26, 2016, http://www.antaranews.com/en/news/102760/govt-to-revoke-passports-held-by-those-wanted-over-terrorism.

34. Alex Matthews, "Extremists 'Are Allowed to Leave UK So They Don't Carry Out Attacks Here': Counter-Terrorism Official Claims Police Face Dilemma Over Whether Terrorists Are More Dangerous 'Home or Away,'" *Daily Mail* (London), December 15, 2015, http://www.dailymail.co.uk/news/article-3359631/We-soldiers-streets-London-contain-Paris-style-terror-attack-multiple-gunmen-says-police-chief.html.

35. Australian Associated Press and Business Spectator, "Citizenship Laws Clear Parliament," *Australian*, December 4, 2015, http://www.theaustralian.com.au/business/business-spectator/citizenship-laws-clear-parliament/news-story/bd0a737b7381eb84002404070ff0245b.

36. *Local* (Paris), "France to Strip Five 'Terrorists' of Nationality," October 6, 2015, http://www.thelocal.fr/20151006/france-to-strip-nationality-from-five-terrorists.

37. *Local* (Paris), "Terrorism: France 'To Scraps Plan to Strip Citizenships," December 22, 2015, http://www.thelocal.fr/20151222/france-u-turns-on-plan-to-strip-jihadists-nationality.

38. *Local* (Paris), Agence France-Presse, "France Sticks to Plan to Strip Terrorists' Passports," *Local* (Paris), December 23, 2015, http://www.thelocal.fr/20151223/france-constitution-emergency-powers.

39. Agence France-Presse, "Fury as Hollande Calls to Strip Terrorist Passports," *Local* (Paris), December 30, 2015, http://www.thelocal.fr/20151230/hollande-under-fire-over-call-to-strip-citizenship-from-terror-convicts.

40. Adam Nossiter, "French Proposal to Strip Citizenship of Terrorism Convicts Sets Off Alarms," *New York Times*, January 8, 2016, http://www.nytimes.com/2016/01/09/world/europe/french-proposal-to-strip-citizenship-over-terrorism-sets-off-alarms.html.

41. Bamzi Banchiri, "French President Drops Plan to Strip Citizenship from Convicted Terrorists," *Christian Science Monitor*, March 30, 2016, http://www.csmonitor.com/World/Global-News/2016/0330/French-president-drops-plan-to-strip-citizenship-from-convicted-terrorists.

42. Carol J. Williams, "Join a Terrorist Group, Lose Your Citizenship," *LA Times*, November 24, 2015, http://www.latimes.com/world/europe/la-fg-militants-security-citizenship-20151124-story.html.

43. Jonathan Owen and Brian Brady, "Theresa May Urges Action on 'Jihad Tourism,'" *Independent* (London), July 6, 2013, http://www.independent.co.uk/news/world/politics/theresa-may-urges-action-on-jihad-tourism-8692590.html.

44. Alison Smale, "Iraqis' Arrest in Finland Highlights Difficulty in Prosecuting Distant Crimes," *New York Times*, December 24, 2015, http://www.nytimes.com/2015/12/25/world/europe/finland-iraq-refugees-isis.html.

45. Colin Clapson, "Terrorist Threat: What's Belgium Doing?" Flandersnews.be, November 19, 2015, http://deredactie.be/cm/vrtnieuws.english/News/1.2500253.

46. *Local* (Stockholm), "Chechen Jailed for ISIS Fight in Syria," November 20, 2015, http://www.thelocal.at/20151120/chechen-jailed-for-isis-fight-in-syria.

47. *Local* (Vienna), "Doubts Grow in Sweden over Seized Terrorist," November 21, 2015, last updated November 23, 2015, http://www.thelocal.se/20151121/doubts-grow-in-sweden-over-isis-terrorist.

48. Stewart Bell, "Windsor Man Who 'Got the Last Laugh' and Slipped Past No-Fly List into Turkey Now Back in Canadian Court," *National Post* (Toronto), October 16, 2015, http://news.nationalpost.com/news/canada/windsor-man-who-got-the-last-laugh-and-slipped-past-no-fly-list-into-turkey-now-back-in-canadian-court.

49. Staff reporter, "Norwegian Syria Fighter Seized on Terror Charge," *Local* (Stockholm), February 14, 2015, http://www.thelocal.no/20140214/norway-jihadi-arrested-for-terror-on-return-from-syria.

50. Agence France-Presse, "French 'Syria Fighter' Arrested in Germany," *Times of Israel*, June 15, 2014, http://www.timesofisrael.com/french-syria-fighter-arrested-in-germany/.

51. Rod McGuirk, Associated Press, "Australian Medic for Islamic State Arrested on Return Home," *Times of Israel*, July 25, 2015, http://www.timesofisrael.com/australian-medic-for-islamic-state-arrested-on-return-home/.

52. Sveriges Radio, "Two Swedes Face Terror Prosecution for Terror Killing in Sweden," November 23, 2015, http://sverigesradio.se/sida/artikel.aspx?programid=2054&artikel=6309251.

53. J. M. Laats, "Trial Begins of Two Men Accused of Aiding Terrorist," Eesti Rahvusringhääling (Estonian Public Broadcasting), November 23, 2015, http://news.err.ee/v/politics/society/db578dad-5abe-423f-b6f8-aced75fd42d0/trial-begins-over-two-men-accused-of-aiding-terrorist.

54. Fiona Govan, "Spain Jails Jihadist Recruiter Gang that Sent Suicide Bombers to Syria, *Local* (Madrid), October 2, 2015, http://www.thelocal.es/20151002/spain-jails-11-recruiters-for-sending-suicide-bombers-to-syria.

55. Agence France-Presse, "Two Returning Isis Jihadists Sentenced to Jail," *Local* (Berlin), December 8, 2015, http://www.thelocal.de/20151208/court-sentences-two-returning-isis-jihadists-to-jail.

56. Farik Zolkepli, "Teen Militant Caught in KLIA," *Star Online* (Malaysia), December 12, 2015, http://www.thestar.com.my/news/nation/2015/12/12/teen-militant-caught-19yearold-malaysian-nabbed-in-klia/.

57. Agence France-Presse, "Denmark Charges First Syria Fighter over Joining IS," Yahoo! News, December 15, 2015, https://www.yahoo.com/news/denmark-charges-first-syria-fighter-over-joining-211827436.html.

58. Sverige Radio, "Two Men Sentenced to Life in Prison for Terror Crimes in Syria," December 14, 2015, http://sverigesradio.se/sida/artikel.aspx?programid=2054&artikel=6325359.

59. Agence France-Presse, "Switzerland to Probe Leading Swiss Muslim," *Local* (Stockholm), December 20, 2015, http://www.thelocal.ch/20151220/switzerland-to-investigate-leading-swiss-muslim.

60. Agence France-Presse, "French Militants Who Visited Syria Given 6, 10 Years' Jail," Al Arabiya English, January 8, 2016, http://english.alarabiya.net/en/News/middle-east/2016/01/08/French-jihadists-who-visited-Syria-given-6-10-years-jail-.html.

61. Agence France-Presse, "Paris Bomber's Brother among Jihadists to Be Tried in France," *Local* (Paris), January 23, 2016, http://www.thelocal.fr/20160123/france-to-try-7-jihadists-including-paris-bombers-brother.

62. Rodolfo Toe, "Bosnian Police Arrest ISIS Suspect at Airport," Balkan Insight, January 21, 2016, http://www.balkaninsight.com/en/article/bosnian-citizen-arrested-after-having-fought-for-is-01-21-2016.

63. Deutsche Presse-Agentur, Agence France-Presse, "Former German 'Islamic State' Fighter Gets Four Years, Six Months in Prison," Deutsche Welle, March 4, 2016, http://www.dw.com/en/former-german-islamic-state-fighter-gets-four-years-six-months-in-prison/a-19093806.

64. Rodolpho Toe, "Austria Jails Bosnian for Recruiting for ISIS," Balkan Insight, March 4, 2016, http://www.balkaninsight.com/en/article/austria-jails-bosnian-citizen-for-recruiting-fighters-03-04-2016.

65. Civil Georgia, "Man Found Guilty of Recruiting for IS Group, Given 14 Years in Jail," March 7, 2016, http://www.civil.ge/eng/article.php?id=29025.

66. *Local* (Stockholm), "Bern Backs Harsher Sentence for Homegrown Terrorists ," March 11, 2016, http://www.thelocal.ch/20160311/bern-backs-harsher-sentence-for-homegrown-terrorists.

67. International Centre for the Study of Radicalisation (ICSR), "ICSR Report: Victims Perpetrators Assets; The Narratives of Islamic State Defectors," (London: ICSR, 2015), http://icsr.info/wp-content/uploads/2015/09/ICSR-Report-Victims-Perpertrators-Assets-The-Narratives-of-Islamic-State-Defectors.pdf.

68. Elizabeth Cohen and Deborah Goldschmidt, "Ex-terrorist Explains How to Fight ISIS Online," CNN, December 20, 2015, http://www.brproud.com/news/exterrorist-explains-how-to-fight-isis-online.

69. Elizabeth Cohen and Debra Goldschmidt, "Ex-terrorist Explains How to Fight ISIS Online," CNN, December 21, 2015, http://www.cnn.com/2015/12/18/health/al-quaeda-recruiter-fight-isis-online/index.html.

70. Peter Neumann, International Centre for the Study of Radicalisation (ICSR), "ICSR Report: Victims, Perpetrators, Assets; The Narratives of Islamic State Defectors," (London: ICSR, 2015) http://icsr.info/wp-content/uploads/2015/09/ICSR-Report-Victims-Perpertrators-Assets-The-Narratives-of-Islamic-State-Defectors.pdf.

71. Dominique Simonnot, "DAECH, c'est pas le Club Med," *Le Canard Enchainé* (Paris) December 2, 2015.

72. Anne Speckhard and Ahmet S. Yayla, "Eyewitness Accounts from Recent Defectors from Islamic State: Why They Joined, What They Saw, Why They Quit," *Perspectives on Terrorism* 9, no. 6 (2015), http://www.terrorismanalysts.com/pt/index.php/pot/article/view/475/html.

73. Andrew McIntosh, "Un djihadiste québécois renie ses liens avec l'État islamique," *Journal de Montréal*, January 6, 2015, http://www.journaldemontreal.com/2016/01/06/un-djihadiste-quebecois-renie-ses-liens-avec-letat-islamique.

74. *Jakarta Post*, "Former Indonesian Terrorists Pledge Support against IS," December 30, 2015, http://www.thejakartapost.com/news/2015/12/30/former-ri-terrorists-pledge-support-against-is.html.

75. *Local* (Vienna), "Missing Vienna Girl 'Beaten to Death' by Isis," November 24, 2015, http://www.thelocal.at/20151124/missing-vienna-girl-beaten-to-death-by-isis.

76. Agence France-Press, *Local* (Stockholm), "Denmark's 'Soft' Model for Converting Jihadists," *Local* (Stockholm), November 23, 2015, http://www.thelocal.dk/20151123/denmarks-soft-model-for-de-radicalizing-jihadists.

77. Elise Vincent, "L'Etat accentue la lutte contre la radicalisation," *Le Monde* (Paris), November 24, 2015, http://www.lemonde.fr/police-justice/article/2015/11/24/le-gouvernement-accelere-sur-la-lutte-contre-la-radicalization_4815998_1653578.html?xtmc=elise_vincent&xtcr=2.

78. Marguerite Afra Sapiie, "Experts Call for Deradicalization of Returning IS Supporters," *Jakarta Post*, November 26, 2015, http://www.thejakartapost.com/news/2015/11/26/experts-call-deradicalization-returning-is-supporters.html.

Chapter Eight

Conclusion

The Road to Damascus

Then Ananias went to the house and entered it. Placing his hands on Saul, he said, "Brother Saul, the Lord—Jesus, who appeared to you on the road as you were coming here—has sent me so that you may see again and be filled with the Holy Spirit." Immediately, something like scales fell from Saul's eyes, and he could see again. He got up and was baptized, and after taking some food, he regained his strength.

—Acts 9:17–19

CHAPTER ABSTRACT

This short chapter provides an overall perspective on the nature of the threat from fighters returning from overseas conflicts. It also seeks to look forward to what we need to do and what we need to keep in mind.

WHAT WILL THE FUTURE HOLD?

This book has been about journeys. We have discovered why some people make the decision to go to war and what drove them to leave, at times, comfortable lives to place themselves in danger. In some cases, their stories have a lot in common with the story of the apostle Paul. Originally known as Saul, he traveled to Damascus and underwent an epiphany or conversion process. Saul became Paul, a new man. It is not an exaggeration to say that young men who go off to war and who survive also become new men (sometimes broken and badly damaged new men). For those who join IS they undertake their own road to Damascus. War seldom leads to good outcomes,

135

at least among those forced to wage it. But do these men pose a threat to their societies?

Some have overtly compared today's foreign fighters with IS to Spanish Civil War veterans. Both sets fought for largely ideological reasons against brutal dictators. Furthermore, since there turned out to be little threat to the West in the aftermath of the Nationalist victory in Spain in 1939, the hype over the threat from returnees from the Levant is overblown, right?

Well, not so fast.

There is no question that of all the foreign, unsanctioned wars in which Canadians and Westerners opted to participate in the twentieth century, ideological motivation was common for the foreign soldiers—or at least some of them—who fought in Spain. Call it communism, call it socialism, call it antifascism, there was clearly a political underpinning to their decision. And of course the struggle between communism and the West was one that both dominated and threatened throughout the century. Both sides used proxy actors in efforts to undermine the other, and some of these actors were terrorists.

And yet it would be a stretch to suggest that returning Spanish Civil War combatants adhered to an ideology that not only hated the West but also sought its destruction through violence and terrorism at home. Indeed, there were no acts of terrorism that came out of the experiences of these men, and the fears and anxieties of governments and security and law-enforcement agencies turned out to be unfounded—fortunately.

The current wave of foreign fighters constitutes a very different beast, however. The ideology that gives IS and AQ and others its raison d'être is inherently hateful and *does* seek to overthrow the West, its institutions, and its culture through violence. Whether or not this goal is attainable—I happen to think it is not—proponents are bent on seeking to kill in the name of that ideology. And that renders them a real and significant, albeit not existential, threat to the West.

We have already seen attacks carried out by returnees, and we will see more. IS veterans will eventually run their course, but the bad news is that other conflicts either current (West Africa, Middle East, South Asia) or future will provide opportunities for more people to travel, acquire skills, and return to wreak havoc. Unfortunately these wars to come are hard to predict, and it will be even harder to prevent or resolve them before hundreds if not thousands see them as viable or mandatory duties to fight. The ideology that drives IS and AQ will long outlast those groups. It will adapt and change to suit the particular circumstances of future Islamist groups.

It is also inevitable that men and women will participate in wars for some time to come. Even if war as a human action occurs less frequently than it has historically (à la Pinker[1]), it will never disappear. And where there is war, there will be a willing cohort.

What we must not ignore in the wake of IS is the new phenomenon of female involvement. In Western societies we have witnessed an interesting debate over whether women should have combat roles. An equally fascinating to-and-fro has occurred among extremist Islamist ideologues. Traditionally women were denied any active part in violent jihad. IS, however, has overturned this custom. As a consequence, strategies to deal with returnees will have to evolve to adequately include measures that have women in mind, something we have not had to do to date. Whether any of these returning women become operational will be an interesting phenomenon to watch for. Nevertheless, the majority who come back disillusioned will require our help.

Wars have always left destruction in their wake. Destroyed cities, countries, lives. Even those who survive war are never the same, and this is also applicable to those we send to fight. Veterans often return broken and need help readjusting to society. Canada has struggled with how to reintegrate veterans, and there has been a disturbing trend of suicides among those that fought in Afghanistan. Future conflicts will bring their own sets of suffering and illness.

And the same goes for violent jihad. Canadians and other Westerners will continue to go, and those not killed will need to be dealt with, whether as returning assailants, radicalizers, patients, or inmates. Regardless, we will have to develop multiple programs to deal with this issue. The vast majority will be citizens of Western states, and unless citizenship-revocation measures gain more traction, they will still be part of our societies: We cannot ignore them.

Luckily we are currently working on such programs. We will learn what works and what doesn't, and we will be in a position to adapt to ensure better results. On the harder end, it is hoped that we will get better at detection and interdiction to prevent extremists from leaving and future attacks from happening. And yet we have to accept that some attacks will take place. Equally of importance is the assurance that our reaction to the few violent incidents that squeak through is measured, temperate, and mitigated. Overreaction will lead to further problems that will only exacerbate the situation.

Let us not ignore the threat from those who choose to fight in ideologically driven wars with groups that fundamentally hate who we are. But let us not assume that every fighter poses a disproportionate threat to the West. With respect to the unprecedented numbers of Westerners who have fought with IS, unnamed French counterterrorism officials have warned of a "generational" threat.[2] Probably true, but let's keep it in perspective. Yes, it will unfold over a generation, but that does not mean that an entire generation poses a threat.

We can handle this, and by *we* I mean the "big" we: communities, law-enforcement agencies, security services, and governments. Working together we can minimize the risks to our countries. The task is laid out for us, and it is time to get to it.

NOTES

1. Steven Pinker, *Better Angels of Our Nature: Why Violence Has Declined* (New York: Viking, 2011).

2. Michel Moutot and Eric Randolph, Agence France-Press, "Jihadist Veterans Pose Generational Threat Even If IS Defeated: Experts," Yahoo! News, December 7, 2015, http://news.yahoo.com/jihadist-veterans-pose-generational-threat-even-defeated-experts-042747808.html.

Appendix

Jihad as War

Fight those who do not believe in Allah, nor in the latter day, nor do they prohibit what Allah and His Apostle have prohibited, nor follow the religion of truth, out of those who have been given the Book, until they pay the tax in acknowledgment of superiority and they are in a state of subjection.

—Quran, sura 9:29

subjugation?

APPENDIX ABSTRACT

We will develop further here the analysis initiated in chapter 2. A number of sources, both historical and contemporary will be examined to demonstrate how religion and ideology are being used to justify violent jihad and to encourage Muslims to join terrorist groups.

NOTE

This section is not intended to be exhaustive: Entire volumes could be written (and in some cases already have) on each individual. I have elected to focus on those who, in my experience as an intelligence analyst, are actively used by extremists as sources of information, sanction, or inspiration. It should also be stressed that my experience was largely focused on Canadians radicalizing to violence: In other countries such individuals may migrate to one source more than another. To cite a small example, in Canada the works of Abu Musab al-Suri did not appear to be influential (perhaps because his opus major, *The Global Islamic Resistance Call*, is more than 1,600 pages long!). In other places his works may be critical. Interestingly, however, the

139

Combatting Terrorism Center at West Point in its 2006 Militant Ideology Atlas did not cite al-Suri as a particularly influential ideologue.

THE QURAN

Here is a more comprehensive list of Quranic verses used to justify jihad:

- "[2.178] O you who believe! retaliation is prescribed for you in the matter of the slain, the free for the free, and the slave for the slave, and the female for the female, but if any remission is made to any one by his (aggrieved) brother, then prosecution (for the bloodwit) should be made according to usage, and payment should be made to him in a good manner; this is an alleviation from your Lord and a mercy; so whoever exceeds the limit after this he shall have a painful chastisement. [2.179] And there is life for you in (the law of) retaliation, O men of understanding, that you may guard yourselves."
- "[2.190] And fight in the way of *Allah* with those who fight with you, and do not exceed the limits, surely *Allah* does not love those who exceed the limits. [2.191] And kill them wherever you find them, and drive them out from whence they drove you out, and persecution is severer than slaughter, and do not fight with them at the Sacred Mosque until they fight with you in it, but if they do fight you, then slay them; such is the recompense of the unbelievers."
- "[2.193] And fight with them until there is no persecution, and religion should be only for *Allah*, but if they desist, then there should be no hostility except against the oppressors. [2.194] The Sacred month for the sacred month and all sacred things are (under the law of) retaliation; whoever then acts aggressively against you, inflict injury on him according to the injury he has inflicted on you and be careful (of your duty) to *Allah* and know that *Allah* is with those who guard (against evil)."
- "[2.216] Fighting is enjoined on you, and it is an object of dislike to you; and it may be that you dislike a thing while it is good for you, and it may be that you love a thing while it is evil for you, and *Allah* knows, while you do not know. [2.217] They ask you concerning the sacred month about fighting in it. Say: Fighting in it is a grave matter, and hindering (men) from *Allah*'s way and denying Him, and (hindering men from) the Sacred Mosque and turning its people out of it, are still graver with *Allah*, and persecution is graver than slaughter; and they will not cease fighting with you until they turn you back from your religion, if they can; and whoever of you turns back from his religion, then he dies while an unbeliever—these it is whose works shall go for nothing in this world and the hereafter, and they are the inmates of the fire; therein they shall abide."

- "[3.121] And when you did go forth early in the morning from your family to lodge the believers in encampments for war and *Allah* is Hearing, Knowing. [3.122] When two parties from among you had determined that they should show cowardice [about *jihad*], and *Allah* was the guardian of them both, and in *Allah* should the believers trust. [3.123] And *Allah* did certainly assist you at [the Battle of] Badr when you were weak; be careful of (your duty to) *Allah* then, that you may give thanks. [3.124] When you said to the believers: Does it not suffice you that your Lord should assist you with three thousand of the angels sent down? [3.125] Yea! if you remain patient and are on your guard, and they come upon you in a headlong manner, your Lord will assist you with five thousand of the havoc-making angels. [3.126] And *Allah* did not make it but as good news for you, and that your hearts might be at ease thereby, and victory is only from *Allah*, the Mighty, the Wise."

- "[3.157] And if you are slain in the way of *Allah* or you die, certainly forgiveness from *Allah* and mercy is better than what they amass [what those who stay home from *jihad* receive—no booty and no perks in heaven]. [3.158] And if indeed you die or you are slain, certainly to *Allah* shall you be gathered together."

- "[3.169] And reckon not those who are killed in *Allah*'s way as dead; nay, they are alive (and) are provided sustenance from their Lord."

- "[3.195] So their Lord accepted their prayer: That I will not waste the work of a worker among you, whether male or female, the one of you being from the other; they, therefore, who fled and were turned out of their homes and persecuted in My way and who fought and were slain, I will most certainly cover their evil deeds, and I will most certainly make them enter gardens beneath which rivers flow; a reward from *Allah*, and with *Allah* is yet better reward."

- "[5.033] The punishment of those who wage war against *Allah* and His apostle and strive to make mischief in the land is only this, that they should be murdered or crucified or their hands and their feet should be cut off on opposite sides or they should be imprisoned."

- "[8.012] When your Lord revealed to the angels: I am with you, therefore make firm those who believe. I will cast terror into the hearts of those who disbelieve. Therefore strike off their heads and strike off every fingertip of them."

- "[8.15] O you who believe! when you meet those who disbelieve marching for war, then turn not your backs to them. [8.16] And whoever shall turn his back to them on that day—unless he turn aside for the sake of fighting or withdraws to a company—then he, indeed, becomes deserving of *Allah*'s wrath, and his abode is hell; and an evil destination shall it be. [8.17] So you did not slay them, but it was *Allah* Who slew them, and you did not smite when you smote (the enemy), but it was *Allah* Who smote

[*Allah* gets the credit for *jihad*], and that He might confer upon the believers a good gift from Himself; surely *Allah* is Hearing, Knowing."

- "[8.39] *Shakir*: And fight with them until there is no more persecution and religion should be only for *Allah*; but if they desist, then surely *Allah* sees what they do."
- "[8.65] O Prophet! urge the believers to war; if there are twenty patient ones of you they shall overcome two hundred, and if there are a hundred of you they shall overcome a thousand of those who disbelieve, because they are a people who do not understand. So when the sacred months have passed away, then slay the idolaters wherever you find them, and take them captives and besiege them and lie in wait for them in every ambush, then if they repent and keep up prayer and pay the poor-rate, leave their way free to them; surely *Allah* is Forgiving, Merciful."
- "[9.12] And if they break their oaths after their agreement and (openly) revile your religion, then fight the leaders of unbelief—surely their oaths are nothing—so that they may desist."
- "[9.029] Fight those who do not believe in *Allah*, nor in the latter day, nor do they prohibit what *Allah* and His Apostle have prohibited, nor follow the religion of truth, out of those who have been given the Book, until they pay the tax in acknowledgment of superiority and they are in a state of subjection."
- "[9.38] O you who believe! What (excuse) have you that when it is said to you: Go forth in *Allah*'s way [to *jihad*], you should incline heavily to earth; are you contented with this world's life instead of the hereafter? But the provision of this world's life compared with the hereafter is but little. [9.38] If you do not go forth [to go on *jihad*], He will chastise you with a painful chastisement and bring in your place a people other than you [to go on *jihad*], and you will do Him no harm; and *Allah* has power over all things."
- "[9.073] O Prophet! strive hard [*jihad*] against the unbelievers and the hypocrites and be unyielding to them; and their abode is hell, and evil is the destination."
- "[22.039] Permission (to fight) is given to those upon whom war is made because they are oppressed, and most surely *Allah* is well able to assist them."
- "[29.006] And whoever strives hard [in *jihad*], he strives only for his own soul; most surely *Allah* is Self-sufficient, above (need of) the worlds."
- "[33.25] And *Allah* turned back the unbelievers in their rage; they did not obtain any advantage, and *Allah* sufficed the believers in fighting; and *Allah* is Strong, Mighty. [33.26] And He drove down those of the followers of the Book who backed them from their fortresses and He cast awe into their hearts; some [Jews] you killed and you took captive another part. [33.27] And He made you heirs to their [Jewish] land and their dwellings

and their property, and (to) a land which you have not yet trodden, and *Allah* has power over all things."

- "[33.050] O Prophet! surely We have made lawful to you your wives whom you have given their dowries, and those [captive women] whom your right hand possesses out of those whom *Allah* has given to you as prisoners of war, and the daughters of your paternal uncles and the daughters of your paternal aunts, and the daughters of your maternal uncles and the daughters of your maternal aunts who fled with you; and a believing woman if she gave herself to the Prophet, if the Prophet desired to marry her—specially for you, not for the (rest of) believers; We know what We have ordained for them concerning their wives and those whom their right hands possess in order that no blame may attach to you; and *Allah* is Forgiving, Merciful."
- "[47.004] So when you meet in battle those who disbelieve, then smite the necks until when you have overcome them, then make (them) prisoners, and afterwards either set them free as a favor or let them ransom (themselves) until the war terminates. That (shall be so); and if *Allah* had pleased He would certainly have exacted what is due from them, but that He may try some of you by means of others; and (as for) those who are slain in the way of *Allah*, He will by no means allow their deeds to perish."
- "[49.015] Verily the true believers [are] those only who believe in God and his apostle, and afterwards doubt not; and who employ their substance and their persons in the defense of God's true religion: These are they who speak sincerely."
- "[61.004] Surely *Allah* loves those who fight in His way in ranks as if they were a firm and compact wall."
- "[66.009] O Prophet! strive hard against the unbelievers and the hypocrites, and be hard against them; and their abode is hell; and evil is the resort."

THE HADITHS

Following on the discussion in chapter 2, here is a listing of hadiths related to jihad:

- "Upon his return from battle Muhammad said, 'We have returned from the lesser *jihad* to the greater *jihad* [i.e., the struggle against the evil of one's soul].'"
- "A man asked [the Prophet]: '. . . and what is Jihad?' He (peace be upon him) replied: 'You fight against the disbelievers when you meet them (on the battlefield).' He asked again: 'What kind of Jihad is the highest?' He

(peace be upon him) replied: 'The person who is killed whilst spilling the last of his blood.'"

- "I asked the Prophet, 'What is the best deed?' He replied, 'To believe in Allah and to fight for His Cause.'"

- "It has been narrated on the authority of Abu Sa'id Khudri that the Messenger of Allah (may peace be upon him) said (to him): Abu Sa'id, whoever cheerfully accepts Allah as his Lord, Islam as his religion and Muhammad as his Apostle is necessarily entitled to enter Paradise. He (Abu Sa'id) wondered at it and said: Messenger of Allah, repeat it for me. He (the Messenger of Allah) did that and said: There is another act which elevates the position of a man in Paradise to a grade one hundred (higher), and the elevation between one grade and the other is equal to the height of the heaven from the earth. He (Abu Sa'id) said: What is that act? He replied: Jihad in the way of Allah! Jihad in the way of Allah!"

- "Allah's Apostle said: 'I have been ordered (by Allah) to fight against the people until they testify that none has the right to be worshipped but Allah and that Muhammad is Allah's Apostle, and offer the prayers perfectly and give the obligatory charity, so if they perform a that, then they save their lives an property from me except for Islamic laws and then their reckoning (accounts) will be done by Allah.'"

- "A man came to the Prophet and asked, 'A man fights for war booty; another fights for fame and a third fights for showing off; which of them fights in Allah's Cause?' The Prophet said, 'He who fights that Allah's Word [i.e., Islam] should be superior, fights in Allah's Cause.'"

- "The Prophet said, 'A single endeavor (of fighting) in Allah's Cause in the forenoon or in the afternoon is better than the world and whatever is in it.'"

- "Allah's Apostle said, 'Allah guarantees him who strives in His Cause and whose motivation for going out is nothing but Jihad in His Cause and belief in His Word, that He will admit him into Paradise (if martyred) or bring him back to his dwelling place, whence he has come out, with what he gains of reward and booty.'"

- "It has been narrated on the authority of Masruq Who said: We asked 'Abdullah about the Qur'anic verse: 'Think not of those who are slain in Allah's way as dead. Nay, they are alive, finding their sustenance in the presence of their Lord' (*Qur'an* 3:169). He said: We asked the meaning of the verse (from the Holy Prophet) who said: The souls of the martyrs live in the bodies of green birds who have their nests in chandeliers hung from the throne of the Almighty. They eat the fruits of Paradise from wherever they like and then nestle in these chandeliers."

- "The Prophet Muhammad was heard saying: 'The smallest reward for the people of Paradise is an abode where there are eighty thousand servants and seventy-two wives, over which stands a dome decorated with pearls, aquamarine, and ruby, as wide as the distance from Al-Jabiyyah [a Damascus suburb] to Sana'a [Yemen].'"

I now turn to a series of scholars who take what we have just discussed and provide their interpretation for those not trained in religious exegesis. Again, the following section is illustrative and not exhaustive.

SCHOLARS

Ibn Taymiyyah

There is a Chinese proverb that says "May you live in interesting times." This could certainly be applied to Ahmad Ibn Taymiyyah, who lived in the thirteenth and fourteenth centuries CE. During his early years, the Mongol wave over Asia made him a refugee (the Mongol leader Hulagu Khan sacked Baghdad, the seat of the Islamic Caliphate and the jewel of the Muslim world in 1258). Much of the Muslim world at the time was also occupied by Christian Crusaders. Both events crucially molded Ibn Taymiyyah's worldview, especially with respect to violent jihad.

He took to religious studies in exile in Damascus and Cairo in the more conservative Hanbali school. He hated Sufism (a brand of Islam) and Christianity and was not fond of Shia Islam. The work he is most known for is *The Book on the Government of the Religious Law*, which in essence a call for sharia law to be applied to all levels and aspects of government.

Ibn Taymiyyah was also known for a famous fatwa (religious ruling) against the ruling Mongols. Although the invaders had allegedly converted to Islam, Ibn Taymiyyah stated that they were not genuine Muslims since they used laws other than sharia to govern; hence, jihad against the foreign occupiers was obligatory. The Mongols, he claimed, were living in a state of *jahiliyyah* (ignorance). Here is an excerpt from that fatwa: "Everyone who is with them (the Mongols) in the state over which they rule has to be regarded as belonging to the most evil class of men. He is either an atheist and hypocrite who does not believe in the essence of the religion of Islam . . . or he belongs to that worst class of people who are the people of *bida '* [innovation seen as heretical]."[1]

These words imply that anyone who supported the state run by the Mongols would be an enemy of Islam and could be targeted for violence. Ibn Taymiyyah viewed jihad as the "best voluntary act" man could perform. As we shall see with later ideologues, he insisted that jihad was a superior act in Islam to the hajj (pilgrimage), prayer, and fasting. Those who fought in jihad would embrace happiness in this life and the next. He also categorically rejected the hadith distinguishing the greater (internal) and lesser (violent) jihad.

Ibn Taymiyyah also spoke of the need for all Muslims to engage in jihad: "Since jihad is part of the perfection of *al-amr bil-maruf wal-nahy an al-munkar* [commanding right and forbidding wrong], it, too, is a collective obligation. As with any collective obligation, this means that if those sufficient for the task do not come forward, everyone capable of it to any extent is in sin to the extent of his capability in that area. This is because its obligation when it is needed is upon every Muslim to the extent of his/her ability."[2]

Ibn Taymiyyah is one of the oldest scholars still cited regularly by extremists and was a particular favorite of deceased Al Qaeda leader Osama Bin Laden. Here are a few excerpts from Bin Laden's statements.

- From "The Betrayal of Palestine" (1994): "The words of the Sheikh of Islam ibn Taymiya apply: 'There is no greater duty after faith than unconditionally fighting the attacking enemy who corrupts religion and the world. He must be resisted as hard as possible.'"[3]
- From "The World Islamic Front" (1998): "The Sheikh of Islam [i.e., Ibn Taymiyyah] when he states in his chronicles that 'As for fighting to repel an enemy, which is the strongest way to defend freedom and religion, it is agreed that this is a duty.'"[4]
- From "Terror for Terror" (2001; published just after the 9/11 attacks): "The scholars and people of the knowledge, amongst them . . . [ibn Tayiyya] . . . say that if the disbelievers were to kill our children and women, then we should not feel ashamed to do the same to them, mainly to deter them from trying to kill our children and women again."[5]
- From "Depose the Tyrants" (2004): "The Sheikh of Islam, ibn Taymiyya, said: 'If the reason for harmony is religion and working for it, then the reason for division is what God ordered of His servant.' He also said that the restrictions and limitations imposed on the umma by its scholars, sheikhs, rulers, and noblemen are what allowed the enemy to gain control over it."[6]

There are a few significant takeaways from Ibn Taymiyyah's works that resonate with violent jihad today. First and foremost is the contention that Muslim leadership is not to be trusted merely because the leaders purport to be legitimate. The Mongols were not true Muslims in spite of their conversion to Islam and had to be opposed by force. Modern extremists will label current leaders the same way: false Muslims. Jihad, Ibn Taymiyyah wrote, is the most important tenet of Islam and surpassed all others. In addition, jihad had to be waged at an individual level since the Muslim leadership could not be trusted to call for it. He also believed that the Islamic world was not being served by its current leadership and should be replaced by true Islamic government. These themes, developed seven hundred years ago, help underscore modern extremist thinking on violent jihad.

Maulana Maududi

Abu A'la Maududi (also rendered Mawdudi) was an Indian-Pakistani Islamic scholar who lived from 1903 to 1979 (he actually died in Buffalo, New York, where he was seeking medical treatment). He was the founder of the Jamaat-e-Islami political party, one of the first to marry the notion of modern governance and Islam.

While Maududi wrote extensively on a variety of topics related to Islam in the modern world, we will limit our focus to two works concerning jihad: *Jihad in Islam* (1927) and a pair of sermons on the topic.

Jihad in Islam

In 1939, Maududi delivered an address in Lahore in which he sought to provide a comprehensive understanding of jihad. He set jihad in the context of Islam, which he termed a "revolutionary ideology and program which seeks to alter the social order of the whole world." Muslims are to carry out this program through revolutionary struggle. He contrasted the term *jihad* with that of *harb* (war), noting that jihad is more forceful and wider in connotation. To Maududi, "war" was what other states and nations do for the achievement of personal or national interests: Islam does not share these interests. Other countries seek hegemony: Islam seeks the welfare of all humanity. It also envisages the annihilation of all tyrannical and evil systems in the world through the enforcement of its own program of reform.

According to Maududi. Islam wants to set up a state based on its ideology and requires the entire planet to achieve this goal, which he wrote will benefit all humanity. A variety of forces need to be pressed into service to this end, and the composite of these forces is called *jihad*. He added that jihad must be *fi sabilillah*—for the cause of God: No selfish motives are allowed. All sacrifice is directed to one end, the establishment of a just and equitable social order among human beings. Those who engage in jihad are contrasted with those who fight in the way of the *taghout* (devil)—that is, he who assumes the position of Lord over others and expropriates more than his due.

As the message of Islam is intended for all, it implies that sovereignty belongs to no one except God. Hence no one can become a self-appointed ruler and issue laws of his own volition. Allowing a ruler to do so constitutes equating the ruler with God (known as *shirk*—idolatry—in Islam) and is "the root of all evils in the universe." Only Islamic revolutionary leaders can attain the correct level of justice and moderation. The Quran speaks of *Hizb Allah* (the party of God), the raison d'être of which is to destroy un-Islamic systems and install an Islamic system of government. To do so it must capture state authority, through jihad, to eventually effect a world revolution. It cannot rest content with the establishment of such a government in one territory.

Maududi rejected the classic distinction between "offensive" and "defensive" jihad. Only those countries engaged in classic warfare are subject to these categories. He wrote, "Islamic jihad is both offensive and defensive at one and the same time. It is offensive because the Muslim Party assaults the rule of an opposing ideology, and it is defensive because the Muslim Party is constrained to capture state power in order to arrest the principles of Islam in space-time forces."

A true Islamic state would allow full freedom of religion but would not allow non-Muslims to administer state affairs, since their system is, in the view of Islam, evil. Under an Islamic system, certain "practices" would be discontinued, including the following:

* All forms of business based on usury or interest
* Gambling
* Prostitution and other vices
* Indecent dress; minimum standards of dress would be imposed on non-Muslim women
* Censorship of cinemas and
* All cultural activities "corrosive of moral fibres."

Once Muslims are victorious, the victors cannot emulate their enemies by assuming despotic powers. Jihad, Maududi wrote, is "a dry labour, devoid of pleasure . . . a sacrifice of life, wealth, and carnal desire."

Khutabat

In a book of sermons on various aspects of Islam, Maududi dedicated the last two chapters to jihad ("Jihad" and "The Importance of Jihad"). In these sermons, Maududi stated that the so-called pillars of Islam (praying, fasting, giving to charity, etc.) are nothing but a preparation for the greatest task—jihad. Reiterating previous points that the world is corrupt and ruled by evil governments, Maududi stressed that the only solution is to "right the mutilated shape of government." The root of this evil is man's rule over man and this must be replaced by God's rule over man.

The aforementioned Islamic tenets serve as a training ground for jihad and divine government. In fact, argued Maududi, pure practice (*ibadat*) is meaningless unless a person has the intent to progress to jihad. In "The Importance of Jihad" he moves on to note that true Muslims must have only one belief (*deen*) and reject the beliefs of others—namely, democracy, monarchy, and non-Muslims. It is not sufficient for Muslims to engage in mere worship while still living under foreign ideologies. Removing these false ideologies will not be simple and will only come about through the steadfast actions of those willing to engage in jihad.

Sayyid Qutb

West Point's 2006 *Militant Ideology Atlas* suggested that terms like *jihad* and *Islamic extremism*, which some might fight offensive, ought to be supplanted with the term *Qutbism*. Their rationale is worth quoting at length: "Label the entire Jihadi Movement 'Qutbism' in recognition that the Jihadis cite Sayyid Qutb more than any other modern author. Muslim opponents of the Jihadis (including mainstream Wahhabis) use this term to describe them, a designation Jihadis hate, since it implies that they follow a human and are members of a deviant sect. Adherents of the movement consider 'Qutbi' to be a negative label and would much rather be called Jihadi or Salafi. Calling the movement 'Qutbism' would also remove potentially offensive words from the lexicon of public officials (like 'Islamofascism') and disassociate the movement from Islam."[7]

While I admire the sentiment and think it has merits, it also has some downsides that are not relevant to this book. What is more interesting, however, is the podium on which Sayyid Qutb is placed and the alleged influence he holds as an extremist ideologue. So, who is Sayyid Qutb, and what did he have to say that was so important?

Sayyid Qutb was a member of the Egyptian Muslim Brotherhood. Jailed and tortured by the regime after a failed assassination attempt on President Nasser, Qutb was hanged by the government in 1966. He was able to use his prison time to pen a number of influential tracts and books, none of which is more important than *Ma'alim fil Tariq* (rendered as *Milestones* in English). This book is a recipe for the perfect Islamic society, one that can only be achieved through violence, and remains one of the most widely read influences on the jihadi mind set.

Qutb spent much of his book discussing why Muslim societies were failing and repeated much of what Maududi had written decades previously. Qutb's prescription matched in part that of the Muslim Brotherhood: *Islam huwa al hal* (Islam is the solution). As experiments with other systems of governance had failed—capitalism, communism, monarchy—it was clear that only within a true Islamic system of government would humanity find perfection.

For our purposes, however, it is Qutb's description, and justification, of jihad that is of interest. In discussing the state of *jahiliyyah* (ignorance, a state where Islam does not govern), Qutb noted that Islam "uses physical power and jihad for abolishing the organizations and authorities of the *jahili* [adjective form of *jahiliyyah*] system which prevent people from reforming their ideas and beliefs, but forces them to obey their aberrant ways and makes them serve human lords instead of the Almighty Lord."[8]

Qutb also took issue with what he saw as a contrived distinction between "offensive" and "defensive" jihad. He twisted the notion of defense to mean the "defense of man" against those elements that limit his freedom (i.e., non-Islamic governance). To attain this freedom, Islam must employ jihad ("Since the objective of the message of Islam is a decisive declaration of man's freedom, not merely on the philosophical plane but also in the actual conditions of life, it must employ jihad"[9]). Qutb summarizes the reasons for jihad as follows:

- To establish God's authority on the earth
- To arrange human affairs according to the true guidance provided by God
- To abolish all the Satanic forces and Satanic systems of life and
- To end the lordship of one man over others, since all men are created equal and no one has the authority to make them servants or to make arbitrary laws for them.[10]

— in Muslim world !

Qutb believed that *jahili* societies would inevitably attack Muslim ones and that thus jihad was inevitable. Even in the absence of an attack from outside, jihad would have to occur to remove these non-Islamic systems of government (Qutb wrote that it was the duty of Islam to "annihilate all such systems as they are obstacles in the way of universal freedom"[11]).

It is worth noting that Qutb's overall obsession was with how to remove illegitimate systems of governance. His remedy was jihad, but he was careful to not explicitly call for violence in *Milestones* (possibly as he was incarcerated while writing it). The intent is clear in any event, as Qutb sees all systems of government as manmade and not God-derived, accepting that the former will not easily embrace the latter without the use of violence. He built on the ideas of Maududi and was deemed enough of a danger to be killed by the state.

Abdullah Azzam

In November 1989, an explosion on a street in Peshawar, Pakistan, blew a car to fragments, among other damage. In that car was a theologian named Abdullah Azzam and his two sons. The bomb obliterated one son and made another's leg fly over a telephone line. Abdullah Azzam's body, however, was intact—save for an internal hemorrhage—and passersby detected the scent of musk (a sign of martyrdom).

The Palestinian-born Azzam was in some ways the spiritual founder of Al Qaeda. He moved to Pakistan in the wake of the 1979 Soviet invasion of Afghanistan and became a major figure in the international jihad that ensued. He was a friend and mentor to Osama Bin Laden, although the two had a falling-out over interpretation of the true intent of jihad.

We will examine two short works by Azzam: "Defense of the Muslim Lands" and "Join the Caravan." Both have been very influential in explaining and justifying violent jihad to subsequent generations.

"Defense of the Muslim Lands"

The first sentence in this pamphlet is a quotation from Ibn Taymiyyah: "The first obligation after *Iman* [faith] is the repulsion of the enemy aggressor who assaults the religion and the worldly affairs." Written probably in 1979, "Defense of the Muslim Lands" had immediate applicability to the situation in Afghanistan. Azzam calls fighting "one of the most important obligations. . . . Because it is absent from the present conditions of the Muslims, they have become as rubbish of the flood waters." He goes on to explain the difference between offensive and defensive jihad—stressing that the former is *fard kifayah* (collective obligation: if enough Muslims engage, the rest do not have to), while the latter is *fard `ayn* (individual obligation on all Muslims). Azzam listed four conditions for defensive jihad:

- If the *kuffar* enter a land of the Muslims
- If the rows meet in battle and they begin to approach each other
- If the Imam calls a person or a people to march forward, then they must march, and
- If the *kuffar* capture and imprison a group of Muslims.

Azzam called upon all Muslims, specifically Arab Muslims, to fight jihad in Palestine or, failing that, in Afghanistan (non-Arabs should opt for Afghanistan because the battle was already raging there and the mujahideen need help).

In differentiating between *fard `ayn* and *fard kifayah*, Azzam noted that Afghanistan represented indeed *fard ayn* (condition #1 above) and that this obligation implied a wife did not need the permission of her husband, or a child from his parents, nor a debtor from his creditor. Furthermore, authorization from a sheikh (or caliph for that matter) is not required since jihad, like other aspects of Islam (praying, hajj, etc.), does not need to be sanctioned. Azzam wrote, "Yes we fight, and we haven't an *Amir* [leader]. None has said that the absence of a community of Muslims under an *Amir* cancels the *Fard* of jihad."

Azzam discussed the possibility of seeking help from non-Muslims. He notes that there are contradictory hadiths on the subject but that some felt such aid would forfeit the ultimate aim of jihad (the United States nevertheless did assist the mujahideen in Afghanistan). Should such aid be sought, the Muslims must retain a position of authority and superiority.

When broaching the topic of peace talks in Afghanistan, Azzam asserted that peace would be possible only if the Soviets were to withdraw from the country, initiate peace talks, and make way for an Islamic state.

"Join the Caravan"

In 1987 Azzam wrote "Join the Caravan" partly to encourage more Muslims to travel to Afghanistan to engage the Soviets. In the introduction he wrote that "anybody who looks into the state of the Muslims today will find that their greatest misfortune is their abandonment of jihad due to their '. . . love of this world and hatred of death.' Because of that the tyrants have gained dominance over the Muslims in every aspect and in every land." He called upon all Muslims to fight, citing eight justifications:

- In order that the disbelievers do not dominate
- Due to the scarcity of men (i.e., the mujahideen in Afghanistan need help)
- Fear of the Hell-Fire
- Fulfilling the duty of jihad, and responding to the Call of the Lord
- Following in the footsteps of the Pious Predecessors (i.e., the Salaf)
- Establishing a solid foundation as a base for Islam
- Protecting those who are oppressed in the land and
- Hoping for martyrdom and a High Station in Paradise.

The sixth justification is interesting, as it may be the origin of the name Al Qaeda (*qaeda* means "base" in Arabic). Azzam also spoke of preserving the earth from corruption, securing Islamic places of worship, and protecting the *ummah* (universal Muslim community) from punishment. Jihad, he wrote, is the "highest peak of Islam" and the "most excellent form of worship, and by means of it the Muslims can reach the highest of ranks."

In part 2 of "Join the Caravan," Azzam chastised scholars, mothers, imams, and all Muslims for failing to promote jihad. According to Azzam, jihad is the obligation of a lifetime, just as prayer and fasting. In part 3 he noted that jihad remains *fard 'ayn* until the liberation of the "last piece of land which was in the hands of the Muslims but has been occupied by the disbelievers."

Azzam is still an influential ideologue. Even if his death arose out of a disagreement with Osama Bin Laden (according to some), the Al Qaeda leader had both of Azzam's works discussed here with him in Abbottabad when he was killed.[12] There is even an Azzam Publications in the UK dedicated to keeping the ideologue's works alive.

Muhammad abd-al-Salam Faraj

On October 6, 1981, the president of Egypt, Anwar Sadat, was in a reviewing stand on the annual Egyptian armed forces day. Sadat had made enemies with his role in the US–brokered peace deal with Israel. At one point in the procession, armed men jumped from a truck and rushed the stand. Thinking them to be ordinary military personnel, Sadat rose to receive a salute. They were not ordinary soldiers: They were from Egyptian Islamic Jihad. Throwing hand grenades and firing from automatic weapons, they succeeded in assassinating the president. The lead assassin, Khalid Islambouli, shouted "death to Pharaoh" as he shot (*pharaoh* is a generic extremist term for un-Islamic rulers).

The chief ideologue behind the group was Muhammad abd-al-Salam Faraj: He was executed in1982 for his role in the attack. Faraj's main work of interest to us is *Al Faridah Al Ghaybah* (The Forgotten [or Absent] Obligation), a work that still resonates today. The title plays on the five pillars or obligations in Islam: the profession of faith (*shahada*), daily prayers (*salat*), fasting during Ramadan (*sawm*), alms (*zakat*), and pilgrimage to Mecca once in one's lifetime (hajj). Faraj, like others before him, elevated jihad to the level of obligation and demonstrates that it is Islam's primary requirement. In his mind, however, Muslims have set aside this requirement and it has become neglected. He blamed modern Islamic scholars for underplaying the importance of jihad to the future of Islam even though they know it is the only way to bring Islam back and cause it to come to the surface again.

Faraj argued that today's so-called Islamic states are anything but Islamic. Laws are un-Islamic, and the rulers themselves have become apostates by allowing un-Islamic practices to thrive in their states. He further noted that the Islamic world has been governed by the laws of the "disbelievers" since the dissolution of the Caliphate in 1924. Citing Ibn Taymiyyah (Faraj cited the thirteenth-century scholar throughout his work), Faraj called upon the apostates (i.e., the rulers of Muslim countries) to be killed and declared that fighting these pseudo-Muslims is obligatory, as they have "snatched" leadership from Muslims.

In a recurring theme, Faraj rejected the argument that jihad is for defensive purposes only. He writes, "So fighting in Islam is to raise Allah's word highest, either offensively or defensively. Also Islam was spread by the sword, but only against the leaders of *kufr* [unbelief]."[13] He went on to cite several Quranic verses that call for jihad and notes that "most of the scholars" agreed that violent verses abrogated nonviolent ones. Fighting, he wrote, is "now *fardh* [obligation] upon every Muslim."[14] He enumerated the conditions for jihad:

- When Muslim and disbeliever armies meet

// • When the disbelievers invade a Muslim country (it is obligatory for Muslims to fight to force them out) and
• When an Imam orders a people to march forth in the cause of Allah.[15]

Faraj also "categorized" jihad as jihad *an-nafs* (the inner self), jihad against the *Shaytan* (Devil), and jihad against the "disbelievers and hypocrites."[16] Jihad, he noted, should not be avoided through fear of failure or an absence of leadership, and abandoning jihad is in fact responsible for the humiliation and division of the *ummah* (global Islamic community).

In discussing how Muslims should wage jihad, Faraj supported deceit and lying (since there is no covenant between Muslims and the present rulers) and even help from a nonbeliever. He concluded by admonishing those that use the term *suicide operations* instead of *martyrdom operations*.

The importance of Faraj's work lies in his meticulous use of Islamic scholars, Quranic verses, and hadiths. He also cites stories from Islam's past to illustrate the justification of jihad.

Abu Muhammad al-Maqdisi

Abu Muhammad al-Maqdisi (b. 1959) is probably best known as the teacher of Abu Musab al-Zarqawi, the particularly brutal extremist killed in a US air strike in Iraq in 2006. Maqdisi has been in and out of Jordanian prisons, and at one point there was debate over whether he had abandoned his extremist ideology.

Dutch scholar Joas Wagemakers published a definitive biography of Maqdisi and his worldview in 2012, and I refer the reader to that volume for a comprehensive view of this important ideologue. Nevertheless, we will examine one of Maqdisi's works, probably his most important, *Millat Ibrahim*, to gain insight into the Jordanian's views on violent jihad.

Millat Ibrahim

The premise behind *Millat Ibrahim* (The Religion/People of Abraham) is to remind Muslims of the fundamental enmity they should have toward the *mushrikeen* (polytheists), up to and including aggression, hostility, and warfare. Abraham (*Ibrahim* in Arabic) considered these people as enemies, and his views should be emulated.

In the introduction, Maqdisi provided a lengthy quotation worth repeating:

> To the transgressing rulers [*Tawāghīt*] of every time and place . . . to the transgressing rulers [*Tawāghīt*]; the governors and the leaders and the Caesars and the *Kisrahs* [Persian Emperors] and the Pharaohs and the Kings . . . to their servants and their misguiding scholars ['*Ulamā*] . . . to their supporters

and their armies and their police and their intelligence agencies . . . to all of them collectively, we say: "Verily, we are free from you and whatever you worship besides Allāh." Free from your retched laws, methodologies, constitutions and values . . . free from your repugnant governments, courts, distinguishing characteristics and media . . ."

We have rejected you, and there has become apparent between us and you, enmity and hatred forever, until you believe in Allāh Alone. I will perform Jihād against Your enemies as long as you keep me (in existence), And I will make fighting them my practice.

Al Maqdisi noted that Abraham was a true Muslim and that the *Tawaghit* have embraced Islam's enemies and forsaken the tenet of *Al Wala' wal Bara'* (Allegiance and Disavowal—remaining true to Muslims and treating all others as enemies). He called upon Muslims to show their disavowal of non-Muslims, openly declare their disbelief in them, and openly demonstrate hatred. A consequence of this hatred is the obligation to wage jihad, a practice that helps draw the true believers nearer to Allah.

According to Maqdisi, organizations such as the police, military, and intelligence services exist to promote falsehood (i.e., by supporting apostate governments that draft un-Islamic laws) and should be avoided. Muslims should openly declare their opposition to their enemies while secretly planning to attack them. Furthermore, the Quran (25:52) states quite clearly, "So obey not the disbelievers and make jihad against them." In his conclusion, Maqdisi noted that he has clearly outlined the path Muslims should take and challenges them to take up this path.

In Maqdisi's world, there is a clear difference between believers and nonbelievers: The former should not associate with the latter. There is no "getting along" or compromise. The only state is a state of jihad.

In recent years there has been some debate as to whether Maqdisi has renounced his views on jihad. While he certainly did distance himself from the actions of his brutal pupil Zarqawi, it is doubtful whether he has truly abandoned the call for violence. Regardless, his works are still available and still inspire others today.

Anwar al-Awlaki

A US drone launched missiles at a target in Yemen at the end of September 2011. Inside the car were four individuals believed to be linked to AQ. One of them, Anwar al-Awlaki, the US–born son of Yemeni parents studying in the United States, met his maker that day.

It is not an exaggeration to state that Awlaki is the most influential contemporary extremist ideologue out there. In my experience with CSIS, it was rare to *not* see Awlaki's works play a role in the violent radicalization of Canadians. He was charismatic, learned, thoughtful, and prolific, and he spoke fluent American-accented English. It was through his efforts in part that we have *Inspire* magazine to deal with.

Awlaki's writings, audio recordings, and videos are too numerous to summarize here. He developed many themes that were solely religious in nature and are still seen as "must-haves" by many. He also worked into his sermons and lectures the topic of violent jihad. For reasons of brevity, we will look at one of his works that was directly linked to this topic.

"44 Ways to Support Jihad"

Awlaki wrote this piece in the late 2000s, and it is based partially on an earlier work: *39 Ways to Support Jihad* by Muhammad bin Ahmad As-Salim. Awlaki introduces his work with the following:

> Jihad is the greatest deed in Islam and the salvation of the *ummah* is in practicing it. In times like these, when Muslim lands are occupied by the *kuffar*, when the jails of tyrants are full of Muslim POWs, when the rule of Allah is absent from this world, and when Islam is being attacked in order to uproot it, Jihad becomes obligatory on every Muslim. Jihad must be practiced by the child even if the parents refuse, by the wife even if her husband objects, and by the one in debt even if the lender disagrees
>
> Dear brothers and sisters, the issue is urgent since today our enemy is neither a nation nor a race. It is a system of *kufr* [unbelief] with global reach. The *kuffar* today are conspiring against us like never before. So could we be heading towards the great battle between the Romans [i.e., the West] and the Muslims . . . which the Prophet spoke about?

Awlaki next provided forty-four ways in which Muslims can support jihad *fi sabilillah*. Here are a few of those ways:

- Jihad with your wealth: "Probably the most important contribution the Muslims in the West could do for Jihad is making Jihad with their wealth since in many cases the mujahideen are in need of money more than they are in need of men."
- Taking care of the family of a Mujahid: "Anyone of you who takes care of the family and wealth of a mujahid will receive half the reward of the mujahid (hadith reported by Muslim)."
- Paying zakat (alms) to the mujahideen: "But if Muslims would rid themselves from the whispering of *Shaytan* [Satan] they would come to realize that the best way to spend their zakah nowadays is by giving it to the mujahideen." Awlaki cleverly links one Muslim obligation—zakat—to another—jihad.
- Contributing to the medical needs of the mujahideen: "The mujahideen are in great need of any medical assistance they can get. They need physicians, they need hospitals . . . and they need medicine."

- Fighting the lies of the Western media: "Can't you see that the Western media is constantly trying to underplay the atrocities committed by the West while exaggerating the violations—which are few and far between—committed by Muslims? . . . A Muslim should not believe Western sources unless they are confirmed by a trustworthy Muslim one."
- Encouraging others to fight jihad: "Encouraging others to participate in Jihad was an act of worship we were specifically asked to do."
- Fatwas supporting the mujahideen: "There are scholars who are willing to speak out the truth. Such scholars should be encouraged to do so."
- Arms training: "This issue is so critical that if arms training is not possible in your country then it is worth the time and money to travel to another country to train if you can."
- WWW jihad: "The Internet has become a great medium for spreading the call of jihad . . . some ways in which the brothers and sisters could be 'internet mujahideen' is by . . . establishing discussion forums . . . establishing e-mail lists . . . posting jihad literature and news . . . setting up websites."
- Raising our children in the love of jihad and the mujahideen
- Preparing for hijrah: "Muslims should therefore prepare themselves to leave when the opportunity arises. Preparation for *hijrah* is not restricted to Muslims living in non-Muslim countries but applies to every Muslim because more often than not Jihad in itself demands *hijrah*."
- *Nasheeds* (songs and poetry): "*Nasheeds* are especially inspiring to the youth. . . . Nasheeds are an important element in creating a 'Jihad culture.'"
- Translating Jihad literature into other languages.

Have we seen Awlaki's work reflected in the mind sets of recent extremists? I can think of no better example than Andre Poulin, a.k.a. Abu Muslim, who left Timmins, a small town in northern Ontario, to join and die for the Islamic State. In a now-famous posthumous video issued by IS, Poulin makes a pitch for more Muslims to join him in Syria. Here is an excerpt from that video: "Every person can contribute something to the Islamic State. It's obligatory on us. If you cannot fight, then you can give money. If you cannot give money, then you can assist in technology. If you cannot assist in technology, you can use some other skills. We can use you."

Much of what Awlaki suggested is mentioned here. The US–Yemeni citizen will live on in the virtual world for a long time, extolling and inspiring others to engage in violent jihad.

Osama Bin Laden

The leader of Al Qaeda from 1989 to his death at the hands of US Special
Forces in Abbottabad, Pakistan, in 2011 was not a religious scholar. He was
the wealthy son of a Saudi construction magnate who was raised partly in the
 West but who radicalized over the Soviet invasion of Afghanistan and joined
the fight. Despite his lack of religious credentials, however, he issued a series
of statements from 1994 onward. These statements are full of religious cita-
tions and encourage the world's Muslims to join the fight against its enemies,
ranging from autocratic or despotic Islamic regimes to the West (which often
supports such regimes).

So, although he did not have the weight of religious education and study
behind him, Bin Laden's statements were seen as important sources of inspiration. Jihad was a constant theme, as we shall see from the following excerpts.

- From "The Invasion of Arabia" (1995–1996): "Honorable and righteous
  scholars, come and lead your *umma*, can call her to God, and return her to
  her religion in order to correct beliefs, spread knowledge, enjoin good, and
  forbid evil. Call her to jihad for the sake of God Almighty, and call her to
  motivate people for it. . . . And if you cannot do so in your own country,
  then emigrate for the sake of God Almighty. . . . Emigration is related to
  jihad, and jihad will go on until the Day of Judgment."[17]
- From "The Saudi Regime" (1996): "Our encouragement and call to Muslims to enter jihad against the American and Israeli occupiers are actions
  which we undertake as religious obligations."[18]
- From "A Muslim Bomb" (1998): "We believe that jihad is now an individual duty on our *umma*. . . . Muslims are obliged to perform their legal
  duty of jihad against what is clearly the biggest unbelief."[19]
- From "Under Mullah Omar" (2001): "Teach them that jihad for the sake
  of God can only be done by a group that listens to and obeys a single
  commander, through which God unites them from their differences and
  disarray."[20]
- From "To Our Brothers in Pakistan" (2001): "Dear brothers, I bring you
  the good news that we are established on the path of jihad for God."[21]
- From "From Somalia to Afghanistan" (1997): "For this and other acts of
  aggression and injustice, we have declared jihad against the United States,
  because in our religion it is our duty to make jihad so that God's word is
  the one exalted to the heights and so that we drive the Americans away
  from all Muslim countries."[22]
- From "To the People of Afghanistan" (2002): "Oh, people of Afghanistan,
  you know that jihad is of the utmost value in Islam, and that with it we can
  gain pride and eminence in this world and the next. You know it saves our

lands, protects our sanctity, spreads justice, security, and prosperity, and plants fear in the enemies' hearts. Through it kingdoms are built, and the banner of truth flies high above all others."[23]

- From "To the Americans" (2002): "Why are we fighting and opposing you? The answer is very simple: because you attacked us and continue to attack us."[24]
- From "Resist the New Rome" (2004): "The West today is doing its utmost to tarnish jihad and kill anyone seeking jihad. . . . This is because they all know that jihad is the effective power to foil all their conspiracies. Jihad is the path so seek it."[25]
- From "Terror for Terror" (2001): "And I swear by God, happy are those who are martyred today, happy are those who are honored to stand under the banner of Muhammad, under the banner of Islam, to fight the world Crusade. So let every person amongst them come forward to fight those Jews and Americans, the killing of whom is among the most important duties and most pressing things."[26]

We can see a number of themes in Bin Laden's words, ranging from the obligation to engage in jihad to the claim that Muslims are merely responding to attacks by the West and its supporters in the Muslim world on the *ummah*. The fact he was not a recognized scholar should not be overemphasized. He was a charismatic figure and seen as a hero within extremist circles. His death did not signify his disappearance from the world stage and did not undermine his continuing influence.

SUMMARY

There is a lot of similarity and overlap in the material just presented. I believe that this is for two primary reasons: (1) all scholars derive their works from the same primary material (i.e., Quran and hadith) on jihad, and (2) each scholar builds on the work of his predecessor.

So, if I were a Westerner curious about jihad, seeking more information about what Islam has to say about it, or seeking final confirmation that traveling to join a foreign conflict was sanctioned, what would I learn from the above? In part, the following would strike me:

- Jihad is a part of worship (*ibadat*) like praying, fasting, and performing the hajj.
- Jihad is the most important form of worship.
- Jihad is required to put Islam back on top.
- Jihad is obligatory, and most Muslims are too weak to perform jihad.
- The distinction between offensive and defensive jihad is a false one.

- Jihad is required since the Islamic world is under attack.
- I do not need anyone's permission or approval to fight in a jihad.
- I do not have to wait for an *amir* or caliph to come along to declare jihad.
- Allah demands and supports jihad.
- And jihad will lead to the end of history and the triumph of Islam over all religions.

Any one of these justifications may be sufficient to convince someone that performing jihad is the most important act a Muslim could perform. And in light of the last four decades of terrorism it is clear that there are many individuals who are so convinced. They have traveled to conflict zones around the world to engage in what is being sold as jihad. Some of those have recently left their homelands to fight with IS.

NOTES

1. Richard Bonney, *Jihād: From Qur'ān to Bin Laden☐*, foreword by Zaki Badawi (London: Palgrave, 2004), 115.☐☐
2. Ibid., 117.
3. From Bruce Lawrence, ed., *Messages to the World: The Statements of Osama Bin Laden*, intro. Bruce Lawrence, trans. James Howarth (London and New York: Verso, 2005), 5.
4. Ibid., 61.
5. Ibid., 118–19.
6. Ibid., 249–50.
7. William McCants, ed., *Militant Ideology Atlas* (West Point, NY: Combating Terrorism Center, US Military Academy, 2006), 10, https://www.ctc.usma.edu/v2/wp-content/uploads/2012/04/Atlas-ResearchCompendium1.pdf.
8. Sayyid Qutb, *Milestones*, trans. International Islamic Federation of Student Organizations (Stuttgart: The Holy Koran Publishing House, 1978), 99.
9. Ibid., 113.
10. Ibid., 127.
11. Ibid., 137.
12. Michiko Kakutani, "Osama bin Laden's Bookshelf Reflects His Fixation on West," *New York Times*, May 21, 2015, http://www.nytimes.com/2015/05/22/world/asia/bin-ladens-bookshelf-reflects-his-fixation-on-west.html.
13. Muhammad Abd Al Salam Faraj, *The Forgotten Obligation* (London: Maktabah Al Ansaar Publications, 2000), 51.
14. Ibid., 60.
15. Ibid., 61.
16. Ibid., 62.
17. Lawrence, *Messages to the World*, 18–19.
18. Ibid., 41.
19. Ibid., 79.
20. Ibid., 97.
21. Ibid., 101.
22. Ibid., 47.
23. Ibid., 159.
24. Ibid., 162.
25. Ibid., 218.
26. Ibid., 129.

Glossary

amir	leader
Amīr al-Mu'minīn	"commander of the faithful," Ar.
AQ	Al Qaeda
AQAP	Al Qaeda in the Arabian Peninsula
bay'a	"pledge of allegiance," Ar.
bida'	"innovation," Ar.
CSIS	Canadian Security Intelligence Service
CVE	countering violent extremism
Dabiq	online magazine of the Islamic State
Dar al-Kufr	"land of disbelief," Ar.
Deen	"faith," "belief," Ar.
DHS	United States Department of Homeland Security
du'a	"prayer of supplication," Ar.
fard `ayn	"individual obligation," Ar.
fard kifayah	"collective obligation," Ar.
fatwa	a religious opinion in Islam
fi sabilillah	"on the path of God," Ar.
hadith	saying of the Prophet Muhammad
harb	"war," Ar.
hijra	"migration," Ar.

HRT	high-risk traveler (RCMP)
HUMINT	human intelligence
ibadat	"worship," Ar.
IDF	Israel Defense Forces
iman	"faith," Ar.
IS	Islamic State
ISIL	Islamic State of Iraq and Levant, another name for IS
ISIS	Islamic State of Iraq and Syria, another name for IS
isnad	a chain of reporting used in hadith verification
jahiliyyah	"ignorance" (i.e., the state of ignorance before the advent of Islam), Ar.
khilafa	"caliphate," Ar.
kufir	"nonbeliever," Ar.
kuffar	plural of *kufir*
kufr	"unbelief," Ar.
mahram	"male relative," Ar.
nasheed	"poem," "song," Ar.
Naskh	"abrogation" (i.e., where a later verse in the Quran supersedes an earlier one), Ar.
RCMP	Royal Canadian Mounted Police
sharia	Islamic law
Shaytan	Arabic for "devil," "Satan"
shirk	an Islamic term that refers to the association of other deities or persons with God
SIGINT	signals intelligence
sura	a chapter of the Quran
taghout (s), *tawaghit* (pl)	"devil," "corrupt ruler," Ar.
TTP	Tehrik-e-Taliban Pakistan
ummah	the global Muslim community
YPG	also known in English as the People's Protection Units; the military arm of the Kurdish group PKK

YPJ   also known in English as the Women's Protection Units; the women's brigade of the YPG

zakat   paying alms

Suggested Reading

Arial, Tracey. *I Volunteered: Canadian Vietnam Vets Remember*. Winnipeg: Watson and Dryer, 1996.

Brown, Stanley McKeown. *With the Royal Canadians*. Toronto: The Publishers' Syndicate, 1900.

Cook, Timothy. *At the Sharp End: Canadians Fighting the Great War, 1914–1916*. Toronto: Viking Canada, 2007.

Gurski, Phil. *The Threat from Within: Recognizing Al Qaeda–Inspired Radicalization and Terrorism in the West*. Lanham: Rowman & Littlefield, 2016.

Howard, Victor. *The Mackenzie-Papineau Battalion: Canadian Participation in the Spanish Civil War*. Ottawa: Carleton University Press, 1986.

Jenkins, Philip. *The Great and Holy War: How World War I Became a Religious Crusade*. San Francisco: HarperOne, 2014.

Maudoodi, Syed Abul 'Ala. *Khutabat = Fundamentals of Islam*. 2nd ed. Chicago: Kazi Publications, 1977.

McCants, William. *The ISIS Apocalypse: The History, Strategy, and Doomsday Vision of the Islamic State*. New York: St. Martin's Press, 2015.

Morris, Ian. *War! What Is It Good For? Conflict and the Progress of Civilization from Primates and Robots*. New York: Farrar, Straus and Giroux, 2014.

Patin, Nathan. "The Other Foreign Fighters: An Open-Source Investigation into American Volunteers Fighting the Islamic State in Iraq and Syria." A Bellingcat investigation. Bellingcat. https://www.bellingcat.com/wp-content/uploads/2015/08/The-Other-Foreign-Fighters.pdf.

Peck, Mary Biggar. *Red Moon Over Spain: Canadian Media Reaction to the Spanish Civil War, 1936–1939*. Ottawa: Steel Rail, 1988.

Petrou, Michael. *Renegades: Canadians in the Spanish Civil War*. Vancouver: UBC Press, 2008.

Shaw, Amy J. *Crisis of Conscious: Conscientious Objection in Canada during the First World War*. Vancouver: UBC Press, 2009.

Zuelhke, Mark. *The Gallant Cause: Canadians in the Spanish Civil War, 1936–1939*. Mississauga, Ont.: John Wiley and Sons Canada, 1996.

Bibliography

Abel, Allen. "Ghost Battle." *Canadian Geographic* 132, no. 1 (January–February 2012): 34–49. Available online under an updated title, "Who Won the War?" http://www. canadiangeographic.ca/article/who-won-war.

Andrews, John. "More War than Peace." In "The World in 2016," ed. Daniel Franklin, special issue. *The Economist* (2015. Entire issue available online at http://www.theworldin.com/ article/10447/world-2016.

Arial, Tracey. *I Volunteered: Canadian Vietnam Vets Remember.* Winnipeg: Watson and Dryer, 1996.

Baracskay, Daniel. *The Palestine Liberation Organization: Terrorism and Prospects for Peace in the Holy Land.* Santa Barbara, CA: Praeger, 2011.

Batrawi, Samar, and Ilona Chmoun. "Dutch Foreign Fighters Continue to Travel to Syria." *CTC Sentinel* 7, no. 7 (July 2014): 11–14. Available online at https://www.ctc.usma.edu/ posts/dutch-foreign-fighters-continue-to-travel-to-syria.

Black, Anthony. *The History of Islamic Political Thought.* New York: Routledge, 2011.

Bonney, Richard. *Jihād: From Qur'ān to Bin Laden☐.* Foreword by Zaki Badawi. London: Palgrave, 2004.☐☐

Brett, Rachel, and Irma Specht. *Young Soldiers: Why They Choose to Fight.* Boulder, CO: Lynne Rienner, 2004.

Brown, Stanley McKeown. *With the Royal Canadians.* Toronto: The Publishers' Syndicate, 1900.

Burke, Jason. *Al Qaeda: Casting a Shadow of Terror.* New York: I. B. Tauris.

Cook, Timothy. *At the Sharp End: Canadians Fighting the Great War, 1914–1916.* Toronto: Viking Canada, 2007.

The Economist. "Caliphate Calling." News. February 28, 2015. http://www.economist.com/ news/international/21645206-how-islamic-state-appeals-women-caliphate-calling.

———. "Fighting Near and Far." Briefing. November 21, 2015. http://www.economist.com/ news/briefing/21678847-islamic-state-may-be-lashing-out-abroad-because-it-has-been-weakened-nearer-home-it-will.

———. "Jihad at the Heart of Europe." Briefing. November 21, 2015. http://www.economist. com/news/briefing/21678840-brussels-not-just-europes-political-and-military-capitalit-also-centre-its.

———. "Locker Hurt." News. August 15, 2015. http://www.economist.com/news/middle-east-and-africa/21660998-generals-blow-away-plan-cut-their-budgets-locker-hurt.

Faraj, Muhammad Abd Al Salam. *The Forgotten Obligation.* London: Maktabah Al Ansaar Publications, 2000.

Gaffen, Fred. *Unknown Warriors: Canadians in Vietnam.* Toronto: Dundurn Press, 1990.

Gilsinan, Kathy. "The ISIS Crackdown on Women, by Women." *The Atlantic*, July 25, 2014. http://www.theatlantic.com/international/archive/2014/07/the-women-of-isis/375047/.

Gude, Hubert, and Wolf Wiedmann-Schmidt. "Back from the Caliphate: Returnee Says IS Recruiting for Terror Attacks in Germany." *Spiegel Online*, December 16, 2015. http://www.spiegel.de/international/world/german-jihadist-returns-from-syria-and-gives-testimony-a-1067764.html.

Hegghammer, Thomas. "Should I Stay or Should I Go? Explaining Variation in Western Jihadists' Choice between Domestic and Foreign Fighting." *American Political Science Review*, February 2013. doi:10.1017/S0003055412000615. Text available online at http://hegghammer.com/_files/Hegghammer_-_Should_I_stay_or_should_I_go.pdf.

Hegghammer, Thomas, and Peter Nesser. "Assessing the Islamic State's Commitment to Attacking the West." *Perspectives on Terrorism* 9, no. 4 (2015). http://www.terrorismanalysts.com/pt/index.php/pot/article/view/440/html.

Hodges, Glenn. "Tracking the First Americans." *National Geographic* 227, no. 1 (January 2015): 120–135. http://ngm.nationalgeographic.com/2015/01/first-americans/hodges-text.

Hoyle, Caroline, Alexandra Bradford, and Ross Frenett. "Becoming Mulan? Female Western Migrants to ISIS." London: Institute for Strategic Dialogue, 2015. http://www.strategicdialogue.org/wp-content/uploads/2016/02/ISDJ2969_Becoming_Mulan_01.15_WEB.pdf.

International Centre for Counter-terrorism (ICCT). "The Foreign Fighters Phenomenon in the European Union: Profiles, Threats and Policies." ICCT research paper. The Hague: ICCT, 2016. https://www.icct.nl/wp-content/uploads/2016/03/ICCT-Report_Foreign-Fighters-Phenomenon-in-the-EU_1-April-2016_including-AnnexesLinks.pdf.

International Centre for the Study of Radicalisation (ICSR). "ICSR Report: Victims Perpetrators Assets; The Narratives of Islamic State Defectors." London: ICSR, 2015. http://icsr.info/wp-content/uploads/2015/09/ICSR-Report-Victims-Perpertrators-Assets-The-Narratives-of-Islamic-State-Defectors.pdf.

Islamic State of Iraq and the Levant. "A Call to Hijrah," *Dabiq*, no. 3 (September 10, 2014): .

———. "Shari'ah Alone Will Rule Africa." *Dabiq*, no. 8 (March 30, 2015): .

Jenkins, Philip. *The Great and Holy War: How World War I Became a Religious Crusade*. San Francisco: HarperOne, 2014.

Keating, Joshua E. "Is It Legal for Americans to Fight in Another Country's Army?" *Foreign Policy*, September 2, 2011. http://foreignpolicy.com/2011/09/02/is-it-legal-for-americans-to-fight-in-another-countrys-army/.

Keshen, Jeffrey A. "The War on Truth." *Canada's History* (August–September 2015): 52–56. Available online at http://greatwaralbum.ca/Great-War-Album/About-the-Great-War/Unrest-on-the-homefront/The-War-on-Truth.

Khan, Adnan R. "A Tale of Two Canadians, Fighting Islamic State." *Maclean's*, August 9, 2015. http://www.macleans.ca/news/world/a-tale-of-two-canadians-fighting-islamic-state/.

Kuntz, Katrin, and Gregor Peter Schmitz. "The Belgium Question: Why Is a Small Country Producing So Many Jihadists?" *Spiegel Online*, January 27, 2015. http://www.spiegel.de/international/world/belgium-muslim-youth-turning-toward-jihad-in-large-numbers-a-1015045.html.

Lawrence, Bruce, ed. *Messages to the World: The Statements of Osama bin Laden*. Introduction by Bruce Lawrence. Translation by James Howarth. London and New York: Verso, 2005.

Liversedge, Ronald. *Mac-Pap: Memoir of a Canadian in the Spanish Civil War*. Edited by David York. Vancouver: New Star Books, 2013.

Maher, Shiraz. "From Portsmouth to Kobane: The British Jihadis Fighting for ISIS." *New Statesman*, November 6, 2014. http://www.newstatesman.com/2014/10/portsmouth-kobane.

Marean, Curtis W. "The Most Invasive Species of All." *Scientific American* 313 (August 1, 2015): 32–39. doi:10.1038/scientificamerican0815-32.

McCants, William, ed. *Militant Ideology Atlas*. West Point, NY: Combating Terrorism Center, US Military Academy, 2006. https://www.ctc.usma.edu/v2/wp-content/uploads/2012/04/Atlas-ResearchCompendium1.pdf.

Morris, Ian. *War! What Is It Good For? Conflict and the Progress of Civilization from Primates and Robots*. New York: Farrar, Straus and Giroux, 2014.

Neumann, Peter, and International Centre for the Study of Radicalisation (ICSR). "ICSR Report: Victims, Perpetrators, Assets; The Narratives of Islamic State Defectors." London: ICSR, 2015. http://icsr.info/wp-content/uploads/2015/09/ICSR-Report-Victims-Perpertrators-Assets-The-Narratives-of-Islamic-State-Defectors.pdf.

Peck, Mary Biggar. *Red Moon Over Spain: Canadian Media Reaction to the Spanish Civil War, 1936–1939*. Ottawa: Steel Rail, 1988.

Petrou, Michael. *Renegades: Canadians in the Spanish Civil War*. Vancouver: UBC Press, 2008.

———. "'You Are History. You Are Legend.' Canada's Last Spanish Civil War Vet Dies." *Maclean's*, September 11, 2013. http://www.macleans.ca/news/you-are-history-you-are-legend-canadas-last-spanish-civil-war-vet-dies/.

Pinker, Steven. *Better Angels of Our Nature: Why Violence Has Declined*. New York: Viking, 2011.

Qutb, Sayyid. "The America I Have Seen." 1949. Available online at http://www.kalamullah.com/Books/The America I have seen.pdf.

———. *Milestones*. Translated by International Islamic Federation of Student Organizations. Stuttgart: The Holy Koran Publishing House, 1978.

Rafiq, Haras, and Nikita Malik. "Caliphettes: Women and the Appeal of Islamic State." Foreword by Baroness Sandip Verma. London: Quilliam Foundation, 2015. https://www.quilliamfoundation.org/wp/wp-content/uploads/publications/free/caliphettes-women-and-the-appeal-of-is.pdf.

Shaw, Amy J. *Crisis of Conscious: Conscientious Objection in Canada during the First World War*. Vancouver: UBC Press, 2009.

Speckhard, Anne, and Ahmet S. Yayla. "Eyewitness Accounts from Recent Defectors from Islamic State: Why They Joined, What They Saw, Why They Quit." *Perspectives on Terrorism* 9, no. 6 (2015). http://www.terrorismanalysts.com/pt/index.php/pot/article/view/475/html.

Stevens, G. R. *A City Goes to War: History of the Loyal Edmonton Regiment*. Brampton, Ont.: Charters, 1964.

Thorup, Mikkel. *An Intellectual History of Terror: War, Violence and the State*. New York: Routledge, 2010.

US Department of Homeland Security, Office of Intelligence and Analysis. "Rightwing Extremism: Current Economic and Political Climate Fueling Resurgence in Radicalization and Recruitment." Report. Washington, DC: U.S. Department of Homeland Security, 2009. Made available through Federation of American Scientists at https://fas.org/irp/eprint/rightwing.pdf.

Westcott, Lucy. "Report: Number of Foreign Fighters in Iraq and Syria Double to 31,000." *Newsweek*, December 7, 2015. http://www.newsweek.com/foreign-fighters-syria-and-iraq-double-31000-86-countries-report-402084.

Zuelhke, Mark. *The Gallant Cause: Canadians in the Spanish Civil War, 1936–1939*. Mississauga, Ont.: John Wiley and Sons Canada, 1996.

Index

About the Author

Phil Gurski served for more than thirty years as an analyst in the Canadian intelligence community. From 1983 to 2001 he worked as a multilingual analyst for Communications Security Establishment, Canada's signals-intelligence organization. In 2001, he joined the Canadian Security Intelligence Service (CSIS) as strategic analyst, specializing in homegrown Al Qaeda–inspired terrorism and radicalization to violence. In 2013, he moved to Public Safety Canada as senior strategic advisor on Canada's Countering Violent Extremism policy. He has presented on these issues across Canada and around the world. He is currently president and CEO of Borealis Threat and Risk Consulting Ltd. and author of *The Threat from Within: Recognizing Al Qaeda–Inspired Radicalization and Terrorism in the West* (Rowman & Littlefield, 2016).